Managing a Construction Firm on Just 24 Hours a Day

About the Author

MATT STEVENS is the president of his own construction consulting firm, Stevens Construction Institute, Inc. He has been working with contractors as a management consultant since 1994. He has more than 30 years of experience overall, including as a specialty contractor and general contractor. Stevens has worked with dozens of clients and conducted hundreds of seminars across the country. He worked as a management consultant with FMI Corporation from 1997–2002. He earned an undergraduate degree in construction management and an MBA. Stevens writes a monthly newsletter for his Web site (www.stevensci.com); his blog, the *Construction Contractor's Digest*, contains 150 articles (www.contractorsblog.com); and he has a regular column in *Contractor* magazine. His e-learning Web site is www.constructioncbt.com.

Managing a Construction Firm on Just 24 Hours a Day

Matt Stevens

New York   Chicago   San Francisco   Lisbon   London
Madrid   Mexico City   Milan   New Delhi   San Juan
Seoul   Singapore   Sydney   Toronto

The McGraw·Hill Companies

Copyright © 2007 by The McGraw-Hill Companies, Inc. All rights reserved. Printed in the United States of America. Except as permitted under the United States Copyright Act of 1976, no part of this publication may be reproduced or distributed in any form or by any means, or stored in a data base or retrieval system, without the prior written permission of the publisher.

1 2 3 4 5 6 7 8 9 0   CUS/CUS   0 1 9 8 7 6

ISBN-13:   978-0-07-147915-8
ISBN-10:   0-07-147915-5

The sponsoring editor for this book was Cary Sullivan, the editing supervisor was Jody McKenzie, the production supervisor was Jim Kussow, and the project manager was Samik Roy Chowdhury (Sam). It was set in Garamond-Light by International Typesetting and Composition. The art director for the cover was Handel Low.

Printed and bound by Von Hoffmann/Owensville.

McGraw-Hill books are available at special quantity discounts to use as premiums and sales promotions, or for use in corporate training programs. For more information, please write to the Director of Special Sales, McGraw-Hill Professional, Two Penn Plaza, New York, NY 10121-2298. Or contact your local bookstore.

This book was printed on acid-free paper.

Contents

Foreword

T hank you for purchasing my book, *Managing a Construction Firm on Just 24 Hours a Day*. I am pleased you chose to read my work, which is for the express purpose of being a resource for construction leaders. I work as a management consultant for the construction industry, and this book is the summary of my research, training, and consulting across the continental United States. My work focuses on the business of construction contracting exclusively.

This book is my interpretation of how to work smarter, not harder, in the construction industry.

I dedicate this book to my two children. They are the ones who show me the importance of the little things.

Olivia Kathleen—one of the truly great women this country has produced. We are not without leadership for the future.

David Matthew—a brilliant and capable young man who will do well in a critical endeavor. He won't spend his time on minor things.

I wish to recognize **FMI Corporation**; this is a great group of people. They continue to be the class of management consultants for the construction industry. I worked from the Tampa office and I especially want to thank them. They taught me many things and they were patient in the process.

Last, I want to thank **Gloria Grabach**, a dear friend who supports me in many ways. I want to say that everyone should have a friend like Gloria, strongly in your corner and quietly suggesting ways to improve.

1

The Business of Contracting

I wrote this book to continue the discussion about the business management of construction contracting. There have been few books written about this subject. Our business, over the years, has evolved from a craft focus to a business focus. It has been slow, but sure. A myriad of changes have occurred, however this is the most significant. This book contains interpretation of business approaches utilized in the industry.

THE BEST INDUSTRY IN THE UNITED STATES

My child Olivia is in college. She is starting to ask about industries and careers. Olivia has made me think further about what construction contracting has to offer her. I have concluded it is the best career a young person could choose. You may not believe it, but the facts will show our business is unmatched. It offers participants long-term tangible benefits. However, many people will disagree. Let me show you the many virtues our industry has and you can be the judge.

The Construction Industry Is Not Going Away

Construction is a basic necessity to human life: shelter, food, clothing, and water. Contrastingly, most manufacturing will be leaving this country over the next few years. Construction cannot be exported.

It must be *in situ* or occurring where it produces the end product. This is unlike service centers, computer programming, or engineering where other countries provide it from afar, and then send it back to the United States. Construction and its sister, demolition, is captive to the site.

Merit-Based

The construction industry rewards hard work. There is no substitute. We are all dissatisfied with the work ethic today. When we find it, we reward it. Let me give you an example: A person (male or female) comes to you and doesn't speak English well, but has promised to work hard. You give him or her a chance, and one year later you are glad that you did. This person kept his or her promise. Now what will you do? Ignore this employee? Or cut the employee's pay? Of course not! You will increase this worker's wages and give him or her more responsibility. Construction contractors reward merit.

In a few years, that same person, having earned the technical understanding and crew following, might start his or her own business. It is almost expected. After working in the field, interacting with clients, and managing labor, it is normal and rational for this person to at least attempt having his or her own business.

Additionally, the industry is also merit based. Question: what is the best advertising in the construction business? A completed project that is on time and on budget. This project speaks volumes about a contractor's savvy and diligence. Good contractors are in the minority. Word of mouth travels fast. Excellent contractors have more opportunities for work than their lesser competitors.

Small Is Big

Construction rewards the small construction firms. That is, they make a higher percentage of profit. This is a variable cost business. In other words, they do not have to have "critical mass" to be profitable. Net profit statistics consistently show that smaller contractors make a higher percentage of profit before tax than their larger brethren do. Construction is one of the few industries where the big don't eat the small; the fast eat the slow.

> Consistently finish quantity takeoff and unit pricing before bid day. This lets you focus on the business of bidding the project, not the technical details.

Tangible

Our industry erects monuments. Our work is visible to everyone. We can see it for decades after completing it. Construction people show friends, relatives, and potential clients these projects. Unlike other industries, we see what we accomplish every day. Likewise, there is little room for puffery, that is, "smoke and mirrors."

Highly Paid

The construction industry for nonsupervisory, production work pays the fourth highest wage of all industries. The current average hourly wage is north of $19. Industries who compensate production workers better are (1) utilities employees and high-voltage workers (they are the highest paid), (2) petroleum and coal (miners and roughnecks), (3) information or computer technicians, (4) construction journeymen. The lowest paid are (1) apparel, then (2) textile, and (3) retail trade workers.

Best Earning Years Later in Life

Statistically, this is difficult to prove. Anecdotally, though, I have seen enough financial statements to strongly believe this is true. The prime earning years appear to be in the 50s. In my travels, working with clients in the United States, the older contractors do have competitive secrets and keep them to themselves. As a trend, a contractor's profitability grows over the years. I have seen increases as either percentage or gross dollars, or both. Construction becomes more profitable with experience.

Why? Because the business is about people and processes. A senior contractor has had plenty of experience with both.

- *People*: He knows more people just from the years he has been in business. He also knows which ones to coddle, to chastise, to put an arm around, and so forth to get the most out of them.
- *Processes*: Experienced contractors know what doesn't work. They have certainly tried a lot of good ideas over the years. They simply know what works and what doesn't. Additionally, they don't make the same mistakes that a younger, less-experienced contractor makes. Hence, they have a competitive advantage.

In contrast, the best earning years of most other industries are the ages between 35 and 50 (professional sports excluded). The reason for this early, high compensation is the energy, and the willingness to travel, to take risks, and to make extraordinary things happen. However, profitable construction is based on consistent and correct processes, somewhat like the manufacturing business. The more consistently a person does the correct things, the better the outcome.

To reemphasize, construction contracting consists of two components—people and processes. Older executives do have a deep understanding and experience in handling people and building projects (and they have the scar tissue to prove it!). My conclusion is that contractors' best earning years tend to be in their 50s and 60s.

> Know the "sweet spot" of the (1) right project types, (2) the right geographic areas, and (3) the right client type for your company. Consistently profitable contractors are on the look out for, and actively seek, these attributes. In other words, they help make their own luck.

No Consolidation

The construction industry is an owner/operator business. Efforts to consolidate have shown the power of the small business—you cannot beat an owner who is risking his wealth every day.

Large firms are at a disadvantage. Again, small is big, and the fast eat the slow. This translates into hundreds of thousands of family-owned businesses that will continue to operate as long as another generation is willing and able to take over.

Local

Where can a construction company be started? Anywhere! Construction expertise is needed in all 50 states. It does not need a port facility or wide open spaces to operate. You can start one where you live and that is family-friendly, which is an important consideration these days for all working professionals who want to stay closer to their spouses and children. Local projects mean less travel and more time with your loved ones.

No College Degree Is Needed

Construction people who have worked in the field for several years have the equivalent of a college degree. A majority of construction knowledge is earned while working, not studying. Technically, you learn how to install quality work with your own two hands. College students studying construction don't go to class with their tool belts on. I strongly believe that someone who has owned and operated a construction business for 20 years has a master's degree or maybe even a Ph.D.

As an example, I have a sister who is a horse trainer and who never attended college. Peggy has been working in the equestrian business since she was of age 11. That makes her experience 30+ years. One of her students (and by inference, Peggy) won one of the highest honors in Hunter-Jumper competition. No small feat. Because of this, I insist she has a Ph.D. in Equestrian Management.

No Large Capital Investment Needed

As is legend, some successful construction firms have been started with no money. In this business, beginning capital is not a major obstacle. This is a cash flow and variable cost business. To start a contracting firm, you do not have to float an IPO or have a rich uncle. What you need is an understanding of the economics and construction craft skills.

Shortage of People Wanting to Be in This Profession

Industry economists agree that we still have a shortage of people employed in construction. Conservatively, the number needed is over 100,000. As we have learned in our lifetimes, the demand/supply curve is powerful. A shortage of anything drives the price up. Competent construction professionals' earnings have outstripped general wage increases in other industries. That is job security, as well as wealth building. Ask a computer programmer or an airline pilot about oversupply of people and the effect on wages and opportunity. Your parents may remember the oversupply of engineers in the 1950s. Oversupply is a danger to any professional, but there is no danger to construction people in the foreseeable future.

What other industry has all these attributes? The answer is none, although, the perception persists that our industry does not have much to offer young people. This is not true. Surveys have shown that people in construction do not recommend our industry to their children.

A major association recently queried its members with the following question: "Would you recommend this industry to your son or daughter?" The answer came back as 72 percent "no." (They must not have read the previous pages!)

A survey by a major newspaper recently asked high school seniors to rank a list of 50 professions as to desirability. Do you know where the construction business came in? As number 49, right next to migrant farm worker.

We must stop this perception. Simply put, we should communicate the facts to the interested parties. I challenge each of us to promote our industry. Let the truth be told.

> Interview the client to confirm the bid format, alternates, and other important proposal factors before quantity takeoff begins. This keeps wasted time and frustration to a minimum.

WHAT IS A CONTRACTOR'S BUSINESS?

Defining a contractor's business is a challenging exercise. There are so many different types of contractors and types of work. We are hard-pressed to write a definite explanation without ignoring several segments of the construction industry.

We observe over 100 market sectors in the construction industry. In its construction permit data, F.W. Dodge reports 30-odd categories and those are just the type of projects. Now multiply that by all the different types of contractors. The old CSI classification methodology outlines 16 divisions of work. Each division typically has several construction firm types occupying each of those.

Regardless of the type of work and the type of projects, all contractors must perform the following:

1. **Acquire Work**   This includes the functions of estimating, pricing, bidding, marketing, and selling. If we estimate and price work, but don't win any work, we would be a pricing service.

2. **Build Work**   This includes the functions of project management, field management, material procurement, and labor productivity. Contractors do and love to install work. In this step, payment is made by the client.

3. **Keep Track**   These functions include accounting, financial management, administration, and tax reporting. A majority of contractors don't enjoy this part; however, it is certainly a necessary evil to be in the construction industry.

After completing steps one through three, we repeat the process. See Figure 1-1. The speed of this cycle is where a competitive edge resides. If you are slower than your competition, you have a disadvantage. The faster you are in this cycle, the bigger your competitive edge. It is that simple.

Take time to build takeoff assemblies in your estimating software. This lets simple dimensional takeoffs convert into extended pricing for multiple parts of a job.

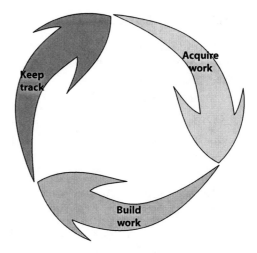

FIGURE 1-1
The business cycle of a construction contractor. The big don't eat the small; the fast kill the slow.

You Have Speed, the Other Guy Doesn't. Who Dies? Not You.

Speed of process gives a competitive edge to any contractor. This is not about working harder every day, but working smarter. Those processes that are faster and just as accurate allow contractors to earn more with less investment. Part of working smart is to address the risk that is wholly evident in the industry. You have to make sure there are processes to keep you covered from the liability that others will surely try to place on you. (There are more lawyers than ever before.)

In this book, you get over 140 of the best practices in the construction industry. Some may not strictly apply to you. However, you can be assured that over 100 will apply. This means, you can find 100 ways to be faster tomorrow in your processes.

As a rule of thumb in a contracting business, you should be turning over your working capital 8 to 12 times a year. As an example, if you have $1,000,000 of working capital, your revenue should be in the range of $8 to $12 million. That is the speed of process.

Read these best practices and take them to heart. They have been researched for more than a decade and their value has been confirmed by dozens of contractors. You will find they are a better approach.

> Give your estimators uninterrupted time for quantity takeoff. This is a tedious exercise. Missing important parts means that the price is less, while the cost is the same to build the project. 0 unit quantity times any unit price is 0. This can be a financial disaster.

Business Trends in Construction

In the 1960s, the name of the game for construction firms was to get it done, deliver the project, and then, at the end of the job, hash out the financial issues with the client. Contractors were comfortable doing this. Clients understood the ethic and appreciated the extra work this involved.

Since that time, owners have slowly changed, but change they have. Clients, mostly owners, view construction firms as a resource to be managed. Owners understand more about the construction process than ever before. They involve themselves deeper in projects. This is the owner's right. However, if the owners manage the details closer, we should expect responsive and reliable partners. If they are not, we should be reasonably expected to hold them accountable.

Another change has occurred for specialty contractors who work for general contractors: the business relationship is different. There are two factors:

1. The desire of managers not to gain field experience
2. The rise of the construction management degree

This has made some prime contractors harder to work with. Let me quickly say that a number of great general contractors in this country understand what I am about to state.

Lack of Field Experience

Most young construction professionals working today do not (and did not) go through the "field." They won't. They don't want to work in the dirty and dangerous environment of a construction project. They would rather be in the office at headquarters. Obviously, you cannot learn how to do construction in an air-conditioned office. This lack of field experience means young construction professionals have less construction knowledge and technical understanding.

More Construction Management Degrees

The other change is the rise in the number of construction management degrees earned. More colleges offer them than ever before and more people have earned them, including this author. They have turned construction into a business. Craftsmanship is now assumed to be the same from contractor to contractor. The contracts are thicker and have more language that protects the owner. The terms "Paid-if-Paid" and "Notify and Proceed" are two examples.

> Review accounting records to confirm or change the unit costs that were bid. Contractors need to bid their actual cost, not what it "should" cost or what we charged years ago.

Because of these two trends, subcontractors now build projects with more paperwork, less coordination, and less leadership than decades ago. We did it better back then.

As stated earlier, the top general contractors are different. They build projects with the help of their subcontractors. They offer leadership and coordination, and they are good business partners. Certainly, they have made it more of a business. These days, being businesslike is imperative, but not to the detriment of important factors, such as craftsmanship.

In practical terms, the construction business is now a tennis match. It is a game. Hit the ball over the net and wait for the return. If there is no return, stop the match and find out why. You cannot continue to serve into an empty court. When you stop the match, you must persuade (or force) the other side to continue to play.

As an example, when you send a request for information, you should expect it to be answered in a timely fashion. If not, you, the contractor, have to address the problem now. To install work without needed clarification is indefensible and there is no clear recourse afterward. It's the same for changed orders, pay requests, changed project conditions, and the like.

Additionally, keeping score has a new meaning. Today, capturing, notifying, and tracking issues on a project are a must. Your primary scoring mechanism is the Critical Path Method (CPM) schedule, but this is augmented by other project documentation. This documentation is the only way you can prove you are right in your claims. *By law, you may be right; however, if you can't prove it, you aren't right.*

The following are items that, if not answered promptly, might be grounds for a contractor to stop work on the entire project or to stop only on the affected part:

1. Monthly draw requests
2. Change order written acknowledgement
3. Request for information (RFI) answers
4. Submittals
5. Product information on owner furnished material
6. Color selections
7. Signed and executed contracts

Each contractor is aware of the problems caused by slow or non-responsive clients. This is just one of the many risks we take, but this is a risk we can control. We can affect this and, therefore, direct the project to a satisfactory end.

In this industry today, every contractor must know an attorney to call. Fortunately or unfortunately, we have no lack of attorneys. Unless you do a tremendous amount of work and are in need of more than construction law, our advice is to find a boutique firm or a small, specialty law firm whose niche is construction. That is, a 1–3 lawyer shop that works with contractors exclusively. This kind of shop won't have to learn about your business on an hourly basis and they should know the other side of attorney's habits and personalities well. This aids in your strategy. Should you litigate or try to settle? Additionally, small legal firms are not rigid about billing and they do treat their fees with you in mind. The last thing they want is bad word of mouth about their expertise or their value.

Contracting has changed from the 1960s to now. That is to be expected. Years ago, the construction business was straightforward; now it is not. Today, business people and lawyers are showing us that leverage is more important than ever. They have put the word "contract" into "contracting." Sadly, construction has evolved into a business, while craftsmanship devolved into a secondary priority.

> The only reason a contractor won't win a good job is lack of qualified leads. Finding many potential clients who have a buying profile means one or more of them will have a profitable job and wants to do business with the contractor. In contrast, having only one qualified lead puts pressure on the contractor not to walk away, even if the price and terms are risky.

CONSTRUCTION ECONOMICS: THE SUPPLY AND DEMAND CURVE OF CONTRACTING

In the study of economics, many models are used to illustrate key concepts. Some of the models were created to explain real-world behavior. One of these practical models, in my opinion, shows the dynamics of the construction industry. The model is the *Supply-Demand Curve*, which is insightful in explaining the business of contracting.

Once understood, the Supply-Demand Curve shows some difficult realities of contracting. It illustrates the problems and opportunities in the industry. That is, how good and bad contracting can be as a market and a profession.

As a concept, the Supply-Demand Curve for construction services shows how both the supply and demand of any industry reacts to a price change. It illustrates how the demand for construction services and the supply of contractors react with a change in the cost of construction. In essence, how clients and contractors behave when the price goes up or down. The Supply-Demand Curve Model can help explain some of the economic issues of the construction industry. First, let's make clear three definitions:

Price Is the Owner's Cost

In other words, when contracting prices are high, we mean that the market sees a high cost to build. When cost is low, then contractors have dropped their bid prices (and, presumably, decreased profit margins). When we use the word "cost," it does not mean the cost of material or labor to the contractor. This use of *cost* means the price of our construction services to the market.

Supply and Demand

Supply means the number of contractors. For the purpose of simplicity, we will keep this discussion contained to this point. However, please understand that the number of contractors drives capacity. Supply is defined as the number of qualified contractors to perform a specific type of work. Hence, a changing number of contractors affects the amount of construction that can be installed.

Demand is the willingness of people to pay the average price quoted by contractors. Clients want construction services at that cost.

We will not discuss current prices, their level, or future pricing movements. What we will discuss is how a price change affects demand and supply.

The purpose of this section is to take a macro or global view of the industry. For business planning, this is an important item. It answers the question: what will I do if demand drops? What is my plan B? Alternatively, how do I take advantage of a price increase, which is an opportunity for more profits?

The supply curve is flatter than the demand curve (see Figure 1-2). That is, the supply or number of contractors does not greatly increase due to an increase in price (profit). Furthermore, it doesn't decrease because of a price drop. People who are contractors will stay in the construction business. They might make their business smaller, but they will still own a construction firm.

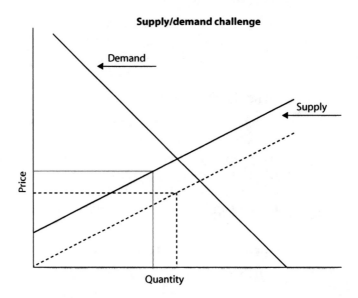

FIGURE 1-2
Supply-Demand Curve for construction services. Demand for services goes up or down quickly (the slope is steep) with a change in cost to clients, but the supply of contractors (the slope is flat) does not change quickly.

> Contractors need to know their breakeven cost (direct cost and overhead) of every bid. They know they can only play the "poker game" of negotiating effectively with this knowledge.

Why?

Unlike real estate, contracting is a long-term skill which entrants cannot learn quickly. Real estate is not an easy profession either, but it is one that is widely understood. If you look at the real estate industry, most of its professionals have owned property or a house before they entered the business.

In construction, the demand curve for services is steep (see Figure 1-3). That is, a change in price greatly affects demand.

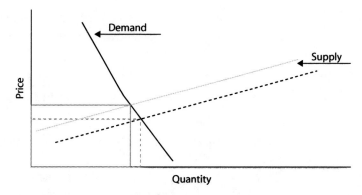

FIGURE 1-3
How supply-demand works in the construction contracting market.

If price goes up, demand lessens. The reason for this is people have options other than building a new office, factory, or home. In the short term, they will stay in the existing facility and, if necessary, renovate what is absolutely essential. If the price goes down, demand rises. The inexpensive metal building (imported) market is an example of this.

You can see how supply-demand works in the construction contracting market. Don't forget, the construction of a home is the largest individual purchase a person will make. Building a new factory or corporate office is a top-three corporate investment. This decision is not an impulse buy. The cost/benefit value is weighed carefully and against other contractors' offerings and against not building at all.

> Use a proven bidding strategy to "leave less money on the table" on each bid. Most bidding strategy is based on quantitative methods. Contractors use the parts of these models that apply to their business and ignore the parts that don't.

Contractor supply (the number of contractors) does not rise or fall markedly due to price (whether low or high profit margins) in the short term.

Construction contracting factors that cause this are as follows:

- Highly technical
- High risk
- Not an attractive professional industry to the general public
- Competent contractors don't grow quickly
- A majority of participants do not desire another field of work

Said another way, the short-term supply of contractors will not increase or decrease greatly. The phrase used by economists is "it is inflexible."

An important point is this: if the supply of contractors does shrink, prices should go up. There is little chance of that. This business breeds people who begin work as employees, and then start their own businesses. It is relatively easy to form a construction company. Also, it is a long-term skill not willfully abandoned.

Furthermore, as you look at the industry from the early 1960s to the present, you can see the following:

- Constant dollar value of construction has stayed relatively flat.
- The number of contractors has increased three-fold.

To state this in a sentence, the number of construction firms has tripled, while the volume of work has stayed the same. The pie has stayed the same size, but more people are at the dinner table. Thus, the following effects:

- Competition has increased.
- Margins have decreased.

All older contractors yearn for yesteryear and with good reason. It was easier to make a profit. Competition was less and margins were stronger.

As a result, ours is the second riskiest business (as a percent of business failures) in the United States and it is becoming more difficult. Right or wrong, this is the situation we find ourselves in.

In contrast, let's look at real estate. Most people have owned real estate and are comfortable with it. However, a majority of people have not owned a construction business and they probably never will. It is not truthful to say most people would be comfortable owning a contracting firm.

The supply curve of realtors is steep. When the market is good, people will jump into the business. The number of real estate licenses in resort towns is approximately 10 percent of the native population (this is more than attorneys).

Reasons for the Number of Realtors

Real estate is a profession that is demanding of a person's time and energy. However, it is very attractive in terms of financial benefit. Many smart people have chosen this as a career. However, it is easier to become a realtor than a qualified contractor.

- The skills demanded are not highly technical. Real estate is a sales business. People can float in and out of the industry.

- The licensing and regulation is less onerous than construction.

- The profits can be superior. Ninety-plus percent of millionaires have real estate in their investment portfolios.

- Speculative money is part of the real estate business. No one will buy a construction firm speculatively.

- The risk is less in real estate. People are only at risk for their time in real estate. The commission is paid if the deal goes through. Typically, an agent doesn't pay out of his or her personal wealth if a "deal" is poorly managed.

The demand curve for real estate is also flat. As you know, the demand doesn't change much due to the price in the short term. There is only one location per parcel and the value of that is subjective. In the foreseeable future, many people believe U.S. real estate is a better value versus other countries'. Thus, domestic and international demand has been steady.

Include people with field experience in bidding projects, planning for next year, and even designing reports and procedures. Contractors make money in the field. All processes, paperwork, and the like reflect this thinking.

In Summary

When prices rise for construction services:

- Demand goes down significantly.
- Supply of contractors is mostly unchanged.

When prices decrease for construction services:

- Demand goes up significantly.
- Supply of contractors is mostly unchanged.

Our conclusion is this: construction service prices will never be driven up wildly, unlike sectors such as gold, Internet stocks, and, in our example, real estate. People have options to building, including delaying, minimizing, or even doing it themselves.

For the contractor, no windfall profits are on the horizon. This means he or she has to be highly focused on the right work and highly disciplined to only accept a profitable price for that work. The market for construction services will never be generous.

Consistently review each site before each bid and use a checklist to make sure all aspects are covered.

THE ATTITUDE OF SUCCESSFUL CONTRACTING: NO WINDFALLS ARE LEFT

We know our business is a tough one, but it has not always been that way. A time or two ago, material prices were stable, people wanted to work, the economy was steady, and legal/political issues were a minor concern.

We all have worked as laborers in the field. Some of us remember how much fun it was. Loud music playing on the radio, our shirts off, and after-work time was ours. What happened? In the decades since, we have moved up in our responsibilities, thus we're having less fun. More to the point, though, the business has changed.

Our industry has increased its demands on us in our quest to make a profit. No windfalls are left. We don't have the luxury of naïve competitors. More information is available to more people. The Internet is one cause and more educational outlets for contractors is another.

Additionally, the clients and suppliers have grown in their sophistication. They know our business deeper and the job of building work better. To them, construction contracting is more transparent and that leaves us with fewer opportunities to make a profit.

Changes in the Last Three Decades

Lets's look at the changes that have occurred in the last 30 years or so. These points are compiled from several groups of contractors at different times. They were asked what has changed in the last three decades. See if you agree:

Rising Age of Workforce   The average age of foremen has risen to the upper 40s. No one is replacing them. As a witness to that fact, the average age of a construction apprentice rose to the upper 20s. Less people want to be in our industry. The young people are seeking other careers first, and then, working in construction. The replacements are not coming. This has made the average age of field managers rise.

Declining Quality of Construction Documents   Designers work under price pressure from owners/developers. This price pressure forces intense cost/labor management. To make a profit, time has to be cut from oversight by experienced design people, thus, plan details and clarity are not there. Frustration by the contractor is the result.

Fast Track Schedules   Years ago, this was a new concept. Now, Fast Track is a standard expectation. We are starting to evolve into "Flash Track" (a fictitious term) schedules. Owner demands are starting to border on the ridiculous.

Material Availability   Between the shortages and the decreased amount of stocked material at suppliers' warehouses, this is another negative change. Material logistics are a greater concern than ever. If you don't have the material, you cannot install it.

Restrictions/Red Tape   Bureaucratic demands on contractors has risen to an all-time high. Permitting, Occupational Safety and Health Administration (OSHA), environmental, and client paperwork requirements make office work more demanding.

Technology   It took this country 30 years to exhaust all the 800 telephone numbers, and then only three more years to take up all the 888 numbers. Wireless, Internet, software, and the like were not standard equipment three decades ago. They are now. We believe if you don't have some technology in your business, you are at a competitive disadvantage.

Design-Build   The advent of Design-Build Construction is a welcome change. More project control by one organization. Contractors are glad to take over, but some liability issues are a concern. Contractors have had to go back to school to learn this new way of contracting. However, with this method, there is only "one captain of the ship."

Risk   With more change and demands by others, contracting has more risk than ever before. Add to that price (profit) pressure and, again, the opportunities are limited. The law of repose or extended construction liability time has not decreased. This still makes all projects built years ago a business risk to construction firms.

Workforce   Fewer American high school graduates and more immigrants work in construction contracting. It is a different workforce and this will not change. The languages and customs of other countries are the norm on the project. We have to gear up and learn to be cosmopolitan.

Competition   Today, the U.S. has three times the number of contractors it had in the 1960s (see Figure 1-4). That speaks volumes

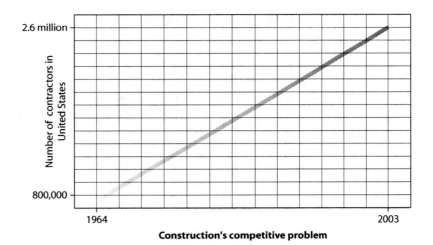

Construction's competitive problem

FIGURE 1-4
The population of contractors has risen to three times the number of the 1960s, while the industry's revenue volume has stayed approximately the same (in constant dollars).

about the lack of profit opportunities. This translates into more bidders on projects and more headhunters for your employees.

We conclude, quite obviously:

The only thing constant in construction is change.

The contracting business will, some day, settle down and become more predictable. We can't say when that is going to happen, but when it does, it will be a welcome change.

The disciplined contractor will survive. The undisciplined contractor will struggle and become extinct. Processes and people make up the construction business. Tighter procedures and careful hiring/ mentoring are the keys to a predictable future.

Take field dimensions using standard templates or worksheets. This minimizes misunderstandings and keeps accuracy high.

Construction Productivity Is Flat

We track several metrics that indicate the general health of our industry, its workforce, and its practices. Our ongoing tracking of productivity has indicated a stagnant state for some time. Our consulting firms review the constant dollar value of construction put in place and divides it by the number of people who work in the industry.

What we have found is unsettling. The overall trend is flat. That is, with all the computer technology, efforts made to improve the industry practices, and other initiatives, we still have not improved the productive rate of work installed each year as an industry. See the U.S. Construction Labor Productivity Chart in Figure 1-5.

Figure 1-5 shows a long-term problem over a number of years. The output of a labor dollar is not rising. You could make the case that we received more from our labor dollar in the 1990s than we do in this decade. The question is this: what can we do about it?

FIGURE 1-5
Labor output for payroll input is slightly declining. (Source: U.S. Department of Labor and U.S. Department of Commerce)

Financially successful contractors don't bid unsuitable work. They use the word "no" or some prefer to use "pass" in telling clients they won't price the work. At a minimum, they discourage clients from unsuitable work. Estimators, craftsmen, project managers, and superintendents are a scarce resource to be conserved and used for profit opportunities.

Supervisory Hours Are Trending in a Downward Direction

Recently released information by the Bureau of Labor Statistics (see Figure 1-6) shows a negative trend for construction supervisors and their crews. In the period from 1979 to 2003, supervisor hours are at almost a 1:1 ratio with a worker's hours. This means supervisors are at more of a leverage point for production. This is certainly good news.

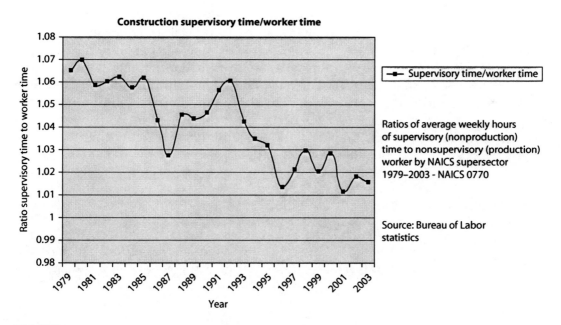

FIGURE 1-6
This downward trend signals a positive trend. Field managers are able to manage larger crews. Both managers and their crews work for the same number of hours, if not slightly more.

Larger Crews

We have lost seasoned foreman due to retirement. Some people call it Too Many Birthdays (TMB). Sadly, we have less-experienced foremen taking over and there are fewer of them. So, the industry has placed inexperienced people in that slot with slightly larger teams. Although this is not a great change downward, in this day of more advanced technology and "smarter" management practices, this is troubling. We would expect it to be even further down as greater efficiencies are implemented by technology, supplier innovations, better construction practices, and client enlightenment about the construction business.

More Paperwork, But Better Systems

Regulators may make the construction business obsolete, but we seem to be keeping it managed. Our paperwork continues to mount for clients and the government; however, our systems have kept up.

Again, this is good news at the field level. In your office, you can beat this trend downward and edge the competition. Clearly, planning processes and technical construction training are the places to start. Each worker must know his duties for the day and how to perform them well. Preferably, the duties should be in written form, so no mistakes occur. Over the long term, each person on a crew must continue to be trained in the ways to do his job better. Remember, the crew will produce the next crew leader and trained crew leaders are critical.

> "Condition" bids by using a standard industry proposal agreement. Attach a schedule of values and rules of acceptance. The bid is based on cost and terms assumptions. Any change to cost and terms changes the bid—thus is subject to negotiaton.

Risk versus Reward

The normal risk versus reward curve is linear and it is positively related. It states that for every risk factor taken, there should be

Risk vs. reward (general business)

FIGURE 1-7
The general business risk/reward makes sense. It gives a premium for risk. The plotting is slightly different for each business, but it is a positive relationship, meaning for every one unit of risk, there is a corresponding unit of reward.

a reward. As Figure 1-7 shows, high-risk propositions that are successfully overcome should pay a handsome sum. We will prove that the risk/reward curves for general business and for the construction business are completely different. In my opinion, this is crucial for all contractors to understand if they are to work smarter.

Strangely, the construction industry is different. For high-risk situations, there is less reward. For lower risk situations, there is more reward. The curve is perpendicular to the normal one, as you see in Figure 1-8.

Why? Two factors determine reward:

1. Percentage of actual net profit
2. Cash-to-cash cycle

Percentage of Actual Net Profit

This is what most people think of when they hear the term return on investment (ROI). We will show it is not the total ROI picture. To figure the percent you know, the percentage of net profit is a straightforward calculation of the simple formula in the box below.

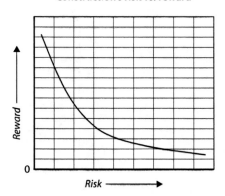

Construction's risk vs. reward

FIGURE 1-8
Construction's risk/reward relationship does not resemble the general business one. It is a negative relationship, meaning for every increasing risk factor, there is a decreasing reward (percentage of profit).

Revenue minus Direct Costs minus Overhead
Divided by
Revenue

Cash-to-Cash Cycle

This is the other critical part of a ROI calculation. There are several ways to think of this in real terms. Here are three explanations.

- We are renting and risking our working capital to the project, and charging interest on the rent and risk (profit). The question is this: how quickly do we receive it back with interest and risk fee (profit)?

- We are waiting for our working capital and our profit to come back to us in each job. If it comes back two times as fast, we have made two times the gross profit on the same percent of profit.

- If we are forced to wait on our cash and have to use a credit line, that immediately decreases our profit due to interest charges. Remember, we are in a single-digit net-profit business.

Combine the two and we have the basis for an ROI calculation. We share with you the actual calculation by showing you one of our standard spreadsheets in Chapter 2. It might surprise you what vastly different outcomes two similar-looking jobs have. It comes down to a great difference of the combination of cash flow and percentage of profit.

Know that the reduction of cost to a contractor from an "Owner Controlled Insurance Program" (and others that are similar) is far less than the Worker's Compensation, general liability, and premium amount. Hidden expenses to construction firms eventually show up in their overhead. Items such as lost premium discounts, agent service, and conflicting goals of light-duty programs, just to name a few. Contractors are careful to calculate the additional cost, which reduces the savings to the project.

High-risk projects typically are larger-dollar volume jobs, so the percentage of net profit bid is lower compared to small projects. The gross profit amount is acceptable due to the project size. Other risk factors are added, such as:

- Project distance from office
- New type of work
- Novice or unknown client
- Unknown building department
- New subcontractor(s)

Several other risk factors could be added to this list.

The net profit can be eroded due to a more difficult business process arising from risk factors such as those in the preceding list.

Larger projects sometimes cause cost overruns in direct cost and overhead due to their size and longer schedule. If your field people are inefficient, the office can spend a lot of time trying to help them.

We want to emphasize that our reward calculation involves only *actual* net profit. This inverse reward curve for construction starts to become clearer when you think about the number of ways and the amounts on which we get "nicked" on the way to finishing a project. For example, are you always paid the full amount of your change orders? Most contractors are not. Sometimes, we are not paid at all and the cost of the extra work comes out of our original budget, thus *decreasing our actual profit* at the end of the job. If the job is larger than we do on average, we bid the job below our standard margins, decreasing the reward compared to our average project size. Size does matter.

High-risk projects as a group tend to have complicated contracts, demanding owners, and unusual construction goals. Conflict between you and others can be high. This ties up your money in retention and/or claims. Low-risk projects tend to be completed quicker, so you realize your profits faster. Put another way, if you complete two like projects instead of one in a given year, your profitability will be much better.

Lower-risk jobs tend to have better gross and net profit margins. They usually are on the small side with clients you know and work you can do with a small crew. Your firm can build the project faster and will be paid in a timely manner. Probably, fewer subcontractors or other prime contractors are involved and the estimated net profit will probably be realized. Your monthly billing will be paid with little delay. The return on the working capital is high.

As a goal, you want to be at the "sweet spot" on the construction risk/reward curve. It is hard to justify being at one of the extremes. Being closer to the middle curve makes sense for most contractors. Handymen are quite happy at one end and international engineering/construction firms at the other. Finding this profitable area is what an older, successful contractor has figured out. For the rest of us, we can utilize a series of statistical analysis tools. This shortcuts years of trial and error. To get to that sweet point earlier in your contracting career, this quantitative method can place you at the right area of the curve.

Give the field manager a copy of the estimator's marked-up bid set of project plans to help speed up understanding of the project details.

Project Risk in Construction

Sometimes a young construction contractor disputes the risk factors that banks, sureties, and others assign to construction projects. He just doesn't believe the risk is there. The confidence the youthful contractor shows is needed if he is to weather all the ups and downs of this business. However, risk in construction is a given. In any town in the United States, you can hear a local story of a bankrupt contractor.

A contractor's risk on a project is caused by two potential events:

1. Unaccepted work by the client
2. Higher than estimated project costs

Most contractor project defaults generate from these two sources. Sureties, banks, and investors know these risks and take conservative financial approaches to manage them.

Unaccepted Work by the Client

Contractors sometimes suffer from a combination of poor craftsmanship or client disputes over work. It leads to unaccepted work, and thus payment is delayed or not made.

Unacceptable Installation   Craftsmanship is what most contractors promise to clients, that the work will be of an acceptable quality and speed. This is clearly a value. Poor quality violates that promise and, if poor quality is the end result, it will lead a client to legal recourse.

Client will not pay for the work   Whether it is changed orders, retention, or a quality issue, the contractor cannot collect his costs, plus overhead, for the installation.

Higher Than Estimated Project Costs

This is the more commonly heard reason for failure. Estimating is where the process starts for a contracting firm. Again, there are subsets to this general heading.

Bad Estimate   Whether this is insufficient quantity takeoff or a mathematical error, the contractor's bid will not cover the costs (direct costs and overhead) to build the job.

Higher Material Costs   Commodity prices skyrocket and the contractor has neither protection from his client contract nor purchase agreements to keep costs within budget.

Poor Labor Management   Labor is most often where a contractor exceeds his budget. This happens most in the labor-intensive trades, such as subcontractors, better known as specialty contractors.

Project Factors Outside the Contractor's Control   This can be a long list if we look at the history of contracting. Weather, latent site conditions, political actions, bankruptcy of subcontractor or client, and so forth. Certainly, these things cannot be prevented, but contingency planning is a step to lessen the impact.

What is the first indication of a contractor who is in financial trouble? It is in cash flow. Decreasing cash flow is the consistent sign among contractor bankruptcies. From the outside, you may see:

1. Outside capital infusion by the shareholders
2. Failure to take early payment discounts
3. Late payments to suppliers, subcontractors, or service providers
4. Lack of bonuses for employees
5. Increased bidding activity and win ratio (to increase cash flow)

Construction is the second riskiest business in the United States and it is easy to see why. People and things seem to conspire against contractors, so construction firms that have longevity are special. Contractors who continue to manage through recessions and booms do so with two incorruptible beliefs: conservative financial habits, and smart and exacting construction methods.

In a nutshell, they don't make many mistakes and, if they do, they certainly have the cash to survive.

> Know the cost of retention and use it as a negotiating point. Industry studies suggest that retention is approximately a 3 percent expense.

We Choose Our Risk Curve

Our *risk curve* is the risk factors that cause us financial harm or reward. Remarkably, the choices we make determine the risk we take.

Contractors are on a risk/reward curve that is much different from the general business as shown in this chapter. There is little similarity of construction to most businesses. Because of its nature, its risk/reward defies some precepts that most other business people hold as fact.

Construction contracting is unlike any other business. It is unique. Take a look at the following list. The combination of factors is found in no other industry.

Our business is:

1. **Craft-driven** It cannot be replicated by machine, only by man. Craftsmen are hard to find and they are our only means of production.

2. **Variable cost-driven** (not fixed cost) You have to make a specific percent of profit with little exception on each job. You don't make money by increasing volume.

3. **Treated as a commodity** Strangely, even though our business lives and dies on the quality of craftsmanship, the customer assumes craftsmanship is a constant. Therefore, they focus on price.

4. **Natural conflict** People expect a minimal price for above-average quality. Add to that time pressure and safety, along with uncontrollable weather, and the inexperienced end user is unhappy.

5. **No road test** Product samples are nonexistent. Naïve customers don't understand what the final product will look like and how long quality takes.

6. **High expectations** The earthmoving and structural work gets naïve end users excited and the detail work afterward makes them frustrated.

7. **All projects are custom** Even though the project may be a cookie cutter, it still is on a different site and at a different time. You cannot be at two places at the same time, hence, the project is custom.

These are risk factors that cause financial harm or reward. Remarkably, the choices we make determine the risk we take.

Our place on the risk/reward curve is of our choice. We choose:

- Large, medium, or small jobs
- Long-duration or short-term projects
- Clients who play fair or not
- Contracts that are onerous or not
- To stick to a niche or not
- To promote managers who are qualified or not
- High-maintenance or low-maintenance crews (see Figure 1-9)

Never accept "Paid–if–Paid" contract terms. To do so is to rely on the credit of the client's client. Your contract is not with that person or organization.

Overhead cost crew comparison

Labor costs	×	×
Crew type	Low maintenance	High maintenance
Overhead dollars needed to manage	Less than average	Higher than average
Behaviors	• Planning • Communicating • Measuring • Feedback • Competing against	• Reacting • Disrespecting • "Painting the target" • Not asking for

FIGURE 1-9
High-maintenance crews increase our overhead cost of construction. Low-maintenance crews do not. If we hire the former, this is one of the risk factors we choose.

Getting on the Right Side of the Risk/Reward Curve in Construction

Risk vs reward is an elemental lesson of business, which states for every increased unit of risk an increased unit of reward should be given. This is a 1:1 ratio. Conversely, if we are taking a minor risk, we cannot expect a large reward.

The construction business is not a minor risk, it is a major one. This is the second riskiest business in terms of percentage of business failures. We certainly should ask for a substantial reward for our efforts.

However, the risk curve in contracting is not similar to the general business risk/reward curve. The risk curve in construction contracting is perpendicular to the normal risk reward curve of general business.

Some of us are on the less risk/high profit side, some of us are on the high risk/low profit side, and some of us are in the middle.

The rewards we are calculating are the returns after the project is complete. This means collected final payments, loss due to claims, unpaid change orders, and other real-world issues.

Common Risk Factors

I have concluded that the construction contracting business is riskier than it has ever been—perhaps the riskiest of all businesses. New risk factors are being added each year. The list below is not complete by any measure, but does illustrate how difficult a business we are in.

1. Longer time—weather, change in financial condition for the owner
2. Unfamiliar governmental agencies
3. Change in laws, material availability, labor availability, supervisor changes
4. Higher than average project size—tighter margins, greater commitment of working capital

Before we start a discussion of risk factors, you need to know that we are assuming the type of work a contractor wants to do and finds interesting has already been decided. From here on, we are focusing on managing the risk factors.

Low-Risk Projects   To review, we know that all construction projects have risk. However, the level of risk, if managed, can produce a better cash-to-cash cycle and a higher actual profit margin:

- Short in duration
- Client who has a history of paying well
- Comfort with designer
- Familiar type of construction
- Contract is standard
- Smaller-than-average job contract size

High-Risk Projects   These factors add to the chance of loss. To be fair, they are of our choice. If we purposely focus on this type of work, we are taking on additional risk:

- Long project duration
- Unknown client or marginal client
- New structure type or architectural design
- Nonstandard contract
- Large job contract size

In the end, once we identify our willingness to take on risk and the type of work we do well, better cash flow and profit margins should follow.

If we choose not to seek the type of business we want, we will be given work we don't want. Our business is managing us instead of us managing the business, which is not an efficient approach to contracting.

To reach the better spot on the curve, you can use a statistical approach. These methods tighten your cost structure and your willingness to take on risk. They are:

1. Focused marketing method
2. Closed project analysis

3. Analysis of estimated versus actual unit costs

4. Job sizing

5. Hit rate analysis

6. Personality profiling (office, field labor, craft, and operator)

7. Bottom-up budgeting

8. Overhead recovery

9. Bid modeling (of competitors and us)

10. Standardization and monitoring of best practices (In other words, everyone executes the work in the same effective way.)

These processes or quantitative methods will drive you to the answer. Notice that marketing is included. The Focused Marketing Method is largely a statistical approach.

In the following chapters, we explain these different processes in some depth. As we stated, the construction contracting business is about people and processes. These are the processes.

The High Cost of Rework

As you can see in Figure 1-10, the cost of installation errors or rework is prohibitive. Review our explanation and see if you agree.

> Monitor the steps completed and to complete on every project. Typically, an electronic means is used to do this, so it is not a paperwork nightmare.

The cost of loss, theft, and mistakes has to be repaid by profit. *Profit* is a function of revenue. This is an illustration of how we must generate a substantial amount of revenue to pay for losses. Some of these losses are easily identified, such as safety, job cost overruns, theft, rework, and so on. Other types of losses are less clear, such as efficiency, morale, lack of paperwork, unrecognized change orders, job site favors, and so forth.

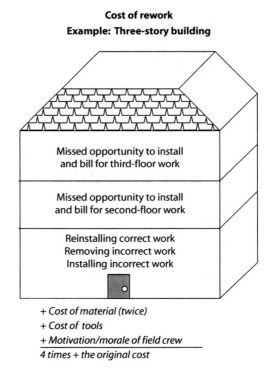

Cost of rework
Example: Three-story building

Missed opportunity to install
and bill for third-floor work

Missed opportunity to install
and bill for second-floor work

Reinstalling correct work
Removing incorrect work
Installing incorrect work

+ Cost of material (twice)
+ Cost of tools
+ Motivation/morale of field crew
4 times + the original cost

FIGURE 1-10
The cost of mistakes is high—three to five times the original cost.

As an example, let's say an employee loses a $1,000 tool. The company's net profit is 3 percent. This means the company has to earn $33,300 of revenue to break even on this loss.

Wouldn't some of your employees act differently if they had this information? And, what if the loss was $10,000? Isn't it time for your construction staff to have some financial education? Figure 1-11 effectively portrays the huge cost that companies must expend to make up for loss.

Know that simplicity means speed. Simple processes are faster processes. The use of sometimes inelegant methods to estimate, build, and financially manage is not objectionable.

The cost of construction mistakes and theft						
Each loss of any kind in construction has to paid for from profit. This is an illustration of how we must generate a substantial						
amount of revenue to pay for losses. Some of these losses are easily identified such as safety, job cost overruns, theft, rework, etc.						
Other types of losses are less clear such as efficiency, morale, lack of paperwork, unrecognized change orders, unrequited job site favors, etc.						
This illustration effectively portrays the huge cost to companies to show the effort that they must expend to make up for loss.						
Mistake/theft	**Profit needed to pay for mistake/theft**	**Revenue needed to pay for mistake/theft**				
$100.00	$100.00	$10,000	**If your company makes 1%**			
$1,000.00	$1,000.00	$100,000	**net profit before tax**			
$10,000.00	$10,000.00	$1,000,000				
$100,000.00	$100,000.00	$10,000,000				
$1,000,000.00	$1,000,000.00	$100,000,000				
$100.00	$100.00	$5,000	**If your company makes 2%**			
$1,000.00	$1,000.00	$50,000	**net profit before tax**			
$10,000.00	$10,000.00	$500,000				
$100,000.00	$100,000.00	$5,000,000				
$1,000,000.00	$1,000,000.00	$50,000,000				
$100.00	$100.00	$3,333	**If your company makes 3%**			
$1,000.00	$1,000.00	$33,330	**net profit before tax**			
$10,000.00	$10,000.00	$333,300				
$100,000.00	$100,000.00	$3,333,000				
$1,000,000.00	$1,000,000.00	$33,330,000				

FIGURE 1-11
This chart is powerful, teaching the problem of loss, theft, rework, and so forth. We equate the dollars of a loss to revenue needed to break even.

The Profitability Challenge

To start this discussion, let's talk about what has occurred over the past four decades. Change is the only constant.

What has changed in the construction business in the last 40 years?

Age of Workforce Has Risen The average age of an apprentice is the upper 20's and the average age of a foreman is the upper 40's.

Quality of Construction Documents   Construction documents have decreased in quality. Architects have to bid the work cheap, and then they don't have money to create the documents well with an experienced designer.

Fast Track Schedules   This is a common term now. Owners continue to be more demanding.

Restrictions/Red Tape   The government continues to control more of our behavior.

Technology/Computers   They have been dizzying in their improvement and applications to construction.

Competition   Since 1964, we have seen an over-300 percent increase in contracting firms, but a steady 400 billion dollar volume of construction work (1996 constant dollars).

Work Ethic   Young people don't believe in the work ethic as strongly as their mothers and fathers.

Design/Build   This area continues to grow steadily as the value of the process is understood by more owners.

Material Availability   Distributors are stocking less and the Great Dragon in China is eating more.

Environmental Concern   We have one more hurdle to jump before we receive our permit.

Perception of Construction as a Career   High school seniors recently surveyed ranked construction lowest, in the bottom 5 percent of all careers (see Figure 1-12).

After winning a bid, do not allow unnecessary subcontractor and vendor interruptions of planning and project review. If subcontractors and suppliers want to know "how they stood," refer them to their unsuccessful competitors. The time after winning a bid is critical for planning, scheduling, and so forth to start the job fast.

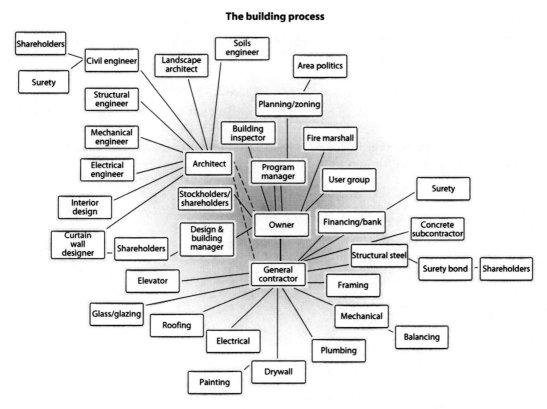

FIGURE 1-12
The construction process is complicated and the team may change often.

Let's discuss one approach to managing these obstacles better than your competitors (and, thus, to making a profit).

Do you enjoy baseball? I do! Have you heard the name Tommy Lasorda? He is the former manager for the Los Angles Dodgers and a well-respected one. He said "When we go to San Francisco and play the Giants, we never focus on anything that is uncontrollable, but we always focus on the controllable, such as looking for pitches we can hit, the pitches we should throw, fielding the ball well, and other fundamentals. We shouldn't worry about the things the other team might do. We can't control their actions, so why waste the time?"

Would you agree this attitude is good for mental health? For less stress? Better for your children? Doesn't it apply to construction contracting? I think it does.

What Are Controllable Obstacles?

I have listed below some typical business issues contractors control or influence. As a contrast, weather is the greatest uncontrollable parameter in construction. The items listed are ones that we should spend time and energy on to manage closely:

- Size of crew
- Training
- Work hours
- Safety behaviors
- Communication
- Planning
- Measuring
- Attitude
- Scheduling
- Saying "no" to a client
- Firing a client
- Many others

These controllable obstacles are the ones we should worry about. We spend our time and energy on these kinds of activities. As we stated, we shouldn't fret over the weather. We are prepared and let it go at that. I heard someone say, "All you can do is all you can do and that is enough." Wise advice for uncontrollable challenges.

We believe the construction process is the problem. Look at the previous list. Wouldn't you agree that most of the items would be better managed with a good, well-defined process we use every time on every job? As you and I have experienced, undefined processes lead to slow execution, rework, and general confusion (see Figure 1-13). Everyone has learned a different way by a trusted mentor. Thus, everyone is approaching the same process differently. No wonder

What can go wrong and its effects

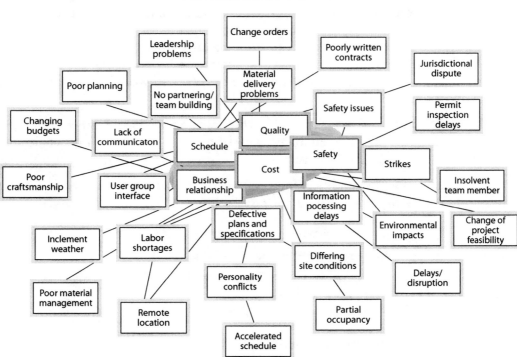

FIGURE 1-13
When things go wrong in construction, many important contracting issues are affected, such as cost, safety, quality, schedule, and business relationships.

the lowest rated productivity metric in my experience is communication. Everyone assumes others learned it the same way.

> Identify long-lead time and critical-path items to make sure they are ordered early and delivered on time. This assures you will not have unnecessary project delays.

The Secret to Profitability

I have been honored to look at dozens of construction companies and work with the finest management consulting firm in the country for five years. Also, I have worked many years in construction contracting. I believe I am qualified to offer an opinion about what makes a profitable construction company. I have seen many companies from their balance sheet, profit and loss statement, and more. The "important few" factors that all contractors cannot neglect are clear to me. To do so would profoundly affect their financial health.

First, let me state that when we make assumptions about any company's profitability, we assume that your company acts legally, morally, and ethically.

Attaining and keeping profitability is a little simpler than you might think. The basis for all profitability is to do the following:

1. Control what you can control
2. Perform the work you are good at
3. Focus on two things: financing and scheduling

This sounds simple, but it works hard.

The Profile of a Profitable Contractor

Many contractors entered the construction business without much capital and without trained people or management expertise. Today, some of these same contractors are leaders in building infrastructure, residences, office buildings, schools, and the like. They are the "go to" people if you want to construct with quality and safety, at a fair price and in a timely fashion. Personally, these same contractors have attained financial security and superior professional reputations.

NASA has quantified many of the qualities needed to be an astronaut. To be accepted in the space program, candidates must have the "right stuff."

What is the "right stuff" to be a successful contractor? We can think of all the successful contractors and it seems they have little in common. Some perform commercial work, others focus on residential, and still others work in the industrial field. One is union, another is not. Some prosper in metropolitan areas and some in a rural location. Some have autocratic styles of management, while others use a participatory style.

To be frank, there is no one consistent profile and I would be wrong to suggest one. However, successful contractors are better than average in one area.

Managing Resources

Construction is a cost-side business. Most contractors cannot receive a premium of even 1 percent over their competitors. They have to price work at the market, while delivering the quality of that same competitor.

This means there is little cushion for inefficiency or mistakes. Added to that is the demand for speed: clients want the finished product faster than last year. Contractors have to rely on (mostly) the same labor pool. Also, they are limited to using the same local material suppliers as everyone else. The contractor has to be excellent at managing resources to meet all these demands. This is the only variable.

What is the key component to being a superior resource manager? It's *information*.

Whether it is labor productivity, cash flow, or return on working capital, timely and correct information is crucial to making the right decisions. Without it, this contractor is no better than the average contractor.

Computers are at the top of the list in gathering, analyzing, and reporting information in a timely manner. There is no dispute about their power.

This does not mean computers are the only tool to use to stay informed. Computers are important tools but, like everything else, they are only as good as the information they produce. In some cases, paper and pencil calculations are far better.

Take, for instance, labor productivity. A contractor is far ahead of the game if his field manager can quickly compare his labor efficiency on his time sheet form, rather than wait for a multipage computer report from the office. (See our best practices listing throughout this book.) We could cite many examples. However, our observation of the industry and our belief is this: excellent contractors are also excellent resource managers, no matter what tools they use.

Labor Is the Greatest Opportunity

Labor is the greatest risk factor and the greatest reward opportunity for construction contractors. Ninety percent of projects that have cost overruns do so because of the labor cost of the job.

Specialty contractors will tell you labor is the single greatest opportunity for them to make or lose the most money. None of the other cost items compare, not material buyout, subcontracting, or equipment utilization. It all starts with labor productivity.

Studies for several years have pointed out that wasted labor time on an average project is over 30 percent. Multiply that percentage by a payroll of $1 million and you will see why labor is such a huge issue.

Analyze an average labor-intensive contractor's profit and loss statement. Calculate a 5 percent increase in labor productivity (the labor cost reduces 5 percent) and the labor savings go directly to the bottom line. Conversely, decrease the labor productivity, and the labor costs increase. You might break even or worse. This is either an opportunity or a problem, depending on how you look at it.

Both specialty and general contractors benefit from a focus on labor. The reason is obvious for specialty contractors: a large part of their costs for any project is dedicated to it. General contractors benefit because, with good labor-management practices, specialty contractors are more flexible in their approach and pricing with general contractors who coordinate well. As you might expect, that same contractor is not as flexible to those clients who do not run organized projects. It is purely a business decision about potential gain or loss.

As an example, general contractors sometimes are given two prices for the same job. One price is given if John (a great coordinator) is the superintendent. The other price is given if Jerry (a poor coordinator) is the superintendent. This sounds logical if you are a specialty contractor.

John does a great job of organizing the job site and keeps people productive. The wasted time on his jobs is probably much lower than 30 percent. On the other hand, Jerry is a good superintendent, but he views his job as being a pusher, not a coordinator. Hence, the subcontractors start, stop, get spread out, and generally become frustrated. Jerry's wasted time approaches 40 percent.

- **Productive Time** is when people are installing work right the first time.
- **Support Time** is time spent gathering information, offloading material, laying out work, and the like.
- **Wasted Time** is neither productive nor support time. It is rework, waiting, smoking and joking, redundant work, and so forth.

The amount of these kinds of time is consistent throughout construction. Figure 1-14 shows averages found in several studies.

Obviously, above-average contractors have more productive time and less wasted time. The business of contracting is fraught with myriad problems, as noted earlier. This is the reason these numbers are what they are. Construction has many stops and starts, probably more than ever before.

For a highly productive job site, there are vastly different financial outcomes. When wasted time is below the 30 percent level, the saved labor dollars go directly to the bottom line.

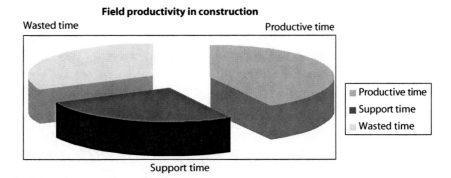

FIGURE 1-14
Productive time is approximately 42 percent, support time is approximately 26 percent, and wasted time is approximately 32 percent.

When bidding organized versus unorganized clients, we should propose different amounts for the same work. The bids reflect the monetary differences of labor productivity expected. This is both logical and rational.

Keep a keen eye on coordinating labor. The better your skill, the more opportunities and financial success will come your way. The benefit is there for both specialty and general contractors. The benefit is obvious for the specialty contractor, who reaps profits and reduces his stress level. For the general contractor, it is simply that your subcontractors can help you in many ways, including competitive pricing and labor availability. As previously said, the quality of a general contractor is largely determined by the subcontractors he works with.

> Aggressively negotiate with your subcontractors and suppliers, but maintain a positive relationship at all times. You may need their help at a moment's notice.

Productivity Improvement

We and our staffs are working hard enough to produce quality projects at a profit. We are competing in a changing market place; it is sometimes fair and sometimes unfair. Furthermore, we have sent our lazy employees (ex-employees) over to the competition. So, how can we improve? How can we make the same profits we did years ago?

Working harder is not the answer. We are doing that and we have the high blood pressure to prove it. Working smarter is the only alternative.

Where do we start? How do we make our staff start to think as we do? There is no easy answer, but there are particular directions you should take and certain milestones you should achieve along the way.

Before we start, let me say this: my observation is that contracting is about people and processes. Good contractors have good people and well-defined, thoughtful processes. Improved people and processes do improve results.

From our studies, a successful construction project has two elements:

- It meets or beats its schedule
- It meets or beats its budget

Quality, of course, is what is satisfactory to the client or what exceeds their expectations.

If you are to consistently win on the job site, senior executives must question and prod people to envision beating the budget (not just *meeting* it). You want to have an attitude of achieving that will most often give the contractor some extra profits and, at a minimum, assure the budget and schedule are met.

You can do this in four practical ways:

First, educate your people.   Show them productivity statistics in the United States. Illustrate how lost time is such a large part of the typical crew day. This is "velvet hand" time. Show them and ask them, don't tell them. Getting their emotional involvement is crucial.

Second, focus your people on the controllable.   This is planning, schedule, buyout, and so forth—not the uncontrollable events, weather, changed conditions, and so forth. Explain that this is where the greatest lasting improvement can be made. You never win consistently against uncontrollable factors, such as weather.

Third, define the major business processes.   These are the processes that most affect the schedule and budget. Map them out and make them clear to all. (See Figure 1-15.)

> Limited time means contracting processes have to be fast and accurate. Today, working smarter, not harder, is a must.

Fourth, follow the productivity improvement cycle.   This applies to getting work, doing work, and keeping score. Improving your productivity is expressed in four steps, and then repeated:

1. **Planning** scheduling the plan and budget.
2. **Communicating** the plan, schedule, and budget.

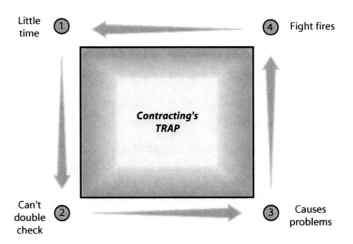

FIGURE 1-15
Limited time means contracting processes have to be fast and accurate. Working smarter, not harder is a must.

3. **Measuring** against the plan, schedule, and budget.

4. **Feedback** performance and adjust the plan, schedule, and budget.

These four steps will help a contractor achieve a lower installed cost with less stress. Once your people have experienced some success, they will own the process emotionally.

> Use a formal pre-job meeting to carefully plan and communicate the project estimate, plan details, and other important factors. The field manager is included in these meetings.

An Important Note to Senior Executives
View the process as one likened to manufacturing: it should be *steady and repeated*. If you experience an upset, go back to your process. If you start having success, then celebrate, but go back to executing those same steps.

Inject your personality in the process and keep it going. Without your involvement, your people will stumble. This is not a management challenge; it is a leadership challenge.

Higher productivity in construction is based on discipline. This is the same efficient process performed over and over again, with attention to detail. Serious contractors do not tire of this.

We cannot ignore the changing of the industry. One of the marked changes is improved productivity. One sector of the contracting market is up 70 percent in the last 10 years. Others are certain to follow. Productivity improvement is not just a practical issue, it's a strategic issue.

> Make sure the field manager meets the client's field manager before mobilization to understand the client's expectations and see if they will be unreasonably demanding. If so, the contractor can get involved personally.

Business Planning

Planning is critical to a construction contractor, but that's no surprise to you. The importance of planning has been stated by many people in many ways as one of the key activities to assure business success. I cannot state it any differently. I agree. Additionally, I believe you are not planning if you make up your plan as you go.

For our purposes, let us clearly outline some of the best ways to achieve planning. Planning must occur at two different levels:

1. **Business** This is the long-term view of how to start and keep your business strong. Once created, your business will need to be updated to reflect changes in the market, industry, client base, and so forth. To keep your business the same invites the fate of the dinosaurs.

2. **Project** This is specific to a construction project, and it addresses the who, what, where, when, how, and why of the job. The project is born on the day of the successful bid and it ends sometime after the project is completed.

In the following, you will find our basic business planning process. We'll address project-level planning in Chapter 3.

A business plan is a contractor's road map at the beginning of his firm's journey. The business plan is similar to a pre-job plan. Both documents are essential in keeping wasted time and adverse situations to a minimum. The reason for planning is simple: it is foolish to make up your process as you go. **In other words, if you don't plan, you don't have a business; you have a job**.

Business planning is not an exciting event. Contractors want to do something now. They are action-based people who like to see something physically built every day. As we said, a business plan is similar to a pre-job plan. However, pre-job planning is energizing because there is a new project to build.

Business planning does not make your heart quiver with excitement. Because we don't have a project to build it becomes an abstract, dull exercise, so we have to sit quietly and think through the details of our new business.

Construction people are visually attuned. We love to see physical progress. A business plan is mostly an invisible thing. It is emotionally hard for a contractor to put one together.

Once we get past the pain of collecting information from others, doing some reading, and writing drafts of our plan, our attention should narrow down the real reasons for this document. Here are the areas of benefit (and risk) that a plan should focus on:

1. **Labor Management and/or Cost Management** Because the firms that have cash stay in business, this is a top priority. A majority of projects that run over on cost do so because of labor. For a general contractor, it is also general conditions (or time). You have to know at the earliest possible moment that you have a "problem" job on your hands.

2. **Cash Flow** This is one of the leading indicators for financial success or failure in construction. How will you keep from using your working capital instead of the client's capital?

Is it by choosing the right clients? Is it by never missing a billing, especially a first one? Is it by creating an aggressive schedule of values? Yes, it is all these and more. See Chapter 4.

3. **Overhead and Profit Margin** These percentages determine whether your business will have money to invest, grow, or harvest. What is the cost of doing business (all costs)? How do you change these margins to reflect a poor-paying and a well-paying client? What is your target ROI for your working capital use and risk? Personal financial considerations should be addressed, such as how much do you need to live on? What will you do with your company's net profits?

4. **Revenue** This is the bane of all contractors. We either have too much work or too little. Too much and we can lose intensity on the profitable details of the business. This will age us far beyond our years. Too little and we have less dollars to pay ourselves and make necessary investments in the business of contracting. We can never get it perfectly tuned, however, we can minimize the wild swings. If you accomplish this, you will consistently give proper attention to operations and greater customer satisfaction. This is a step ahead of the average construction company.

5. **Your Market** What is the perfect job? What is the worst project for you? It is worth the time to answer these questions: what type of work, what geography, and what type of customer? To figure this out might take some time. But, once you are in the sweet spot, you will be nicely rewarded. A niche that has volume is never a bad place to be.

6. **Tools/Equipment Needed** Planning asset purchases is the best practice. Impulsive buys have left several contractors with a "dead" asset. Software is one of the greatest culprits. Plan to select office and field tools, especially high-end technology. Today, the right technology enables you to hire fewer people, which isn't a bad trade-off. Every one of your competitors is using tools and equipment today that make their process faster, while keeping their head count down. This is a reality.

7. **Personnel**   These are the people who you need to bid, build, and administer the work. Hire people who are strong where you are weak. Define the process of how you will find and hire people who won't unpleasantly surprise you. More analysis tools of human behavior are available now than ever before. Review what is available and carefully think about the people issue. This is one-half of your business.

8. **Office Location**   Travel greatly affects the number of job visits a construction supervisor can make. Safety managers, project managers, and executives need to keep a watchful eye on all projects. This is sometimes a moot point, especially if you are small. Most smaller contractors work from their homes. If you do lease an office, consider where your type of construction is. Think about the location of trusted suppliers, service providers, and clients. Again, your physical presence has an impact and the frequency of your presence lessens with distance.

9. **Administration**   Paperwork can be the death of you and your business in time, importance, and stress. Try to collect all the forms, checklists, and other time-saving tools you can. These things help keep you effective and productive. Map out how paperwork will be handled. Just as a pilot never takes off without reviewing his checklist and having a plan B, you should never allow administration of your new company to be undefined. It can be fatal. Any software that eases this demand may make sense for the long haul.

This is a basic treatment of business planning for a construction contractor. It is complicated, and it does take time and energy. Be smart, start early. Think through the business you envision. Do this and keep your emotions as distant as you can. Objective thinking makes your business plan less prone to changes later.

Remember, this plan is never final. It is a living thing. A contractor should revisit the plan every year. Review it, and then contemplate it in light of lessons learned from last year and potential opportunities for next year. Some parts must be visited anyway—areas such as budgeting, dual overhead rates, technology, and targeted markets. These, by their nature, are never stagnant. These parts will benefit from your attention. You have to work *on* the business as well as *in* the business if you are to build serious personal wealth.

If I had to choose one thing to focus on above all others, I would say be brutally honest in the creation of your plan. The construction industry is not a business for hope, wishes, or guesses. The construction business deals in the real world and enforces reality severely.

> Use scope checklists and standard contracts/purchase orders to minimize oversights, as well as missed terms and conditions.

Planning—Market Research

A healthy construction industry suggests that contractors are making profits. Construction health can be gauged by trends in key factors of the supply and demand for the industry's products and services.

If the economy is growing, then construction should be growing. Construction worker employment should be increasing and unemployment should be declining. Housing starts and building permits should be rising at the front end with utility hookups and certificates of occupancy increasing at the backend.

These kinds of statistics, especially construction payrolls, starts, permits, hookups, and certificates of occupancy are monitored closely by, and reported frequently in, most state and local news media. Construction reporting services and government agencies also monitor these statistics.

A strong market is exciting, but the number of contractors chasing that work is the missing piece. Counting potential competitors is literally as easy as downloading business licenses, reading the Yellow Pages, or talking with the local contractors' association(s).

Not only the size of the market and the number of competitors determine whether you should enter it. Consider these questions:

1. Do you have the skills to build this work? If you don't and you still want to compete in this market, start with small projects and learn your way.

2. What is the growth of the market? It is easier to skim off the top of growth than take away a job from an established competitor in an existing, no-growth market.

3. What is your cost structure? Does it fit with the service demands of clients? Is the competitor's cost structure the same? Are they working out of their truck?

4. Do you have existing clients who you know and who trust you? Trust takes a long time to build. Without trust, clients use price as their primary decision-maker. Don't underestimate the importance of trust in getting profitable work.

> Understand the billing and payment process of the client fully. Use the first pay request as an indicator of the client's willingness and ability to pay.

Documenting Your Processes

Without a doubt, the lack of documented processes is the greatest shortcoming of construction companies. Many leaders learned how to build work and make money by experience. Some of this was bad and some of it was good, but all of it is valuable. As a contractor hires others, the communication starts breaking down immediately. There is no time for long training sessions. Work has to be built and time is of the essence. Writing down the major business processes is the only way to communicate well with employees without long telephone conversations.

All construction professionals want to do a great job. Their goals are to make more money, garner a promotion, earn the respect of their peers, be the "go to" person, and generally enjoy a better work environment. Your employees are no different.

However, if this was all that mattered to make profits, most construction contractors would be better off than they are now. We would just have to hire hard-working and well-intentioned employees. Certainly, a majority of construction supervisors give the necessary effort working hard every week, and they want to earn a raise, more time off, and so forth.

So, why does this business work us so hard (late nights, early mornings, and a lot of stress)? Why is it so frustrating?

The answer: it is the process. Casual and assumed processes are in every construction company. That is, there is no clear or written set of procedures. What is to be performed and what behaviors are expected are not obvious. Only through months of working with a company, can you understand all the major processes. Subsequently, many processes are left unstated and, thus, are not communicated (see Figure 1-16).

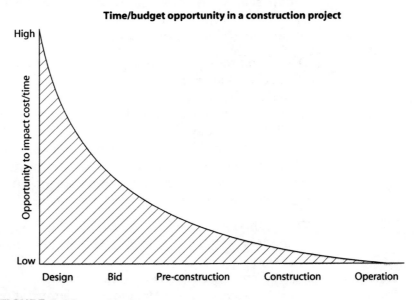

FIGURE 1-16
This identifies a great opportunity for all construction projects. Proactive processes reward contractors with more speed and cost savings.

Some companies have no single defined process and no standard procedures manual. If equipment has a reference book, why shouldn't business processes have one?

Furthermore, if all your processes are undocumented, then your profits are dependent on a strong personality, namely the owner. Clearly, a risk if he or she should falter. Don't leave your company's future in this situation.

Productivity studies place lost labor time at 30+ percent on construction projects. Most of this wasted time is due to inefficient and absent management practices. In a home office, lost time is said to be at an even higher level. In both places, consistent procedures provide efficient and profitable operations.

Smart contractors define and document their major processes. They typically have superior processes to start with, but they don't leave them to chance. Their processes are written down and are a basis for managing the business. This leads to better training for new hires, as well as better monitoring and measuring of performance overall. Because the processes are documented, there is no mystery.

Documenting a company's procedures provides significant benefits. A manual gives supervisory personnel a definitive guide for running a department and/or projects the way management wants them run. A manual also pulls together the cumulative experience of all the company's key managers, so future projects and managers benefit. This boosts competence and profitability, and it allows top management to avoid the trial-and-error method of instructing managers. This is especially important as you hire and initially watch over a new staff member. See Figure 1-17.

The methodology, which we call Interactive Mapping and Planning Methodology (IMPM), is the best practice in construction contracting in two areas:

- Business Process Mapping, as Figure 1-17 shows, for administration.
- Project Schedule Creation (see Interactive CPM in Chapter 3)

ABC contracting				
President	Set budgets, overhead allocation for departments with accounting manager	Determine target markets with company personnel	Set job sizing formula	
Project manager	Search for qualified subcontractors/update list			
Foreman				
Estimator	Download cost/productivity information from accounting and analyze - update labor rates			
Estimating group				
Purchasing manager	Update suppliers & database	Take inventory at yard		
Accounting manager	Set budgets, overhead allocation for departments with president	Review billings for client, change orders, retainage, job cost	Match cash receipts, reconcile billing, & apartment /diem expenses	Creates A/R borrowing balance report

FIGURE 1-17
This is an example of Interactive Mapping and Planning Methodology (IMPM), which shows part of an administration process. It clearly shows responsibility (via rows) and sequence (left to right).

The process map is organized as follows:

1. Left to right for time. The left side is the start of the process with subsequent step-stretching to the right.

2. Swim lanes. Each row is the swim lane of responsibility for the designated person, such as the accountant or project manager.

Many times in group settings, we use sticky notes and paste them on a wall. This method enables everyone to plainly see what steps we are discussing, changing, and so forth. These paper notes can be rearranged on the wall as different ideas are floated.

When creating a schedule, you may use this process in the same way, although it is a bit more complicated. (See Chapter 3.)

The Case for a Contracting Business Manual

A good company process manual demonstrates to employees that management is concerned about doing a consistent job. In addition, it represents a mechanism for internal communication. This communication is structured through the forms, process maps, and written details contained. Specific individual responsibilities become more defined. Then, it is easier to develop consistent practices among the people involved.

In addition to benefiting tenured personnel, the manual can serve as a training tool for new employees. With a company process manual in place, new employees can learn the company's approach to construction step by step. They receive a formal introduction to the company's philosophies, and they learn the specific work steps and concerns associated with each construction phase.

In another sense, the manual serves as a reference for all personnel: it is a minimum standard. The manual addresses specific concerns and outlines consistent, proven methods for dealing with common problems and issues.

A procedure manual is also an impressive document to present to external parties. Most surety agents, for example, would be comforted to know that a company has developed a uniform means of addressing production issues and procedures. They know a manual that defines the structures of an organization, and outlines an approach for dealing with each job phase, demonstrates business expertise. A manual also can be an important marketing tool because it can impress prospective clients and offer a structured way to introduce them to both the construction process and the company's approach to it. See Figure 1-18.

Perhaps the greatest benefit of creating a business process manual is the self-examination necessary to produce it. Current practices and documentation must be thoroughly analyzed, and this process inevitably uncovers some bottlenecks and inefficiencies. The structure of the company is defined, while roles and responsibilities within the company are clarified.

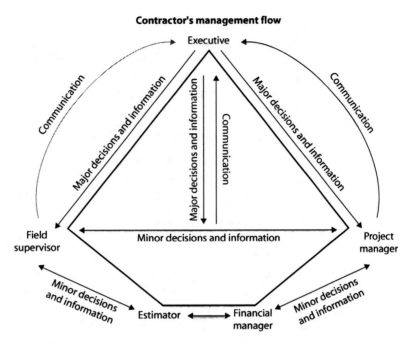

Contractor's management flow

FIGURE 1-18
A procedure manual specifically defines how to communicate major decisions and information to others, so they may make minor decisions.

Some contractors have found that the use of a virtual management manual works as well, if not better, than a paper procedure manual. Computers are fast distributors and efficient organizers of information. Typically, this is done on a company's server and is used to instruct project managers, operations managers, superintendents, and the like to take the same thoughtful steps to plan and control the project. Additionally, they serve as tools for executives to monitor these steps and their timely completion.

There is a correlation between careful, documented management and profitability. It is more anecdotal, but enough subjective evidence exists to conclude the correlation.

Don't leave your processes undocumented. Commit them to writing. You should have a "standard of care" in your business. This can keep quality, efficiency, and cost consistent from project to project and department to department. More predictability occurs from year to year. Your company's unique process manual makes managing less strenuous and it provides senior executives more time for leadership, rather than handholding and firefighting.

Go Past Documentation—Now Improve Your Processes

The construction industry demands that contractors constantly improve. If a contractor chooses not to, he is penalized with less work and more headaches to build that work.

Any improvement program is based on change. That is, where we are now is what we would like to leave behind. Said another way, we currently are at Point *A* and we would like to go to Point *B*. Our current productivity level is Point *A*. This is what we expect, this is what we know, and it is dependable. Some people in our organization have this attitude: this is all that is possible, and there is no great leap we can make without extra people, expensive technology, or outsourcing (at a cost). They feel there are no real opportunities to make things run faster with the same amount of accuracy.

Part of any change in an organization is in the change of attitudes. That people believe there is a better way. How do we change those vital attitudes? Do we have senior management's commitment to accept it? Do we give people a personal shock to make them want to change, such as layoffs or a threat to take away part of their trappings? Or, do we give them the information to make an informed decision about the potential time saved through a process?

Most good and loyal employees just need the endorsement of the construction company owner(s) that the change is needed and the owner(s) will follow through. Giving the employees information about the program is the missing link.

Don't be mistaken, in any change, some people will lag behind. Those people are known as "late adopters." They will have to be reminded. In some cases, saboteurs will emerge and will have to be dealt with strongly. Again, there will always be a need for senior management to emphasize the importance of any initiative, especially one that directly addresses work habits. See Figure 1-19.

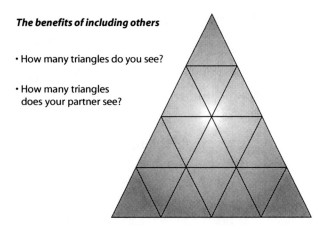

The benefits of including others

• How many triangles do you see?

• How many triangles
  does your partner see?

FIGURE 1-19
Asking others their opinion always leads to better insights. Ask others why they see more or less than you and learn.

> Build a smaller, less-risky job with an unknown client first. This enables you to experience the pay habits, organizational ability, and general capability without a large risk.

As you go through the process of this change, you will have to overcome what I call *habit momentum*, or people doing the things they have always done. This is inherent in all organizations. In some cases, people have learned their particular way of doing things from a respected person many years ago. They don't think there is another way. In other cases, people would rather not go through the stress of changing their habits and take the chance of making a mistake.

These habits have solid reasons why people do them. They are real to each person and not worth the risk of change. Senior management must directly confront how this will be overcome. If they don't, the change will not happen. In some cases, it will occur, but it will not be permanent. Thought has to be given to how this resistance will be overcome.

We have found that a substantial part of implementing change is educating each person. The education has to happen first. To do so, present overall facts that give the person a picture of what is wrong, such as error rates, lost time, and dollars spent.

For people to trust the proposed change, two items have to be established:

1. Predictability
2. Capability

In any organization, people want to know what to expect. They want predictability. In the old psychological contract still in force at some contracting firms is a subtle agreement that people trade loyalty and years of service for predictability. In the wild swings of the construction market and in the era of downsizing, we have seen less loyalty than ever before. The old contract has been broken.

Capability is that emotion that states "we can change this and we will see it through." Said another way, this is not the flavor of the month and senior management is serious about implementing this.

An old parable says that trust is hardest to establish when you need it most. Trust should already exist between a contractor and his employees. In the contracting profession that is almost a proverb.

Think about these questions. Do you know people in our business who have purposely not paid a subcontractor or supplier without cause (or have reduced the final payment)? Or people who have paid people straight time on their overtime hours? What about those who fight even a legitimate worker's compensation claim? The question is this: how much do the employees of these companies trust their owners? How much would you trust them? Would you willingly help with change if your boss acted like the ones in question?

The price of change is high, but the payoff can be enormous. Contractors who are faster with their processes with the same amount of quality and safety have a competitive edge. All contractors are faster now than ever before. Contracting is a cash-flow and variable-cost business. Financial success partly relies on speed, but

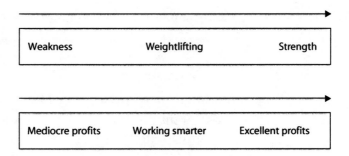

FIGURE 1-20
The process is the secret to a better performance. Personally, or in the contracting business, performing the necessary steps consistently gives a brighter future.

a disciplined process approach wins every time over talent acting inconsistently. See Figure 1-20.

Complete buy out (subcontractors and suppliers) of major cost items within the first 25 percent of project time. After that, aggressively manage delivery times and site logistics.

Measurement Is Not an Opinion

All contractors measure their business. Some use accounting software, while others use a paper-based method. Whatever method, the intent is clear: to identify areas of loss quickly and act to prevent further loss. Whether it is financial, schedule, safety, or quality, measuring helps contractors see facts clearly.

Why should you measure?

- Gets people focused
- Motivates employees
- Monitors improvement and confirms success
- Improves performance

What happens when you rely completely on downstream reports?

- Budget variances
- Experience survey
- Estimated versus actual schedule milestones
- Gross profit per man-hour or man-week (this is a powerful downstream measure)
- Overtime

We are viewing history and we cannot fix what is past. Contractors across the country find upstream measures give a proactive view of the project.

Here is a sampling of proactive measures that give the contractors more comfort.

- Business process steps
- Weekly planning
- Schedule precursors
- Resource forecasting

How should you proceed?

1. Determine what measurements will be used to track improvement (six or less).
2. Baseline the measurements—what is your standard performance?
3. Chart the progress—create a chart and post it.
4. Share the results or the score.
5. Track trends in performance.

You make more money on the cost side of the project than on the sales side.

Clients won't give us great prices, no matter what our niche. Why? Because three times the number of contractors are chasing the same amount of volume (in constant dollar terms) in this country. When you do discover a niche and sell some work at a premium, it isn't long before another company or an ex-employee starts competing against you.

They, many times, use a lower price in their sales pitch and there goes the market. You can see several examples in all 16 divisions of contracting. It doesn't take long for others to figure out what you are doing and replicate it.

We are in a service business and the service cannot be patented. How you do it cannot be protected. Hence, the barrier for others to compete is low, if not nonexistent.

So, except for the first month(s) of any new service offering, the market price will be the client's basis for evaluating bids. What opportunity does that leave you with? On the direct cost side, if you keep your efficiencies better than your competition, you'll win. The market doesn't allow for a 50 percent higher price—you will have to sell at or near the market. Remember the supply-demand curve for contractors, but no curve regulates how efficient you are. Only you can do that.

Every competitor has the same obstacles to building work as you do. Sometimes this is unfair, but if you are better at overcoming these obstacles, then no one can beat you. A low-cost producer has many options and, thus, power in the market.

In real estate, the old saying goes, "you make money on the buy, not the sale." In other words, you make money on buying the property, rather than selling it. If you buy it right, such as in a distress sale, in *lis pendens* or foreclosure proceedings, you buy it at a discount. When you sell it later at the market price, you make the most margin on the discounted price at which you bought it.

This type of analogy is the same for construction. The acquisition or installed cost makes or breaks a project because there are no windfalls in construction.

> Put your best people on the riskiest job, regardless of their availability. This gives you the best chance to make profits and stems the chance of a large loss.

What Approach Works?

Given the previous information, it is clear that contractors don't enjoy many competitive edges. We are certainly at the mercy of the government, the client, and uncontrollable events. We don't need a defense, we need an offense. Contractors need a way to earn more with less risk. One of the most powerful ways to do that is to find and establish yourself in a *niche*, a specialized area with less competition and, thus, more profit opportunity.

This is not a new idea. Older contractors have known this for years. They first thought of it when a young competitor bid low and worked for wages. They knew they couldn't compete and they shouldn't because the risk is too great. So, they had to find a market(s) with less competition.

Niches are everywhere. They aren't just work types (low voltage or hospitals), but also the other two critical factors to finding good work: geography and client type. See our Focused Marketing approach in Chapter 2.

Let's look at geography. There are locations, such as the local city or county, where the building official may be tough on codes. This keeps out some competition. Your challenge is to know what these inspectors want, so you can deliver that to them.

Client types can be multinational corporations, regional developers, doctors, and the like. Again, they are a client type that others might shy away from. Engineers have a detailed approach to everything. Another client type might be Spanish-speaking immigrants. If you can deliver what they want (and charge them a little more), you have established a niche for yourself.

You don't start your business one day and go into a niche. In general, this is a two-step process. First, do the things you know, whatever that is. It may be a humble beginning, but you are establishing yourself as a trustworthy and competent person. Clients are looking for you. The only requirement is that you can pay your bills. Money in the bank keeps a company in business. When you are young, you don't know as much, which is logical. What you can do when you are young is simpler than when you are older, such as houses with four corners versus high-rise apartment buildings. Later in our careers, we learn enough and start building custom homes, that is, houses with double-digit corners. Whatever your course, there is no shame in building work and making money at the same time.

One last word of advice. When you do occupy a solid niche, profits will be good and life might also be good. As a client from California said, "Make money alone and in the dark." In other words, don't tell others where the ducks are flying. Otherwise, you will find someone occupying your favorite duck blind.

> Focus on starting out well-organized and coordinated in the first 25 percent of the project. Contractors know this is the biggest opportunity to cut time and save money during construction.

Work Smart Management Techniques

Any $99 management course can tell you there are several steps for better utilization of your people and resources. They are simple, effective, and a little tedious for those of us who are busy. However, we must make time to manage the business. As many others have said, "Take a break every little while and sharpen the saw. You will cut more trees."

The Steps to Increase Utilization

Small improvements over a long period of time yield significant results. All professionals do well when they compete against themselves. Review the list below and see what you could do to make your time management skills better.

- Plan your week.
- Keep track of that plan.

- Keep track of interruptions to your plan for that week.
- Look at the major causes for not making your plan and for interruptions.
- Take actions to minimize or eliminate those leading causes. In other words, take control of the controllables.
- Later, once the major causes are addressed, look at the minor causes and address them.
- Repeat the previous steps periodically. You never finish. This process is iterative.

Where does the time go? Twenty-four hours is never enough time. However, there are those contractors who do a great job in managing what limited time they have.

As a general statement, resource management is about the following:

- Planning
- Measuring
- Communicating
- Feedback

and this is the essence of self- and business improvement.

Contractors do have interruptions and they can never eliminate them. Controlling what time you do have and making sure you are good about that time is what is important.

> Make sure the estimator and/or salesperson tells the field supervisor and project manager all their bid day promises before mobilization.

Work Smart Time Tactics

One List   Use one list of to-do items in a dedicated place. Many contractors use day books. They are popular because they have daily pages on which contractors can list items, take notes, and refer to often. Keeping Post-it notes on walls, mirrors, and dashboards may work, but keep the same information in a dedicated book. You can carry it with you and refer to it more often.

Planning Time   Make your day's plan at the same time every day, preferably the first thing in the morning before the phone rings and you hit the job site. Look at the previous day's plan, roll over those to-dos not accomplished, and write down the day's new items. Studies have shown a minimum of a 4 to 1 return on planning time. This pays off.

Best Work Time   Know yourself and your optimum work time. Don't fight it. If you are more focused when you work late at night or early in the morning, find a way to take advantage of it. Make your schedule fit that best performing time. The result will be more work done with a higher level of detail. As an aside, this translates into less rework, thus time saved.

Think Before   As you rush to accomplish your list, you sometimes don't plan the little things, such as a phone call. Generally, rushing leads to mistakes. Specifically, it leads to miscommunication. Take time before each phone call to plan what you will say and how you will say it. Confusion will be reduced on the other end.

Be Proactive   Studies of time in the construction industry conclude that, at a minimum, one man-hour of pre-job planning saves four man-hours later. The field and the office both benefit from looking at problems early, making decisions before they need to be made, and so forth. Proactive thinking has other benefits. Less emergencies means reduced stress and frustration.

Be Sensitive to Your Compliance   If you are constantly missing deadlines and commitments, this is a signal that you are scheduling too much to accomplish. This habit has many hazards, including your health and credibility. Be sensitive to this and schedule to 80 percent of your capacity. You can always do more if you meet your schedule.

Know Yourself   We suggest you to take a Time Mastery Assessment, which is a personality profile that analyzes your approach to time. It is simple and takes about 10 minutes to complete. We have them in English and Spanish. Our Internet link for the English version is stevensci.com. The profile is available both online and by U.S. mail.

Use an action plan template and write down all commitments during meetings. This keeps everyone accountable for their promises.

Tips and Tricks

Good time management is about good techniques, technologies, and tricks. It does not matter where it comes from; all that is important is that it works for you.

Use a Fax to E-mail Service   This is a great piece of technology that coverts your incoming faxes to e-mails. No more running to the fax machine. Just wait until the e-mail comes through. Additionally, you don't have to waste toner on unwanted parts of the fax. Just print those desired pages from your computer.

Use an Action Plan Template Pad   Efficient contractors have printed a pad of two-part action-plan templates. From their local copy store, they have made up an action plan form that lists "What is the task," "Who is responsible," and "When will it be done." The contractors fill in this form when they have a meeting with any client, supplier, or other third party. As they conduct the discussion, they simply note on the pad what was agreed on as a needed action. One copy goes to the other party and one stays with the contractor. When the time comes for the action to be finished, it is clear who is responsible. In those cases where the action was not done, there is no argument about who dropped the ball. This kind of system keeps everyone focused on those needed actions to accomplish the project or just to make business go smoother.

Use the Delivery Notification on Your E-mail Software   I'm familiar with Microsoft Outlook. When an important note is sent to a client, Outlook notifies you when it was opened, and then you can call your client immediately. In cases that need documentation, the notification can be printed and filed. Don't forget your client's computer is under his control, so there is less chance of mishandling. Unlike a fax, with Outlook, there is little room for argument.

Use Adobe Acrobat Distiller   For billing, proposals, and other purposes, use Adobe Acrobat Distiller. These files are graphics and, therefore, they are difficult to change. This means you can send those highly important documents to others with confidence. As you know, the Adobe Reader is free, so everyone has it to read your correspondence.

Use Colored Paper for Faxes   When you use colored paper for your fax machine, it identifies a fax as an original and indicates it should be filed in the master job folder. Yellow is a popular and highly visible color, and it copies cleanly. Additionally, any yellow faxes sitting on someone's desk can be seen easily. Again, faxes should be kept in the master file, but that doesn't always occur in a contractor's office. Using yellow paper can help keep communication high and lost faxes to a minimum.

Send (Fax) the Client Your Promised Delivery Date Confirmations from the Manufacturer   This is an effective technique to keep the client informed. It shows the delivery dates the client is relying on. This certainly helps in the cases where delivery was delayed and, somehow, the client thinks the contractor is to blame.

Use a Work List with a Punch List   Some construction contracts specifically call out for one punch list on a project. Other contractors work to discourage multiple punch lists. Typically, the architect coordinates such a document with the engineers, owner, and so forth. Project managers have found that the earlier they start identifying items to be corrected on a project, the more efficiently the close-out process will proceed. If the contract you signed does spell out one punch list by the owner, then start a work list at some point during the job. This will keep the focus on areas that need rework. Working on the punch list at the last part of the job only makes it more difficult. With retention at 10 percent, the average contractor's net profit is in retention, along with his overhead cost.

Place Your Computer on Standby Every Night (Instead of Turning It Off)   This will save your hard drive and enable you to reboot quickly in the morning.

Use Text Messaging on Your Cell Phone for Quick Messages   You don't have to say hello, good-bye, or anything in between. Of course, you only use this for those one-word or one-sentence answers others may need.

Use Computer Hot Button Software   To keep key strokes to a minimum, hot button software is linked to a set of letters/numbers, and then acts when the hot key is pressed, such as **F8**. This saves minutes and hours. If you use Microsoft Excel, once it's set up, this program automatically goes to Excel after you press the link button(s). Personally, I type **xl,** press **F8**, and, in less than five seconds, I have a blank spreadsheet on my screen. It is applicable to all files, Internet, and e-mail records. Combinations are almost unlimited. My digest publishing site is **mt** and, again, I press **F8**. This type of software is inexpensive (less than $100) and keeps us productive. We don't need to take the long cut of Microsoft Windows and increase our chances of suffering from carpal tunnel syndrome.

Don't Allow Salespeople or Vendor Interruptions   After contractors win projects, they are inundated with a flurry of phone calls from interested suppliers and others. This is an unnecessary interruption and it should be stopped. The golden time to plan the job is then, when everyone's mind is fresh and the project is "top of mind." To stop these momentum-decreasing acts, write a letter to all suppliers, service providers, and others stating the new policy: there will be neither unplanned visits nor phone calls concerning a recently won job. You might have to send the fax more than once to get the message across. If someone violates this policy, you can quickly dispatch the wayward person who will then think twice about doing it again.

Backing Up Your Computer   Use a computer-sharing software. Many contractors have more than one computer. Making a duplicate of your company's computer records on a second computer makes a lot of sense. Financially, the subscription is less than $100 a year. It uses the Internet to transfer the files from one computer to the other. On a personal note, I have two computers that have identical files on them from using this software. If one goes down, I can work without interruption in minutes.

Use Data Phones to Save Time   These days, technology products deliver speed. As an example, e-mail sent to your phone is a time saver. We are in a time-sensitive and information-critical business. E-mail is a leverage point. Receiving information as soon as it is sent keeps you better informed. If you travel and/or are involved in multiple meetings, this keeps you actively managing your business during those times. Don't worry, all data phones work with your office computer. All e-mail goes through and will also reside on your laptop or desktop. It is a tandem system, in case you inadvertently delete an e-mail or misplace your phone.

> Use a company-wide schedule and forecast to manage resources, including labor and equipment. This keeps productivity/utilization high and surprises low.

Computers

We live in an age when we can work smarter and don't have to work harder. That is, if we use current construction-related software, hardware, and service providers, we don't have to do as much clerical work (collecting data and compiling information). This allows us more time to do management work (analyzing, planning, and thinking). If you are not taking advantage of this phenomenon, it might be an oversight. Your competitors will show you technology's power at one time or another. You will see it in the way they bid/sell or build work against you.

As you know, electricity travels at 187,000 miles a second. It can certainly speed up the information gathering, analysis, and transfer functions that are a substantial part of a manager's duty.

Some software programs have been around for more than 30 years. They contain many work smart functions learned over the past three decades. Again, the power of technology in construction is indisputable.

Because of the development of integrated software information systems in recent years, much of the financial, estimating, and project management process has been automated for contractors. Available from a number of software vendors, these systems combine accounting, estimating, project management, purchasing, equipment management, on-site labor management, and other critical functions.

This integration feature includes such things as software's automatic updating of job costs when purchase orders or subcontracts are created. Committed costs in the job-cost module are automatically converted to actual costs when a vendor is paid through the accounts payable module. In addition, invoices are automatically created when the project manager updates the percentage completed on a project.

From a management perspective, the advantage of such integrated systems is that companies may continuously update project information. A side benefit from the use of such software is a more standardized approach to management when compared with other manual systems. In other words, the management process can be hardwired.

Some of these systems incorporate remote job entry, which allows job-cost information to be entered from job sites. Thus, labor productivity and accurate job costs are instantly available to on-site personnel. Conversely, some companies have found that using common suites of software and integrating them is an effective course.

Two prime examples are Microsoft Office or Intuit's QuickBooks. Both are dominant in market share. Some clear benefits are (1) Most people who have used computers have used them and many new hires today are competent users. They are ready to use the software now with no training needed. (2) These software packages integrate with other construction-related software, which is especially important when communicating with your clients or suppliers. (3) Because many people use them, you won't need to call customer support. You can just call someone you know in town.

Some older contractors are still not using e-mail. This is a missed opportunity. Net profit before tax margins are single digits (versus decades ago). Competition is greater, cost pressures are more, and uncertainty is the highest it's been in some time. Small efficiency improvements, such as technology, are the only opportunities left. No great windfalls remain.

Again, anyone would be wise to start using a computer to begin organizing, transferring, and analyzing information. Certainly, construction is neither immune from technology's power nor is the competition unobservant of its utility.

> Smart contractors overmanage their projects. They focus on winning the cost battle instead of the overhead battle. Labor coordination, change order opportunity, and risk management are three primary reasons. They know more money is gained (or lost) in these three areas than in the cost of extra overhead.

Software

What software makes sense? This is a great question that is loaded with all sorts of controversy. As you well know, there is some good technology in our industry. Contractors mostly swear by it (although, some swear at it). All contractors are unique and no single software package covers every person's needs.

As an aside, I don't work in the software industry or sell software products. As a client from Texas says, "I don't have a dog in this fight." Our firm does not benefit from the sales, service, maintenance contracts, or upgrades of software.

We live in a world where there is constant change and innovation. Software companies come and go. Some stop supporting certain software while developing others. This has left a few contractors in a bind. Microsoft is a viable company, financially and otherwise. I feel we won't see Bill Gates's company go away in our lifetime. If the company does fold, the new software leader will have to make his program bridge to Microsoft's program (because there are millions of users).

We use less than 10 percent of the available utilities. From several studies, the conclusion is that the average is 6 percent. We buy the bells and whistles, but we use the basic functions. All software looks great in the sales presentation, but it loses its luster in the contractor's office.

People have to use the computer software; it doesn't run by itself. Excel is a straightforward and simple software that helps both new hires and tenured employees to use it effectively. Software that is common has a wide user base. Your new hire might have used it in a previous job. The more common the software, the more likely someone will already have used it.

For several previously listed reasons, we recommend Microsoft's Office Suite, which includes Excel, Word, Outlook, and Access, among other software packages. We know of several situations where contractors have integrated Microsoft Office as their main management software package.

Specialized software has to be used sometimes. For scheduling, only a couple of viable software packages are made for construction. For serious accounting, more packages are available. However, for most day-to-day applications, you will find Microsoft has value.

If you are new to the construction industry, think about using MS Office and integrating it. The benefits and the reduced cost over your career are too great to ignore.

> Be a superior negotiator. Contractors can make or save the most money per hour negotiating than any other business activity. It is the highest and best use of a professional's time.

Using Computer Spreadsheets in Construction

Spreadsheets have been around since the 1980s. They were the first software to which most of us were exposed (I used VisiCalc back then). Since those years, not much has changed in the look of spreadsheets, but the power has risen dramatically. Today, the uses are many and far-reaching, from simple estimating to the data analysis of thousands of labor codes. In addition, they are the base calculator for several software packages. Presently, spreadsheets have grown with our industry and are as common as cell phones in a contractor's office.

Spreadsheets are simple in their layout of rows and columns, but powerful in their use of functions, commands, and so forth. Professionals in the construction industry use them for such basic tasks as number calculation, as well as for their more advanced features, such as database functions and goal seeking. The proper use of a spreadsheet can produce a fast and accurate result. Names of commonly used spreadsheets are Quattro Pro, Lotus, and Microsoft Excel.

A *spreadsheet* is the computer equivalent of a paper ledger, and it consists of a grid made from columns and rows. It is an environment that makes number manipulation easy. The math required with a paper ledger can be overwhelming because if you change the amount, you have to start the math all over again (from scratch).

The nice thing about using a computerized spreadsheet is you can experiment with numbers without having to redo all the calculations. As an example, if you change an overhead rate, and then change the profit margin, we can let the computer do the calculations! Once you have the formulas set up, you can change the variables that are called from the formula and watch the changes. Do that on paper and you had better get your calculator out again, find an eraser, and hope you punched all the right keys in the right order. Spreadsheets are instantly updated if one of the entries is changed. No erasers, no new formulas, and no calculators!

Spreadsheets are valuable tools in business. They are often used to play out a series of what-if scenarios or goal seeking. Spreadsheets are also a great organizer of items, whether they are numbers, text, formulas, or the like. They help us do less redundant work and more thinking. Because of a spreadsheet's power, though, sometimes we use it excessively. As a friend said: "When you have a good hammer, every problem looks like a nail."

We utilize spreadsheets in the construction industry in the following areas:

- Acquiring work (estimating)
- Building work (project management)
- Keeping track (accounting)

These areas cover the total activities of what a contractor does. As previously stated, the contractor must perform these tasks faster than competitors to have an advantage.

Why would it be to our advantage to use a spreadsheet in our construction business? Several well-accepted software packages are certainly available.

- No software is created for your specific business. You will have to customize anything you buy. Because this is the case, why not start with something you can work with that is to your liking?

- We use less than 10 percent of the total utilities in a software package. The sizzle that a specific software offers is nice, but not vital to our business.

- Software companies make the most money on software upgrades, for example, selling the next version. Also, maintenance fees are a yearly annuity for them. In contrast, once spreadsheets are programmed, they continue to produce for years without customer support, they don't have any significant bugs, and they don't have to be upgraded to work.

- Spreadsheets integrate with word processors, databases, Internet, and e-mail, especially if the software is from the same software developer. So, there are no time-consuming and awkward bridges. Don't forget, your clients, suppliers, and subcontractors can read or use a spreadsheet readily.

Break up cliques. Allowing cliques on the job site does little to enhance teamwork and learning. As we move people around to work with others, we do a service for ourselves and to our people. A new partner does add perspective to performing tasks in different ways. In addition, this practice gives a person an understanding of different personalities. In summary, he will learn a greater sense of people. It is inexpensive management training for your next foreman, superintendent, or project manager.

17 Scars (Hard-Won Lessons) from a Spreadsheet User

Spreadsheets will be used in the industry as long as there are computers. They are simple, easy to understand, and powerful. No one disputes this. They are widely used for these reasons. Improving your skill with spreadsheets has a great benefit. See some of our suggestions below:

1. **Commit your work to disk consistently.** Make it a habit to use the CTRL+S or the File | Save command at every major change. As a further safety measure, engage the Auto Recover function. Click on Tools | Options. Instruct Excel to save every 10 minutes. You will thank yourself at least once in your career for doing this.

2. **Name the workbooks logically and place them in a folder that will still make sense to you in six months.** Our memories fade and confusion takes over. You have much latitude in naming your file—255 characters—and also nearly unlimited folder-naming flexibility.

3. **Keep all data in a small space as is practical.** Placing the data over many rows and columns only adds to the memory drain. Keep your data in a small area. Only skip columns and rows if doing so makes the data intelligible.

4. **All formulas must begin with = or +.** Forgetting to use the correct sign can lead to unnecessary frustration.

5. **Make certain you select the cells before engaging a command function.** Again, you will avoid needless frustration.

6. **Use the Undo command when you make a mistake.** Do not try to remember the last steps. Choose Edit | Undo or CTRL-Z to perform the Undo command. This will take you through the exact formula/command reversal without unnecessary steps to correct your error.

7. **Be careful when inserting or deleting rows/columns.** Be sure the worksheet will not be erased, changed, or otherwise affected by your placing/eliminating columns or rows. This can be tricky when using complex formulas and several worksheets at once.

8. **Use File | Preview before printing.** This will give you the actual printed look without wasting paper. As an example, headers and footers will show. Also, large spreadsheets will show print margins and truncation.

9. **Use Manual Recalculation with large spreadsheets.** This will keep productive time high as you make changes to the worksheet. Otherwise, the spreadsheet will not be active for several seconds (or minutes) at a time because Excel is recalculating the changes. *Caution*, be very careful to recalculate often.

10. **Use Protection Command for important work and databases.** When showing or sharing worksheets, it is possible for inadvertent changes to be made, thus change the result. Lock down areas in a spreadsheet, such as a cost database or an estimating assembly.

11. **Do not work on your spreadsheet past 10 P.M.** I have made my largest errors after that time. But don't take my word for it. Ask anyone who has worked with Excel for more than a week.

12. **Building a spreadsheet is always better than buying one.** You have to know intimately how your spreadsheet works. If not, mistakes will happen.

13. **Always triangulate or have double checks for numbers and accuracy.** This prevents input errors or programming flaws from becoming problems.

14. **Use intermediate totals in long strings of numbers.** When an error exists, you don't want to have to recalculate dozens of cells. Intermediate totals enable you to focus on a problem area quickly, resolve it, and move on.

15. **Run dual systems as you work with any new process or template.** Use your current process with the new process until your confidence is built with the new process.

16. **If you do buy a template, remember that all templates must be customized in some way to your particular construction company.** The commercial templates you can buy are great, but they are not perfect for your unique contracting firm.

17. **Digitizers and spreadsheets do mix.** Using digitizers for quantity takeoff conservatively reduces takeoff time by 60 percent. Quantity surveys account for the largest time

investment in the bidding process. If you estimate with a spreadsheet, look closely at linking the powers of spreadsheet and digitizer. This is working smarter.

> Attempt to hire field laborers, craftspeople, and operators who are (1) Safe—workers' compensation and OSHA fines are costly. (2) Efficient—rework and waste is prohibitive. (3) Loyal—so the investment in training and management grooming doesn't leave with the person after a few months. Building work successfully is about keeping cost managed in the field. Seeking these three attributes in crew labor gives you the best chance of doing that.

CHAPTER SUMMARY

The contracting business is a frustrating and unfair industry at times. We can't control many things. We must focus on what we *do* control to make better profits, meet deadlines, and keep our health.

Construction is not a generous business. Competition is great and clients are increasingly demanding. Net profits before taxes are less than 5 percent.

The business aspects of construction contracting are unique. There is little similarity to general business models.

Three things are certain in construction contracting: (1) taxes, (2) death, and (3) change. Be ready for different demands, they are coming in a steady stream.

The project players are changing constantly. Your partners are not the same individuals over a year of jobs. This adds to the chaos that you experience in building projects. Someone new is always working with you.

The secret is the process. A well-defined, thoughtful, and executed process will give you a better outcome. You can minimize miscommunication, time delay, and financial errors.

Process discipline is a huge opportunity for any contractor. Wasted time across the industry is over 30 percent. Multiply this by your payroll dollars or by the hours you work, and you can see the number is enormous. This can be viewed as a problem or as an opportunity. I believe this is an opportunity for you.

Some large-volume contractors have exceeded the 5 percent net-profit barrier consistently. This isn't luck. One year is luck, two years is a trend, and three years is evidence. These contractors have booked higher profit margins over years by using a disciplined and focused approach. It works.

Because of the competitive and economic nature of construction, you must constantly be on the lookout for a niche. This can enable you to charge more due to less competition. In your first years, though, you have to do what you know—to pay the bills. Then, you can start migrating toward specialized pieces of work.

Making the most of your time gives you a business edge in construction. Having more time to plan, negotiate, and trouble-shoot gives you a higher payoff than tasks such as answering the phone, writing notes, and doing other clerical chores. The challenge is to minimize these small-value items and focus on the larger ones.

Time management starts with analysis. What things are you doing now and what things should you be doing both in importance and percentage of time eliminate? You can never control your time and be doing important things every minute. Unimportant items will find ways into your day, but you can keep them to a minimum and do better than some of your competitors.

Basic technology is now a minimum standard for contractors. Its inherent speed provides an undeniable competitive edge.

Use technology to your advantage. It is fast, and it can be organized and portable to wherever you are. Cell phones, laptops, field-to-base units, and personal digital assistants can easily be carried and set up quickly.

Spreadsheets have too many uses to be ignored in our industry. Some contractors have tried to outlaw their use in their companies, but, later, they had to change their minds. Ready-made spreadsheet templates are available in the market. They are too practical a tool not to use.

Software allows smooth calculation of data and timely transmission of that data to other parties. Windows-enabled software makes using software as easy as point and click. The contractor does not need to know any programming to make it function.

Be careful about software purchases. Industry studies show we use less than 10 percent of the functions in any software. Filter the sales pitch from the fact when you consider a purchase. Several construction-specific software packages are available and you will need one or more of them due to their specialized function. Remember, Microsoft cannot be denied as the leader of business software. Its products are simple, powerful, and well-accepted. Certainly, hours of work are needed to make MS Office functional for a construction firm but, once accomplished (by you or someone else), it will be usable for years to come. Microsoft will be one of the last software companies to go out of business. It is too well-accepted and well-managed. Microsoft's successors will bridge to its system.

Well-accepted software has a triple value:

1. It has proven itself in the construction industry and, thus, won't tie you up with problems or bugs.

2. Because many people use it, it is likely you have several friends who use it and can be helpful if, or when, you have a problem.

3. Your new employees will likely contribute much quicker due to their understanding of common software.

2

The Acquire Work Process

The first step in making a profit for any contractor is to acquire work. Without work, the trucks, people, office, and so forth are a waste. A construction contractor without anything to build is a pricing service. Work acquisition is the key to starting the process of a profitable construction business. See Figure 2-1.

As I said previously, the speed of the total process is critical to have a competitive edge (we assume accuracy is the same). A faster cycle time in work acquisition has two basic components.

1. The time to execute all the Acquire Work duties
2. The time to transfer this information to the Build Work phase

First, let's review the general picture of the work acquisition step.

GETTING WORK MEANS BUILDING WORK

The ability to acquire profitable work differentiates successful contractors from their unsuccessful counterparts. This is the primary step for turning a profit. Consistently submitting a profitable, but competitive, price is critical to success. *If a construction company cannot get work, it must be a pricing service.*

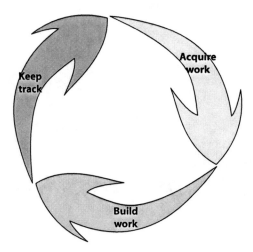

FIGURE 2-1
Work acquisition is integrated with the build work and keep track phases of the business cycle. Now more than ever, what we do in one phase certainly affects the other two.

> **Average net profit before tax is approximately 3 percent for all contractors**

Specialty contractors hover around 4 percent and general contractors are south of 2 percent. This means a flawed process can lead to financial ruin. Too high a price means indifference from the client and no work. Too low a price takes owner's equity out of your company to finish the project.

The following are the steps of a superior estimating and pricing process. Most construction firms must follow this kind of process to arrive at an acceptable bid for both the contractor and the client.

At the beginning of the Acquire Work process, let us point out a key determinant of your bidding success. This is one of several, but if you ignore it, you will find yourself in a weaker position.

> **The number of qualified leads is the key factor to winning profitable jobs.**

Take the example of a rookie salesperson. He can lack essential skills to be a great salesperson, but if he has cultivated 1,000 qualified leads, he will sell something next month. He certainly can find people in this prospect list who would like to do business with him.

Conversely, a savvy salesperson who only possesses one qualified lead is not assured of selling anything next month.

The number of qualified leads is critical. How do you judge them?

1. **They have a deadline.** The client wants to start and build sooner rather than later. Tire kickers have lots of time, so they can shop (your price) around.

2. **They are the decision makers.** This person has the final say. Typically, they have the title president, CEO, or wife. These folks have most of the power.

3. **They have the funds to build.** No sense in dealing with people who don't have money. They can't pay you and you can't get rich by dealing with poor people.

4. **They have a need.** A typical example is their lease is up in six months. Some business development people say they look for cars parked in fields next to plants or stores. This clearly indicates a need for more space.

5. **They let you build a personal relationship.** Marines feel comfortable working with other Marines. So do University of Michigan alumni or people from Texas. There is some level of trust versus an outsider. With no relationship, they might treat you as "just another contractor" and price could become a primary consideration.

6. **They have an identifiable want.** Most men want to have their confidences kept and, in addition, they want the project to go well. If you are a contractor who can be both these things, the client's loyalty to you will be extremely good (some say over 90 percent). This has nothing to do with price and it has everything to do with your relationship skills. Again, make the client look good to his boss, spouse, and so forth and you will win. People also have other wants, such as a contractor who participates in the community or has enviable relationships the client wants. Whatever the wants, identifying them can help you acquire work.

It's important to remember that if a prospect has all six of these attributes, they should go to the top of your list. People who have four or five of the six attributes should be prioritized accordingly.

Find and cultivate dozens of qualified leads and you should be able to receive a decent price for your work.

If you don't have the lowest price in your market, you can still win projects. How? First, let's agree that all customers don't receive the lowest possible price for work. Why?

- Other contractors are busy.
- Some clients are in a rush to get the job built.

Therefore, you can win projects just by bidding and being able to begin construction. You can find customers who like you personally and who find a reason to work with you. See Figure 2-2.

The average contractor in the United States makes 3 percent net profit before tax. Given these tight margins, doesn't it make sense

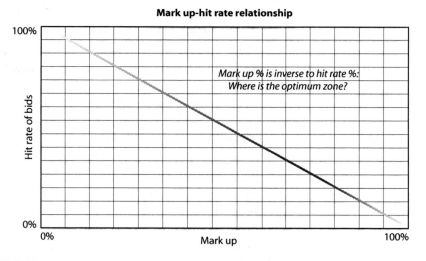

FIGURE 2-2
Hit rates are inversely proportional to profit margin. The higher the profit margin, the lower the hit rate. Financially successful contractors win less than 20 percent of their bids.

to use superior estimating and bidding processes to increase net margins by 1, 2, or 3 percent? Construction firms have found they can increase profits at the bid table. See Figure 2-3.

> Executives lead the recruiting process effectively. To hire quality people in construction, senior people are the only people who can communicate the vision and make commitments to a potential employee. No one else can or should.

Figure 2-4 shows the process of finding your sweet spot. You might be surprised to know that this is a largely quantitative process. After working with this method, clients report more clarity of why they go after certain work, clients, and geographic locations. Being in and around your optimum target, improves your chances for greater profit while exposing you to less risk. Said another way, it reduces your chances of a bad job.

If this is done jointly with your managers, buy-in will result. Your people will subsequently have a greater understanding of what a good job looks like. Subsequently, they will be alert to looking for projects that meet your criteria.

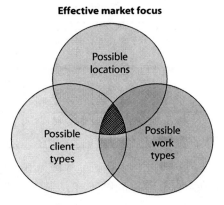

FIGURE 2-3
The focused marketing method answers the question: what are the possible projects, work types, and locations to build?

Type of customer									
Criteria	**Criterion weight**	**$50 million + GC**		**$10–50 million GC**		**<$10 million GC**		**Mechanical**	
Honest-provides factual information about needs, etc.	10	4	40	6	60	2	20	1	10
Relationship-characterized by mutual trust	9	7	63	6	54	4	36	1	9
Reputation-known for quality work	8	7	56	5	40	4	32	1	8
Team attitude-treats us equal member of team	6	6	36	7	42	5	30	4	24
Time to execute-adequate time to effectively deliver a quality job	4	4	16	3	12	1	4	2	8
Time to bid-prefer 2 weeks for adequate planning	3	6	18	5	15	3	9	1	3
Pays timely-progress what payments and retainage	5	5	25	3	15	2	10	1	5
Recognizes our value-we bring to project-quality and professionalism	7	7	49	6	42	4	28	3	21
Past experience-past project success	1	7	7	6	6	5	5	4	4
Quality & desirability of projects-we get good projects as well as poor	2	7	14	6	12	5	10	2	4
Totals			324		298		184		96

FIGURE 2-4
This is an example of using a quantitative method to determine the best customer type.

The following is an example from a specialty contractor who, in determining and scoring the type of customers that are best for them, found who they should not pursue. This is not the right answer for you, because this process is unique to each contractor. They "fired" the right two customer types. Conversely, they pursued more aggressively the customers in the first two columns ($50+ million GC and $10–50 million GC). The total scores tell the story.

To execute such a method, the previous sheet must be created for:

- Customer type
- Geographic location
- Work type

These make up the sweet spot for every contractor and it is worth the effort to determine yours.

> Savvy contractors use best practices in training of their employees.

Estimating Overview

The following are steps for an accurate cost and appropriate profit margin on a bid proposal.

Quantity of Work   Quantity takeoff is one of the most tedious and risky steps of contracting. It demands that the quantity of work be derived from pictures and written words. It has to be accurate. As you know, words can be inaccurate. A picture (or a set of plans) is worth a thousand words, but words are inaccurate. In addition, plans are becoming less clear and detailed.

Technology has helped tremendously to improve accuracy, consistency, and speed. Digitizers, software, CAD, and so forth all contribute to cut hours from the quantity takeoff process. Some studies show that digitizers reduce time spent to half, others report even more time is cut, but it is still a human endeavor. To ensure excellent performance, a thoughtful and disciplined process must be followed.

The quality of plans and specifications over the last two decades has diminished. Unfortunately, this trend will continue for many reasons. One is that design groups are forced to design faster with lower fees. This lends itself to less time spent in the creation and review of the bidding documents. Designers feel the same pressure contractors do—to produce at a lower price and a higher speed. Construction professionals must have a process to address this issue.

Cost of Work Without accurate cost numbers, a company will be either too high or too low. Either way, this leads to undesirable consequences. The contractor will get work at a loss or will not win any work due to a high price. Solid and predictable cost data can be derived from several sources:

- Field experience
- Company cost records
- Observation of crews

Certainly, your cost figures should be unique to you. The use of costing services, such as RSMeans or Walker's, is a last resort. These services can be valuable and should be used in certain circumstances. However, on a daily basis, your cost structure cannot be public information. See Figure 2-5.

> Make sure people are trained formally at least one day a year. Having someone from outside the company to teach can keep the new ideas flowing.

Remember, unit pricing must be what you do work for, that is, your actual cost or productive rate. Never bid what it should be or what you did in the past years. The margins you work with don't allow for that.

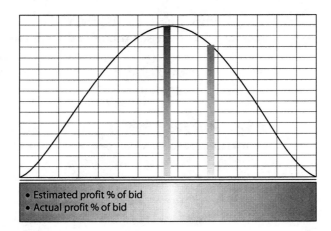

- Estimated profit % of bid
- Actual profit % of bid

FIGURE 2-5
This is a cumulative measure of all jobs for the past year. Profit results like this point to further investigation. It could be that unit costs bid are too high or the field management is better than previously thought. This is from all jobs.

Overhead   The labor content of a project directly affects overhead costs. In other words, field labor causes companies to hire payroll clerks, safety professionals, and operations managers. With it are associated office space, vehicle, technology, and miscellaneous costs.

How to allocate this overhead can make the difference in taking projects cheap or with the appropriate amount of overhead. A company's cost has to be recovered; otherwise, it pays for finishing a project.

Overhead allocation depends on several factors, the most important of which is an accurate budget. Besides the overall numbers, it must delineate the labor/material/subcontract/equipment content. An accurate budget leads to better bidding results. Only a handful of formulas capture the realities of overhead recovery for contractors.

At this point, a contractor knows his breakeven cost or a bid with no profit. If he has done the work of knowing his costs and checking his counts, he can be confident of this estimate. From here, the poker game starts. The client negotiates for a better price, among other things. The contractor is weighing the proposed construction contract. He assesses the speed required, the price requested, and the quality or scope demanded. As you know, furnishing all three leads to bankruptcy. If you provide two of the three, it makes for a reasonable agreement.

Profit Margin   What is a reasonable markup on a project? What factors increase or decrease it? How can we determine this before a bid? You have several factors to consider. The following list is a sample:

- Length of project
- Your backlog
- Competitor's backlog
- Labor content
- Which competitors are bidding?
- How many competitors are bidding?
- Client's character
- Subcontract content
- Location of project
- Intangibles

With each factor, you should be increasing or decreasing your price. Improper pricing makes you miss opportunities or win jobs you later regret getting.

Beware, contractors who do use bidding models give themselves the best opportunity to win consistently. In other words, you can never predict what will happen on one particular project, but you can predict on a group of 100 projects. Over the long haul, good practices can give you superior results.

As an example, contractors used to (and still do) take three envelopes with them to a bid opening. One to submit if there are less than six bidders, one to submit if there are more than six bidders, and one if there are no other bidders. That basic system, done consistently, has netted construction companies additional net profit without opening the toolbox. Quite simply, profit dollars are added to each bid as the number of competitors decreases.

The result of a solid estimating and pricing process is:

- More of the work that the company does well
- Less money left on the table
- More predicable profits

Perform informal training through interaction, such as sharing of technical and business knowledge with employees. Ten minutes a working day equals a 2 percent investment of time (a general business standard).

The Estimating Process

Estimating is part of the three big critical activities of all contractors. Be they large or small, from the north or south, from the Left or Right Coast, construction contractors have to do these three functions as well or better than average to stay in business. To receive a failing grade in any of the three is certain to spell doom for a construction firm.

The three functions a contractor must perform well are:

1. Acquire work
2. Build work
3. Keep track

The secret is to perform each of these faster than your competition. If you do, you have the edge. Anything that retains accuracy, but increases speed, gives you an advantage.

Estimating is a large part of acquiring work. Also, a contractor must use bid strategy and selling skills if they are to acquire profitable work consistently. *Estimating* means determining the accurate cost of proposed work through reviewing and analyzing construction documents, economic conditions, the physical location of the work, and the parties involved.

Some estimating is art and some is science, but it is more science than most people think.

The process of estimating is several steps in this order: the review of plans, specifications, and other contract documents that affect the work.

After becoming familiar with the project documents, quantity take-off is the next step. This is where many mistakes happen. If you count it, you have it covered. If you miss it, it doesn't matter that you have the right unit price. Zero units times $10 a unit is *still* zero. See Figure 2-6.

> Profitable contractors have the ability to resolve conflict. Keeping the communication alive among all parties gives the project the best chance of being built on time and on budget without involving lawyers.

An Estimating Job Description

Estimators are becoming more of the project team. This is in contrast to years ago when the takeoff and pricing was done in a relative vacuum, and then presented to a senior manager—usually the chief estimator—for review and discussion. With the advent of increased competition and the design build concept, companies are making the estimator more a part of their ongoing business process. Their tasks are more varied, such as helping to sell projects and interacting with the field, including verifying effective construction techniques at the time of bid.

As an estimator, you are responsible for:

- The quantity survey of the work
- The unit pricing of that work
- The general conditions' cost of managing that work

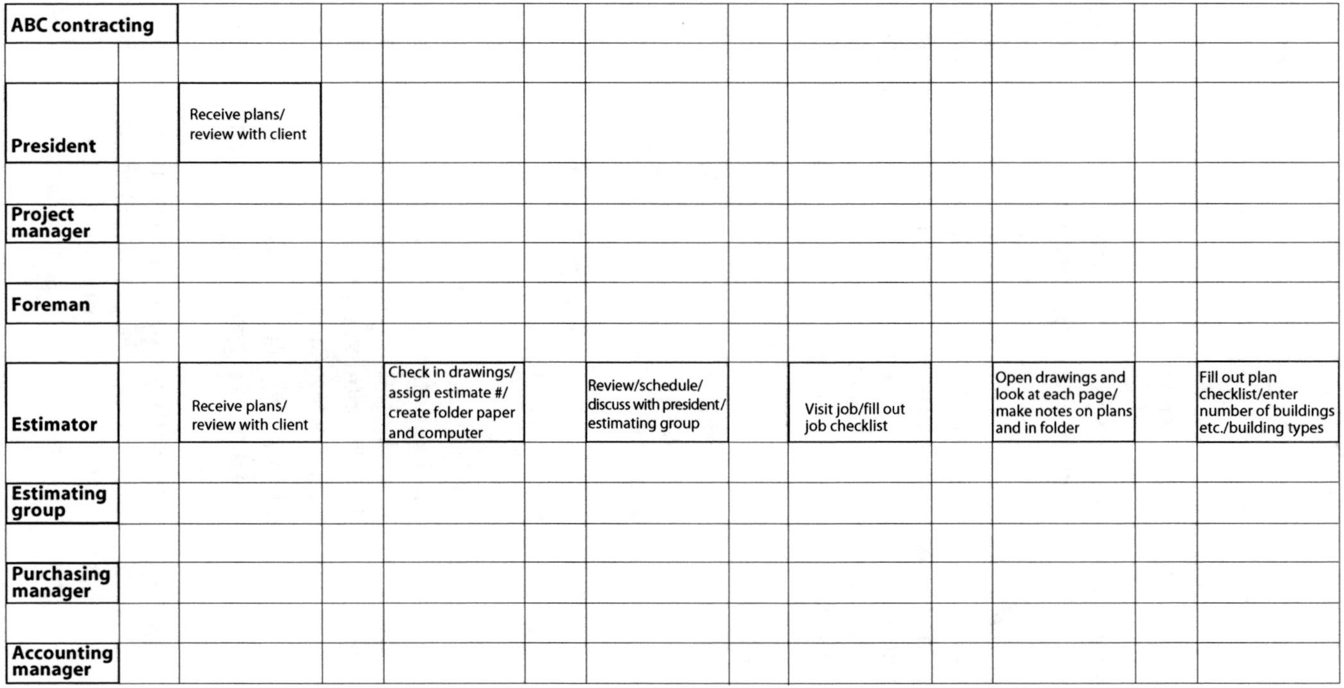

ABC contracting																	
President	Receive plans/ review with client																
Project manager																	
Foreman																	
Estimator	Receive plans/ review with client		Check in drawings/ assign estimate #/ create folder paper and computer			Review/schedule/ discuss with president/ estimating group		Visit job/fill out job checklist		Open drawings and look at each page/ make notes on plans and in folder		Fill out plan checklist/enter number of buildings etc./building types					
Estimating group																	
Purchasing manager																	
Accounting manager																	

FIGURE 2-6
This is a work smart process for estimating. Contractors need to define each major business process and measure for compliance.

- The application of the overhead (office cost) recovery to support that work
- Assisting your supervisor in setting the profit for that work
- Setting the proposal language or terms and conditions for building that work

An estimator assists the project manager in the initial sequencing of construction activities, outlining components such as labor, materials, and equipment. As an estimator, you are responsible to ensure that the work environment is productive among the project manager, others, and yourself. Finally, you are responsible for improving ABC Construction processes overall and you are to support that effort. Never forget, you make or lose money in the field. Your role is to support the field operations in the ways outlined: that is where your risk of loss and/or opportunity for gain resides.

Key Duties

What are the few critical management responsibilities of every estimator. Besides the technical aspects of the job, these business aspects are as important to growth and profit.

- **Represent** your company in a professional manner to clients, architects, consultants, subcontractors, and the general public.
- **Manage** the process effectively from the initial handoff of plans to the handoff to the field after winning the bid. This includes managing the takeoff, pricing, and bidding process along with subcontractor relations, cost, and budget issues, as well as client demands.
- **Administer** the contractual aspects of the project bidding process to maximize profitability and minimize the risk for your company.
- **Proactively communicate** information to immediate supervisors, as well as to field personnel, subcontractors, and vendors to enable them to work toward the successful start (and completion) of the project schedule.

Profitable contractors give their managers the authority to get their job done. They don't make their company "a run it past the boss" bureaucracy.

Sample Checklist of Duties

Please find below the technical steps that could be part of an estimating job description. Review this list and see if this improves your current one.

- Fill out a new bid information form by the person acquiring the bid opportunity. This is faxed or delivered to the estimator with, or in advance of, the plans and specifications delivery.
- Log in plans and assign a project number.
- Physically visit site before each bid.
- Fill out project visit checklist.
- Interview one of the field managers and capture their perspective/work smart ideas.
- Fill out the Project Review form.
- Identify critical path items and long-lead items.
- Estimate/bid/budget the same way you build your work.
- Demand uninterrupted time to take off and price work.
- Say no or pass to unsuitable work.
- Download a map of job location, review, and file.
- Use marks/color coding to count off quantities/alert the field to special conditions.
- Use digitizers or other mechanical/electrical means to take off quantities.
- Make sure you double-check the scale on the digitizer versus plan scale.
- Use takeoff assemblies to take off quantities.
- Finish takeoff and pricing the day before the bid.
- Use triangulation to double-check your bids.

- Do not allow yourself to be interrupted by aggressive sales people and curious subcontractor estimators.
- Check on your actual costs of similar projects to keep bids accurate to your bid cost.
- Obtain a client schedule of milestones and contract completion.
- Prepare a bid schedule and prospective manpower loading.
- Identify weather and seasonal impacts.
- Identify key operational constraints—supervision, equipment, engineering, and so forth.
- Use the overhead recovery process to make certain the job's overhead cost.
- Arrive at your breakeven costs for the job.
- Run a return on investment (ROI) calculation.
- Use market, competitor, and client information to approximate profit margin justified (to leave less money on the table).
- Use margin, not mark up, in calculating the profit.
- Fill out a profit opportunity assessment.
- After the bid is won or lost, furnish information on the bid tracking form.
- If you win the project, meet with the project manager within 48 hours and transfer to him your knowledge, notes, cost information, and other critical information. Do not delay in organizing this information. You must start your pre-job planning immediately.
- If you win the job, transfer a color copy of the bid set to the field manager and the project manager.
- Attend bid coordination meetings weekly.

Typical Forms

See our list of typical forms below that your firm might use. Each has a distinct purpose to keep bids well communicated to others.

- New bid information form
- Focused marketing method

- Dual overhead rate recovery
- Profit opportunity assessment
- Successful bidder letter
- Bid tracking form
- Job sizer
- Return on investment (ROI)

Folder Requirements

On completion of the bid to the client, the estimator should have the following information contained in the job folder:

1. Estimate
2. Subcontract, suppliers, and service providers pricing
3. Soils report
4. Client project information form
5. Project checklist
6. Project specifications, if any
7. Changes, alternates, and addendums
8. RFIs and client's responses (if any) to them
9. Cut/add sheet
10. Estimator's notes of unusual project features, traps, rocks-in-the-road, and client conversations
11. Project location map

On winning the bid, the estimator should include the following list in the folder. This folder should be ready at the preconstruction meeting with the project manager and field supervisor. The handover of this information will be most efficient if documented information is given to both of them.

1. Budgeted costs
2. A preliminary schedule of values (project manager to finalize with client)
3. A supply list—for field and purchasing

4. Material breakdown sheet

5. Any promises or last-minute deals made

Superior contractors know the best and worst suppliers, and then act accordingly. They work with the better ones. Good suppliers will keep you abreast of the latest cost-saving methods of supply.

Determining Unit Costs

Unit costs can be derived from several sources. Labor and equipment production can be determined from the following:

Public Price Books Means, Walker's, National Construction Estimator, and others are all useful tools when looking for some idea of the cost of a work activity. Each has their own strengths. However, most are voluntary cost averages in one large database. Each are well-reasoned and contain thousands of data points, but they are not *your* cost information for *your* unique company.

The value of these pricing services to most contractors is when they need a *plug* number, that is, say at the last moment before a bid, you need to cover the cost of an unfamiliar item. You look to these solid sources of information to get an approximate cost of that work. And, don't forget to use the modifiers for your geographic location, job site factors, and so forth.

Additionally, when documenting and pricing change orders, public price books can be of value. They can help for two clear reasons:

1. Cost data is well accepted by the industry (3,000+ estimators can't be wrong).

2. The descriptions of the work tasks make for a clearly defined and priced change order. In other words, a 12-page cost proposal tends to have more creditability than a 1-page proposal.

Observations   No legal or ethical reason forbids you from observing your competitor's crews and making some determinations. Some contractors who branched out into the marine/lake dock business have perfected this. They simply go fishing around a worksite on a fresh or saltwater bay. While relaxing and catching a few fish, they keep a record of the number of people, probable pay scale, productivity, tasks, and so forth. They do this by taking hobby time to watch that crew on intervals over time. Walks in the park don't have to be leisurely.

You can do the same thing. This activity can give you a more definitive idea of what the production costs should be. Because no one contractor knows everything, this might be a good exercise to sharpen your pencil.

Testing   Nothing prevents you from installing work on your own in a test and measuring the productivity. This gives you special insight into crew productivity. Knowing the wage scale you pay, unit cost is just a calculation away.

Field Experience   Superintendents, foremen, and project managers can be invaluable in giving installation rates, crew sizes, and the like. They know the details involved in the work. You can interview your field people at length to understand completely the work involved.

Your Accounting Records   This is the best source of unit cost information for any construction firm. Your company performance showing cost-per-unit information is reality. With dozens of data points, a contractor can know what the cost of work is for his company.

The challenge for some construction firms is initially capturing this information. It requires a process where field work is inputted into a database. This data must compare units completed to cost expended. As you can see, this is why we believe the acquire work, build work, and keep track cycles are interrelated. See Figure 2-7.

> **Compare**
> **Actual unit cost vs estimating unit costs**

FIGURE 2-7
Bidding your actual costs is imperative, not how much you should build work for or how we did it years ago. Construction is a 3 percent net profit before tax business. There is no room for guesses.

Here's an honest question. Some contractors can use a square-foot cost to acquire work and they have been successful. I know a custom homebuilder who uses $90 a square foot sometimes to bid to a client. He has used this figure in the past and it has been enough to keep him profitable. Why shouldn't we learn a quick method of costing or estimating to make our speed even faster? Quicker estimating has to be an edge, right?

Here are the reasons—they are repeated in different ways throughout this book.

1. **The industry has three times as many competitors** as it did in the 1960s, while the dollar-adjusted volume has stayed flat. You don't have the luxury of excessive margin in your business. The typical owner is getting three times the number of bids.

2. **Material prices and other costs are no longer stable.** You have and will continue to face price uncertainty. Knowing what and how much material, as well as other items, are in your bid allows you to know what your cost risk is on a job.

3. **The risk of contracting is in the field.** The estimate must give the field supervisor and project manager a clear idea of labor hours, material content, and other factors so they can manage the project with facts, not guesses. Great project staffs will not stay with your firm for long if they have to manage in the dark. You will certainly have project losses from this loose way of estimating.

All accounting software exports cost records. Figure 2-8 shows an example of installation cost codes over several projects.

Crew hour/production analysis				
Description	Units	Crew hours	Production	
Installation	700.00	233.33	3.00	
Installation	553.00	177.81	3.11	
Installation	1156.00	387.92	2.98	
Installation	1892.00	896.68	2.11	
Installation	1699.00	542.81	3.13	
Installation	109.00	22.85	4.77	
Installation	822.00	238.95	3.44	
Installation	1322.00	411.84	3.21	
Installation	1072.00	332.92	3.22	
Installation	1307.00	450.69	2.90	
Installation	972.00	332.88	2.92	
Installation	1740.00	591.84	2.94	
Installation	833.00	257.89	3.23	
Installation	1212.00	371.78	3.26	
Installation	855.00	276.70	3.09	
Installation	857.00	266.98	3.21	
Installation	1296.00	437.84	2.96	
Installation	1920.00	650.85	2.95	
Installation	1546.00	518.79	2.98	
Installation	1157.00	386.96	2.99	
Installation	1631.00	522.76	3.12	
Installation	1480.00	469.84	3.15	
	Median		**3.10**	
	Average		3.12	

FIGURE 2-8
Making sure you are bidding your production rates is critical. The only way to determine this is from analyzing your accounting records.

The previous example is from the accounting records downloaded in ASCII-delimited language into a spreadsheet. Note that the consistency of the numbers—except for one—is abnormally high and one is low. Typically, you would delete these numbers from your crew-hour calculation. They are outliers and might make your average inaccurate. We recommend using the *median,* not the average of the production rates.

At this point, the chief estimator would review what is typically bid. This is valuable information if the production basis is used: let's say this is 2.7 units/crew hour or 3.4. This is a significant step because construction companies average less than 5 percent net profit.

In one instance, a company performed masonry and concrete subtrades, along with prime contracting. In the industry, they are known as a self-performing general contractor. They found their bid numbers were significantly different from their actual production numbers on projects with brick. On further review, they saw their bid competitiveness increased in brick-intensive jobs.

On CMU.-intensive jobs, they were bidding a production rate that was lower than reality (their job-cost records). They changed the numbers to their actual production. Their bidding success rate was lowered, but the profit percentage improved.

Other costs are easier to determine. Receiving material costs and subcontractor pricing is as easy as sending a fax or an e-mail.

Subcontractors should submit bids to the contractor. To plug numbers is a dangerous approach because this will catch up to you.

1. **General conditions** This cost is the amount of non-direct field cost to build job. Items such as job site trailers, toolboxes, field engineers, and so forth. On the forms we provide is an extensive list of possible expenses.

2. **Overhead costs** We define this as the amount of office cost to build job. The estimator might use a formula, such as dual rate, or an executive might cost this himself.

   At this point, the contractor adds these costs and, once this is done, he knows his breakeven cost or the cost of building the job with no profit. Knowing this is extremely important and, now, the poker game starts.

3. **Profit margin** This is known as many things. The construction firm adds a markup (or margin) for the risk and return it believes the work deserves. The *profit* is the added dollar amount of what both the client and the contractor will accept. Some contractors have what is called a *walk-away number,* which is the lowest price at which the contractor will sell his work. If the client is unhappy with this last price, then the contractor should be, too, and walk away.

The estimator is not done. If the bid is accepted and the company is awarded the work, the contractor must meet directly with the field manager, the project manager, or both and download all the information about the project to them. He should give them his notes, his takeoff drawings, takeoff sheets, and RFIs. The contractor needs to tell them all he knows: his promises, concerns, or ideas. Now is the time—directly after the award. Memories fade and, if he involves himself in another bid, his memory will fade even more. The time to perform a turnover meeting is, without fail, immediately after the project award. See Figure 2-9.

A determination must be made to see why there is profit fade. Two possible reasons are high-field costs or a low-bid price.

> Weigh the field manager's input in the project schedule. Field experience keeps a CPM schedule practical and real world.

Dual Overhead Cost Application

The right application of costs makes a contractor's financial picture improve greatly. Not knowing costs has serious business consequences. Too many costs and the contractor won't win the project.

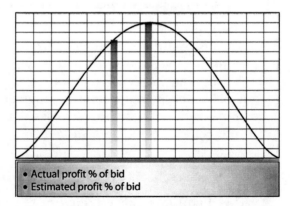

- Actual profit % of bid
- Estimated profit % of bid

FIGURE 2-9
A difference in cost indicates a disconnect between the cost bid and the cost delivered by the field. This measurement is from all jobs. The actual profit is less than the bid profit.

In fact, he might not win any projects, which can be a slow death. Too few costs and he pays to finish the job. The contractor might even be bankrupted on the way to completing the project. This may be sudden death.

Part of getting work is to know the final costs of the project. If you know your final cost, then the poker game starts. In a negotiation or bidding situation, good contractors play a great game if they are certain. Without certainty of your total costs, though, you are in a weak position in this game of cards.

How do you arrive at an accurate cost? Two crucial steps among several are:

1. The proper application of overhead costs for the project
2. Job sizing to proportion overhead and profit the volume of the job

Using a single-rate application for all costs on a job works for a contractor doing identical projects, week in and week out. They are the same slice of bread, white not pumpernickel. Few contractors have a repetitive project type. That is, if all the projects have consistency in the amount of labor, material, subcontracts, equipment, and other direct costs to each job, then the contractor can use a single rate with confidence. See Figure 2-10.

The use of a single rate works for projects with the same kind of costs, but the construction world is dynamic. The construction world is never the same and it will continue to experience new demands in regulations, labor management, technology, and the like. Especially in the areas of commercial, multiresidential, custom home, industrial, highway, and so forth there will be completely different job requirements for each bid letting.

Let's use a single rate and look at three projects with a different labor-to-material/subcontract ratio. You can see the fault immediately.

The High-Labor Content Project:

The high-labor percent job is one where you know a lot of home-office support is needed. This means overhead costs are high, but

	Project A	Project B	Project C
Labor	$10,000	$50,000	$90,000
Material	$20,000	$70,000	$90,000
Equipment	$5,000	$7,000	$20,000
Subcontractor	$169,000	$76,000	$2,000
Other	$2,000	$3,000	$4,000
Total	$206,000	$206,000	$206,000
Overhead - 10%	**$20,600**	**$20,600**	**$20,600**
Profit - 12%	$24,720	$24,720	$24,720
Total bid	$251,320	$251,320	$251,320

FIGURE 2-10
The use of a single rate does not discriminate between a high-overhead cost job and a low one. High-labor content means the office has more functions to perform and, thus, more cost is incurred.

we are costing it at a single average of total office overhead to labor/material/subcontracts direct costs.

When you bid this high-labor content project, you would apply less cost, which would make you low bidder. You will win this job, but it will be more costly to build. Most of your competitors would add cost and have higher bids.

The Low-Labor Content Project:

The low-labor content project shows the other failing of using a single rate. You can use the same average overhead percentage, but this project will be simpler (less costly) for the home office to support. Your average-cost application will be disproportionately higher, so it won't be competitively priced and it won't draw attention (or an interested phone call) from the client. See Figure 2-11.

To summarize, you want Project A, because of its ease of administration and reduced risk. In reality, though, you win Project C, which is a lot more work to earn the same profit of $24,720. See Figure 2-12.

	Overhead cost comparison		
Project	1	2	3
Labor content			
Labor quotient (labor $ / material $)	4	1	0.5
Overhead needed to manage	High	Medium	Low

FIGURE 2-11
This shows the concept of higher overhead costs due to higher labor content.

		Project A	Project B	Project C	
Labor		$10,000	$50,000	$90,000	
Material		$20,000	$70,000	$90,000	
Equipment		$5,000	$7,000	$20,000	
Subcontractor		$169,000	$76,000	$2,000	
Other		$2,000	$3,000	$4,000	
Total		$206,000	$206,000	$206,000	
Dual OH					
Labor/equipment		$2,700	$10,260	$19,800	18%
Material/subs/other		$13,370	$10,430	$6,720	7%
Profit - 12%		$24,720	$24,720	$24,720	
Total bid		$246,790	$251,410	$257,240	

FIGURE 2-12
Dual rate is a more realistic application due to the nature and behavior of construction costs. The dual-rate model is derived from banking information, that is, the financial relationships experienced by real-world contractors, not as a theory represented as a practical solution.

> Use checklists of important processes, such as job review or weekly planning. This keeps people working with speed and fewer errors.

Our firm performs this kind of work with construction contractors nationally. We assist firms in applying dual-rate methodology to their business. Dual-rate methodology does not solve:

- Estimating errors
- Costing problems
- Field productivity issues
- Financial management missteps

The value of *dual-rate methodology* is accurately applying overhead expenses to project costs for bid-price determination or job-costing analysis. The proper application of costs to a bid can be done in two different ways. Both of these result in a dual-rate recovery method, but they arrive at it in a different way.

1. **Analysis of contracting industry cost data**—the use of industry data to derive the proper application of overhead to labor, material, equipment, and subcontractor costs.
2. **Analysis of your own company cost**—a method that lets you self-determine your cost application using your judgment and experience.

Many people prefer to use market data. There is a simple reason for this. To compete, we have to know and use what is normal application. This keeps our cost close to the same as our peers. This information is from banks. As you might guess, the data is neither voluntary nor is it massaged in any way. Banks require complete and forthright information or there is no approval of credit lines, equipment loans, and the like. In other words, you can trust the banking industry's data concerning other contractors as a group. The information is an accurate portrayal of costs. We consult and teach dual-overhead rates. The math and analysis is intense, and it must be carefully executed. Please contact us for this information at mstevens@stevensci.com.

However, a population of contractors like to use their own analysis of costs. Certainly, you have more trust when you determine your own application. Because this is your information, you know both where it comes from and how it is derived.

If you choose to analyze your own data, you will have to do some work and make some assumptions as to the application. Figure 2-13 shows a worksheet with a fairly typical set of overhead-cost categories.

In this example, the contractor determined that 13.95 percent is the coefficient for labor/equipment cost. So, for an individual job, the contractor would add 13.95 percent to the labor/equipment cost. Following that premise, we would add 4.2 percent to the material and subcontract cost total for the job.

The previous sample contains many typical overhead line items. Yours is certainly different. No matter what the list, a proper application lets you conclude a breakeven cost. As stated, this is essential in determination bidding and/or selling strategy.

As you can see, each line item of cost is broken down into two categories:

- Labor/equipment
- Material/subcontracts

One hundred percent of the cost must be accounted for in either of these two buckets. We chose to limit choices to 0 percent, 25 percent, 50 percent, 75 percent, or 100 percent. This keeps the determination quicker. Our view is this: because this is a minor amount of the cost of a bid, these broad-brush percentages do not have a great effect. They will be comfortably close, if not exact. There are more substantial items to work on, which will have a greater impact of bidding success. This self-determination method of overhead application is a practical approach. It lets the contractor become intimately familiar with the overhead amounts and then determine the causes of the costs.

This methodology certainly applies to the cost of a project, so a true profit picture may be determined. We don't want anyone to sue or be sued. However, a prudent contractor should understand this methodology.

			ABC construction			
			Overhead application			
Question to ask: What causes us to have this expense? L/E or M/S?	**Labor/ equipment**		**Material/ sub contract**		**Total company overhead**	
	1,675,000	100.00%	1,900,000	100.00%	$3,575,000	100.00%
Overhead costs categories						
Advertising	2,000	100%	0	0%	2,000.00	0.06%
Bonuses	10,000	100%	0	0%	10,000.00	0.28%
Cell phone	15,000	75%	5,000	25%	20,000.00	0.56%
Commissions	28,125	75%	9,375	25%	37,500.00	1.05%
Computer expense	4,500	75%	1,500	25%	6,000.00	0.17%
Depreciation - G&A	50,000	100%	0	0%	50,000.00	1.40%
Discounts given	750	50%	750	50%	1,500.00	0.04%
Donations	2,500	50%	2,500	50%	5,000.00	0.14%
Dues & subscriptions	1,850	50%	1,850	50%	3,700.00	0.10%
Employee recruiting	3,750	75%	1,250	25%	5,000.00	0.14%
Insur - W/C, office	3,750	75%	1,250	25%	5,000.00	0.14%
Insur - auto	11,250	75%	3,750	25%	15,000.00	0.42%
Insur - other	22,500	75%	7,500	25%	30,000.00	0.84%
Interest expense	2,500	50%	2,500	50%	5,000.00	0.14%
Legal and professional	11,250	75%	3,750	25%	15,000.00	0.42%
Licenses, permits & plans	1,000	50%	1,000	50%	2,000.00	0.06%
Meals & entertainment	4,000	50%	4,000	50%	8,000.00	0.22%
Mileage	750	75%	250	25%	1,000.00	0.03%
Miscellaneous	750	75%	250	25%	1,000.00	0.03%
Office exp. & supplies	15,000	75%	5,000	25%	20,000.00	0.56%
Oil & gas	30,000	75%	10,000	25%	40,000.00	1.12%
Postage & freight	1,125	75%	375	25%	1,500.00	0.04%
Propane	3,750	75%	1,250	25%	5,000.00	0.14%
R&M - building	7,500	75%	2,500	25%	10,000.00	0.28%
R&M - trucks & equip.	21,000	75%	7,000	25%	28,000.00	0.78%
Rent	9,000	75%	3,000	25%	12,000.00	0.34%
Safety incentives	3,500	100%	0	0%	3,500.00	0.10%
Salaries & wages	161,250	75%	53,750	25%	215,000.00	6.01%
Shop supplies tools	18,750	75%	6,250	25%	25,000.00	0.70%
Taxes - other	188	75%	63	25%	250.00	0.01%
Taxes - payroll, office	14,250	75%	4,750	25%	19,000.00	0.53%
Taxes - property	750	75%	250	25%	1,000.00	0.03%
Taxes - franchise	3,750	75%	1,250	25%	5,000.00	0.14%
Telephone & Pagers	6,750	75%	2,250	25%	9,000.00	0.25%
Training	3,750	75%	1,250	25%	5,000.00	0.14%
Travel	1,875	75%	625	25%	2,500.00	0.07%
Uniforms	7,500	100%	0	0%	7,500.00	0.21%
Unapplied labor & overhead	3,750	75%	1,250	25%	5,000.00	0.14%
Unapplied materials	7,500	75%	2,500	25%	10,000.00	0.28%
Utilities	1,500	75%	500	25%	2,000.00	0.06%
	$498,663		$150,288		$648,950	18.15%
Percentages to apply	13.95%		4.20%			18.15%

FIGURE 2-13
This worksheet shows an example of self-determination of overhead application to direct cost. The contractor will use his knowledge of his overhead costs. In this example, we keep the increments to 0%, 25%, 50%, and so forth for simplicity. The contractor may use different percentages.

In conclusion, this is one of several business processes that drive the contractor's business to an appropriate place on construction's risk-reward curve. With it, the contracting business will produce a better financial reward and, in addition, it should be less stressful.

The Steps to Determine Your Dual-Rate Cost Coefficients

Dual-rate overhead analysis contains several key steps. Each is crucial to determine the proper amount of overhead recovered from each project. Once the appropriate rates are calculated, the contractor has a superior model for knowing his overhead costs in each bid.

- Collect and analyze your financial statement for the last three years.
- Create a pro forma (profit and loss statement) for the next fiscal year based on your previous year and any changes you plan to make.
- Break out the five direct-cost areas (labor, material, equipment, subcontracts, and other) of this budget.
- If you have two or more departments in your company, break out the direct cost and overhead cost to each.
- Project revenue, direct costs, and overhead expenses for each department.
- Calculate the coefficients for labor, material, equipment, subcontracts, and others.
- Test on sample projects and pro forma budget for accuracy and reasonableness.

Superior project managers focus on the financials and the schedule of the job. These are the two major areas of risk in a construction project.

Project Sizing

Competition is the greatest it has ever been. Since the mid-1960s, the domestic construction market has not grown by any measure.

In constant dollars (inflation adjusted), we have the same size construction market today that we did back then. This is significant because we now have three times as many contractors. Our industry is crowded with more construction firms, all eating from the same size pie. Statistically and anecdotally, there is no mistaking that the fight to win the next job is greater.

We need every edge. Contractors must consistently price work accurately. There cannot be any air in our pricing to the client if we expect to consistently win good projects.

Using a project-sizing process is one way to size project bids right and, thus, leave less money on the table.

All seasoned contractors understand that larger projects have economies of scale. Material can be purchased in large quantities, therefore, low-unit prices are offered by suppliers. Equipment can be rented for longer periods, so rates will be lower from the rental yards.

With this in mind, the cost of office support or overhead on a job should also have an economy of scale. For large projects, payroll (once it is set up), becomes easier and faster to administer. After a few weeks, the project is easier to manage, cost codes become more familiar and clerical errors are less. Pre-job planning costs are spread over a greater volume. In addition, executive supervision becomes more efficient.

Once smaller projects are set up, they are almost over. The momentum that builds on a large project never has time to form on a small one. Small projects are more costly on overhead as a percentage of direct cost. Therefore, it makes sense to execute some sizing of overhead in our estimating process.

This is a simple process of the following:

1. Adding overhead costs to a smaller than average job.

   or

2. Subtracting overhead costs on a larger than average job.

Obviously, calculating your average job size is simple math. But, it must be done and, once done, it must be inputted as part of this process of project sizing. The average job size is for the coming year, not the past or historical average. Thus, it needs to be calculated each year. See Figure 2-14.

Job sizing is not a huge adjustment to the costs of a job. Your bid amounts will not wildly fluctuate. However, bids with accurate breakeven costs provide you with a greater chance to win a good project. The following example of multipliers can give you an idea of the range of possible values.

- 3x for a project 1/100th the size of your average project
- .8 for a project ten times the size of your average project

This is just one process in dozens that a contractor must use to keep his estimating tight. Construction does not have a silver bullet. The consistent use of many best practices is what drives the contractor's business to a better financial place.

Job sizing makes a lot of sense if you consider the thousands of projects a contractor might bid over their career. Just as in baseball,

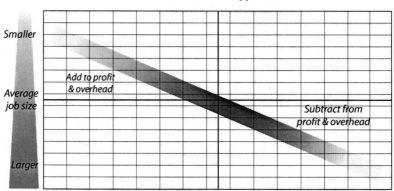

FIGURE 2-14
The size of the job does affect the overhead application and the profit calculation. The percent of the overhead cost varies with the job size.

one more hit over a week makes a .250 hitter a .300 one. And, one more job a month makes a contractor highly profitable.

> After winning a project, name staff to that project within a week, so they can start the process of planning, coordination, scheduling, and so forth.

Bidding

Let's spend a few paragraphs on a critical subject for all contractors: bid conditioning.

In this day and age, you need to make sure you clearly state what terms and conditions your bid is based on. As previously said, if you have a choice, you have more economic power in setting the terms and conditions than in setting a payment amount.

We suggest using bid proposal forms from any of the major contractor associations along with some added language stating that "the terms and conditions contained will be part of any agreement between the parties."

The right bid strategy can add profit to the bottom line and you can approach bidding strategy in several ways. One such approach is to bid a job strictly on financial factors.

To introduce bidding strategy, let's use a straightforward financial example. Let's assume that we will use only financial factors to determine our final bid price. The calculation of ROI will be the only consideration in our profit determination.

Figures 2-15 and 2-16 show our job selection template. You can use this template as a guide to place the appropriate amount of profit on each project. This template has two pages: the first page is the input page (the shaded area) and the second page is the output page.

The project-selection process gives contractors the financial return on a project(s). This is a key step to keep away from a bad

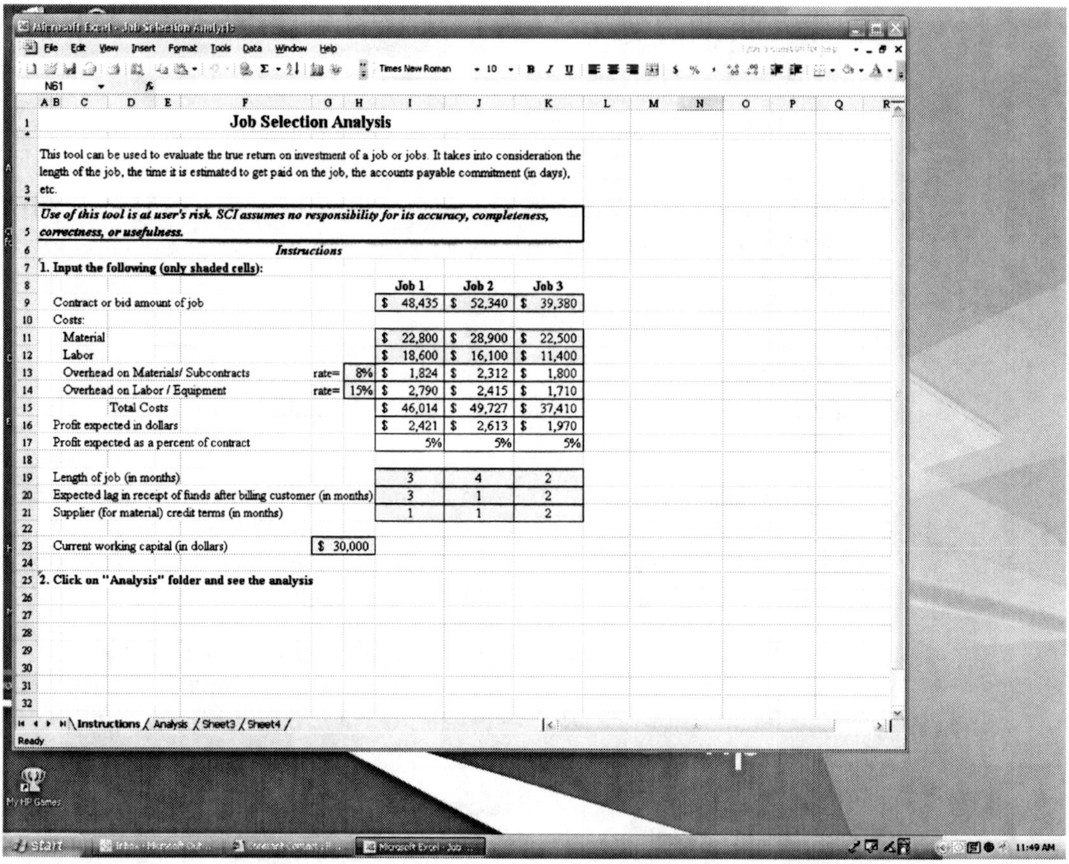

Job Selection Analysis

This tool can be used to evaluate the true return on investment of a job or jobs. It takes into consideration the length of the job, the time it is estimated to get paid on the job, the accounts payable commitment (in days), etc.

Use of this tool is at user's risk. SCI assumes no responsibility for its accuracy, completeness, correctness, or usefulness.

Instructions

1. Input the following (only shaded cells):

			Job 1	Job 2	Job 3
Contract or bid amount of job			$ 48,435	$ 52,340	$ 39,380
Costs:					
Material			$ 22,800	$ 28,900	$ 22,500
Labor			$ 18,600	$ 16,100	$ 11,400
Overhead on Materials/ Subcontracts	rate=	8%	$ 1,824	$ 2,312	$ 1,800
Overhead on Labor / Equipment	rate=	15%	$ 2,790	$ 2,415	$ 1,710
Total Costs			$ 46,014	$ 49,727	$ 37,410
Profit expected in dollars			$ 2,421	$ 2,613	$ 1,970
Profit expected as a percent of contract			5%	5%	5%
Length of job (in months)			3	4	2
Expected lag in receipt of funds after billing customer (in months)			3	1	2
Supplier (for material) credit terms (in months)			1	1	2
Current working capital (in dollars)		$ 30,000			

2. Click on "Analysis" folder and see the analysis

FIGURE 2-15
This template is useful for determining ROI for different projects. We use a simple version in this example.

financial job. Check the numbers in Figure 2-15 and see which project you think has the highest ROI.

Before you decide, be aware of two key points:

1. We assume you personally estimated these jobs. In other words, we assume the costs are accurate and there are no hidden savings.
2. The answer will be decided on the best ROI. No other factors are in this exercise.

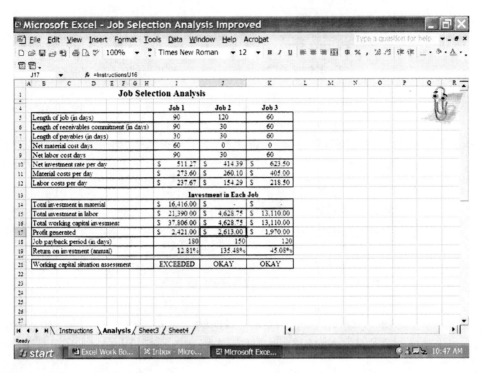

FIGURE 2-16
The result may surprise you, but upon reviewing the calculation the result should make sense.

Below we have listed the factors that determine the ROI for a project. Another way to look at project ROI is that it is the return on working capital that you have invested in a project. From the top of this example:

1. **Revenue.** The proposed bid amount of the job.

2. **Costs.** These are the direct costs to build the project.

3. **Overhead.** The cost of the office, management salaries, and computers to support the field operations. We are using a dual rate, which we discussed earlier.

4. **Profit.** Five percent markup on cost. This percent is for example only.

5. **Length of job.** The total length of construction.

6. **Client pay.** How long the client takes to pay after billing.

7. **Supplier credit terms.** When the payment is due to the supplier.

8. **Working capital.** This is the amount of funds to pay for costs before payment. Exceeding your working capital means you will have to borrow funds and, thus, reduce your ROI. Note: no contractor has unlimited working capital (only the federal government has that).

Which project has the best ROI? Certainly not Job 1; more contractors unanimously agreed in seminars that this project has little to make it attractive. That is the right answer. By executing this step, we never bid this project or bid it at a higher amount. The client pay lag of 90 days is never attractive to any business person.

The second page is the output page. Because this template is a spreadsheet, the numbers can be manipulated. In other words, "what-if" scenarios can be inputted. You can see what different profit and cash flow situations produce financially.

The best ROI seems to be between Job 2 and Job 3. The answer, as shown in Figure 2-16, may surprise you.

Job 2 is the correct answer. You might be wondering how this can be true. Let's look at the calculation. Because the profit margin is the same for all three jobs, it must be another factor.

The other factor is commonly known as cash flow. To most people, *cash flow* is the speed at which a client makes a payment. At least that is part of it. The other part is the speed at which cost is accumulated. More specifically, labor must be paid weekly in the construction business. Thus, high-labor jobs have a high speed of cash outflow.

As an example, a job that has no labor and all subcontractors is typically cash-flow neutral to the contractor, except for general conditions cost and the overhead in the office. From a financial perspective, a job that is paying well and demands less working capital is the best job a contractor can wish for.

The basis calculation for ROI is:

Annualized Profit
Divided by
Working Capital Dollars Required

Jobs that require the contractor to build with his own money are jobs that have risk and take away from ROI.

ROI = ($2,613.00 ÷ 5 month payback period) × (12 months)) / ($4,628.75) = ($6,271.2) / ($4,628.75) = 135.48 %

Job 2 has a low working capital demand of $4,628.75. This shows that we should be able to build at least six of these kinds of projects without borrowing. On Job 2, we can only build two at a time.

Run the same calculation for Job 3 and Job 1. You will find the answers shown in Figure 2-16.

This is not the end of the discussion about project selection. Certainly, if Job 2 is 1,000 miles away, or with a new client or a new type of construction, it does not look as promising.

Job 3 is also a strong one. As a general rule, returns over 40 percent are exceptional and should be a business goal. If this project is next door to your office, it looks even stronger. Those types of projects are visited by the project manager, safety director, and the president every day. This job type tends to be efficient and it is not hard to understand why.

However, Job 1 is a poor candidate for a contractor because it has a modest return. We have a job that will demand $37,000 of working capital before we are paid. This means we will have to borrow, adding debt to our business and interest payments to our cost of work. The beauty of a spreadsheet is we can change the variable and see the what-if result.

Let's do that. We can add profit to the job and see what the return will be. Again, a higher bid is an option. We can input $55,000 as a new bid price, a 16 percent markup on cost. See Figure 2-17 and Figure 2-18.

Now, let's see the result of our new bid price for Job 1.

Now, we can go forward and think about bidding on this project. Again, we raised the profit margin to reflect an ROI goal, but it is clear that the major hurdle of exceeding our working capital still exists.

This represents a significant step in working smarter. We will be cautious about taking on projects that can cause us financial difficulty.

								Job 1	Job 2	Job 3
1					Job selection analysis					
2										
3					This tool can be used to evaluate the true return on investment of a job or jobs. It takes into consideration the length of the job, the time it is estimated to get paid on the job, the accounts payable commitment (in days), etc.					
4										
5										
6					Instructions					
7	1.	Input the following (only shaded cells):								
8								Job 1	Job 2	Job 3
9		Contract or bid amount of job						$ 55,000	$ 52,340	$ 39,380
10		Costs:								
11			Material					$ 22,800	$ 28,900	$ 22,500
12			Labor					$ 18,600	$ 16,100	$ 11,400
13		Overhead on materials/subcontracts			rate =	8%	$ 1,824	$ 2,312	$ 1,800
14		Overhead on labor/equipment			rate =	15%	$ 2,790	$ 2,415	$ 1,710
15				Total costs				$ 46,014	$ 49,727	$ 37,410
16		Profit expected in dollars						$ 8,986	$ 2,613	$ 1,970
17		Profit expected as a percent of contract						16%	5%	5%
18										
19		Length of job (in months)						3	4	2
20		Expected lag in receipt of funds after billing customer (in months)						3	1	2
21		Supplier (for material) credit terms (in months)						1	1	2
22										
23		Current working capital (in dollars)			$ 30,000					

FIGURE 2-17
We have changed the bid amount for Job 1.

Job selection analysis

	Job 1	Job 2	Job 3
Length of job (in days)	90	120	60
Length of receivables commitment (in days)	90	30	60
Length of payables (in days)	30	30	60
Net material cost days	60	0	0
Net labor cost days	90	30	60
Net investment rate per day	$ 511.27	$ 414.39	$ 623.50
Material costs per day	$ 273.60	$ 260.10	$ 405.00
Labor costs per day	$ 237.67	$ 154.29	$ 218.50
Investment in Each Job			
Total investment in material	$ 16,416.00	$ -	$ -
Total investment in labor	$ 21,390.00	$ 4,628.75	$ 13,110.00
Total working capital investment	$ 37,806.00	$ 4,628.75	$ 13,110.00
Profit generated	$ 8,986.00	$ 2,613.00	$ 1,970.00
Job payback period (in days)	180	150	120
Return on investment (annual)	47.54%	135.48%	45.08%
Working capital situation assessment	EXCEEDED	OKAY	OKAY

FIGURE 2-18
This shows a 47.54 percent ROI for Job 1.

My opinion is that this template needs to be run on every project. It can determine the starting point for final price decisions or if we should bid the project at all.

Real-World Bidding Strategy Approaches

Can we make any sense out of bidding results? Is there a way to use the results to our advantage? Would it be a worthwhile profitable) endeavor? The answers to all these questions is yes!

From Marvin Gates's breakthrough work in the 1960s to today, bidding smart has evolved from mostly art to mostly science. As you know, science is teachable.

The following are factors that bidders use to derive the best price:

- Bidding strategy is not derived from "gut feel," but from facts. The list below is a sample of the factors that a contractor might use to determine a bid price on a particular job.
- Number of bidders
- Backlog
- Bidding history

- Location
- Speed
- Labor content
- Type of work
- Several other factors

Could we use these factors to place the appropriate price on a job? A time-dated example is this: a contractor takes three envelopes to the bid opening. One envelope is to be used if less than three contractors are there, one is for if more than three contractors are there, and the last is if no other contractors are there. This is pricing according to the competition.

Some factors decrease your bid price and some increase it. However, good statistical practices, with an understanding of your cost, can lead you to higher and more consistent profits.

As an example, the most profitable insurance product is life insurance. Why? When the average person will die is not a statistical mystery. Current actuarial tables project men passing away in their late 70s and women a few years after that. Insurance firms use modifying factors to raise or lower life expectancy, such as tobacco use, alcohol consumption, family health history, and so forth. From this statistical work, the underwriter estimates the years of life left for that person.

As part of the business calculation, we subtract the person's current age from that life expectancy. The next step is to reduce the policy amount to the present value (the inverse of the expected growth of a premium investment) and add a commission cost by the salesperson. Then, divide this present value by the years of life left and that is your yearly premium. Certainly, each life insurance application is subject to some modification based on unique circumstances, just as a contractor's bid is.

Las Vegas offers another example of using statistics to our advantage. Sin City knows exactly what percentage advantage they have on each type of game. That is, they will win more than the typical customer by some percentage. Depending on the game, how much the house takes varies, but it is in their favor.

Las Vegas cannot predict if you, as an individual, will win or lose, but they do know that if a thousand of people like you gamble on an average day, they will win (profit) by some amount.

The value of these examples is this: if we use statistics, we consistently win on jobs we want and leave less money on the table by doing so.

The linchpin of the equation is information. This is true for insurance companies, casinos, and construction contractors. Each bid contains valuable information for construction to capture and use. See the columns in Figure 2-19.

1. **Competitors.** They are your like-minded and capable equals. They approach the business much as you do, with ethics, qualified crews, and a reputation for superior work. They, like you, will be around for a long time.

2. **Bid price.** If bids are on public work, this is easily available. If not, a friendly owner or contractor might give you the bid tally (if not now, maybe later).

3. **Cost of the work.** You will never know your competitors' true cost, but you do know your cost for the project.

4. **Margin $.** This is the gross amount difference between your cost and their bids.

5. **Margin %.** This is the percentage difference between your cost and their bids.

	Bid price	Cost	Margin $	Margin %
Desker	$150,000	x	$18,433	14.01%
Triangle	$155,000	x	$23,433	17.81%
Symmetry	$152,430	x	$20,863	15.86%
Galvins	$149,678	x	$18,111	13.77%
Vertical	$151,000	x	$19,433	14.77%
Our company	$154,000	$131,567	$22,433	17.05%

FIGURE 2-19
This comparison shows some overall history of your competitors. This basic information can be used to determine your next bid price.

In the next section, let's look at the rules of bidding that many high ROI contractors observe. This is certainly a section where you can make extra profit by working smarter.

Use estimating digitizers to speed quantity take-offs. Some studies show that using *digitizers* cuts takeoff time in half, while other studies suggest it cuts even more. The power of digitizers is they measure/count quantities quickly.

The Five Rules of Bidding Strategy

The guidelines listed below are the basics for bidding strategy. Violate them at your own peril.

First Rule You *cannot* compete against irrational behavior. If you do, *you* have to become irrational to win against it, and then you will suffer business consequences. What you *can* do is pick the opportunities until the competitor changes. That is rational.

Second Rule Because the most profitable industries use statistics to predict long-term behavior, you should also use them to predict your competitor's moves.

Third Rule Competitors have different values and, thus, they have different strategies. Most people will be consistent in these strategies, however, even if they're flawed. This is one of your competitive edges.

Fourth Rule Don't ever forget that the *higher* the price, the *lower* the hit rate. This is a business rule that can reward you. If you can increase the amount you bid accurately, you can increase your amount of profit.

Fifth Rule Your competitors who are equal to you will raise/lower their price, with many of the same factors, like you do and they will be consistent about them.

So, what about these rules? Can you use them to make more dollars? You know the construction business is a tough one. It has been tough historically and it will be tough for some time. The only conclusion I can make is, while we can't control it, we can change it. We can try to make a healthy profit as we work hard and endure hardship.

Tomorrow's bid should consider the history of your competitors.

1. **Median % of margin.** We don't use averages because of mistakes and plug numbers. A median is calculated by not using the highest bid(s) and the lowest bid(s). Competitors have bid errors, such as missed quantities and math errors, but these are not qualified bids. The same could be said for quotes where your peer is busy and submits a high number.

2. **Least is the median least (not the average).** This is the lowest responsible bid they submitted and it's good information to have if you want a job.

3. **Most is the median most (not the average).** This is the highest responsible bid and it's good information to have if you don't want the job. See Figure 2-20.

	Median margin %	Least	Most
Desker	14.15%	13.10%	17.00%
Triangle	15.78%	14.22%	20.10%
Symmetry	14.34%	13.00%	18.88%
Galvins	13.90%	12.90%	17.76%
Vertical	14.50%	13.50%	15.50%
Our company	N/A		

FIGURE 2-20
Least and most bid history give you the information to bid below your competitors or above them. Either is necessary in certain situations.

1. **If I want the job today, what should I bid?**   You will bid below the lowest percentage markup of all the competitors. You should bid 12.89 percent. As in all statistical situations, you don't have a lock on the bid, but this can give you a high probability of winning the job.

2. **If I don't want the job, what should I bid?**   To give yourself the least chance of winning the job, you should bid above the highest median bid. In this case, the markup should be above 20.1 percent. As a friend once joked, if you happen to win the project, you can always subcontract it to the Galvins.

3. **What is my best guess of the projected final cost?**   The projected final cost is your overall estimate. Our estimators know unit cost, but we should add or subtract cost on a macro view. Factors to consider might include:

    - The ability to work with the client
    - The number of potential change orders
    - Business environment
    - Regulatory problems
    - The ability of the client to coordinate

4. **What is the business opportunity for profit?**   This is when the poker game starts. What should I do and how will the competition act? This is where the statistical work comes in. You won't use statistics completely to make this call, but statistics should be over 50 percent of the decision. Good, solid information can tell you some of the following:

A. What is the lowest markup the project competition has ever bid (against my cost)?

B. What is my chance of success against this number of competitors?

C. What is the current backlog of these competitors and, therefore, do I have a chance to add a percent on to my usual profit?

D. What is the safest low bid? That is, if I don't want the project, but I don't want to insult the client by saying "no bid."

Again, you will have other questions to be answered. These are just an example.

Contractors in this country have used this bidding approach and won in two ways:

    A. Priced projects appropriately for the risk involved and, there-fore, they don't involve themselves in losing propositions.

    B. Taken advantage of windfall opportunities.

This adds up to wealth building for contractors and their families, which is a worthy reward for all the hard work involved in the construction business.

> Use a proven method to apply overhead cost accurately to bids and to profitability analysis. The dual overhead approach is one method that gives the contractor a realistic cost of overhead.

Unbalanced Bidding

We believe strongly that contractors make the most money in the field. Building work on time and on budget is the hallmark of great contractors and, also, of profitable ones. But this is not the only place a construction firm makes money. The bid table is another place. Contractors can add margin to his bottom line in many ways by using work-smart strategies when they propose profitable work.

Examples, such as the use of the Gates Model, Dual Overhead Rate Recovery, and job sizing, are winning methods to keep risk lower and profit higher while estimating, pricing, and bidding work. *Unbalanced bidding* is another process that helps construction firms make an extra margin on certain types of bids.

With the advent of job order contracts and other unit price contract-ing methods, opportunities arise. Owners have attempted to further control costs by creating these contract terms. Business-minded contractors know that for every change, they have some chance to profit from it.

For owners to use job order contracts and other unit price methods, they must first have a count or quantity takeoff of the work. In other words, they have to know the amount of work, so they can compare total costs of Contractor A versus Contractor B, and so forth.

The count is performed by someone working for the owner. This could be the engineer, the architect, or an outside firm. As contractors know, the count is sometimes inaccurate, which makes it an inexact takeoff. Unbalanced bidding is a way to approach an inaccurate count by the owner or client. Here is the basic approach:

- On undercounts, use a higher-than-market unit price
- On correct counts, use an average market unit price
- On overcounts, use a lower-than-market unit price

Let's look at undercounts and overcounts. These are the two areas to which unbalanced bidding applies. This project has both undercounts and overcounts.

Overcounts: Overcounts occur when an owner estimates more quantity than what is actually needed.

- The owner thinks the quantity is 100 units.
- Contractor A *knows* there is X work of 50 units.
- Contractor A bids $9 a unit, while others bid $10 (the market price). The bid margin is cut to 18 percent. This makes sense because we aren't going to do much of this work.
- The owner sees Contractor A's bid at $900 and others' bids at $1,000. Contractor A's price is low.

Undercounts: Undercounts occur when an owner estimates less quantity than what is needed.

- The owner *thinks* the quantity is 100 units.
- Contractor A *knows* there is a quantity Z work of 150 units.
- Contractor A bids $10.90 a unit, while others bid $10 (the market price). The margin is raised to 22 percent. This makes sense because we are going to do a lot of this work.
- The owner sees Contractor A's bid at $1,090 and others' bids at $1,000. Contractor A's price is high. When you combine the total bid, though, Contractor A is lower that the other bidder: $1,990 versus $2,000.

At the End of the Job Is Where This Strategy Makes Sense

The quantity of X work installed is 50 units at a bid price of $9 = $450 revenue at a margin of 18 percent.

The quantity of Z work installed is 150 units at a bid price of $10.90 = $1,635 revenue at a margin of 22 percent.

The total revenue is $2,085 at 21 percent margin. This is a more profitable job than if we bid it "balanced."

Unbalanced bidding is an effective way to benefit from careful estimating of actual quantities. A thoughtful site review and/or good quantity takeoff are essential. The job cost of the work is the same for both contractors, but you have taken an entrepreneurial approach and profited greatly. You are being compensated for our careful, thoughtful takeoff.

We work in the second riskiest industry in the United States and we are underpaid for it. The approximate average of net profit for construction firms is 3 percent, so this is not a lucrative business.

Using a business approach to contracting is a rational choice. Unbalanced bidding is one of those business approaches that make sense to unit-price contracting methods. A thoughtful site review and/or good quantity takeoff are essential. Figure 2-21 shows another example:

Work item	Estimated count by owner	Actual count (estimated by you)	Unit price by competitor and total bid ()	Unbalanced bid by you and total bid ()	Actual revenue to you at end of job
Type A	100	100	$5.00 = ($500)	$4.50 = ($450)	$450
Type B	100	1000	$15.00 = ($1500)	$15.40 = ($1540)	$5,400
Total bid as estimated by owner			$2,000	$1990	

FIGURE 2-21
Unbalanced bidding is an effective way to benefit from the careful estimating of actual quantities. The job cost of the work is the same for both contractors, but you have taken an entrepreneurial approach and profited greatly.

> Require the estimator and the project manager to meet within a week or less of winning a job. They know the estimator's memory is fading fast about the project and its details. Also, the project manager can start planning at an earlier stage.

Markup versus Margin

Markup and margin are confusing terms in the construction contracting industry. They only seem to be slightly different, but these concepts produce widely different results. If you care about profits, then you should be interested. Let's look at how they can affect your profit and, thus, your wealth building.

Markup Is Profit Percentage as a Factor of Cost   Cost is the basis for the profit calculation. As an illustration, if you have a cost of $100 and you want to make a 10 percent margin, then you multiply .10 by $100 and add the result—$10—to your cost of $100. Your price to the client is $110.00. We have all performed the math thousands of times, so it's no mystery. Most professionals were taught this as the only way to calculate profit.

Margin Is the Use of a Profit Percentage That Is a Factor of Revenue Revenue is the basis for the profit calculation. Financial pro formas relate all costs as a percentage of revenue (not of cost). To accurately follow your financial planning, you have to keep all expenses clearly defined and easy to follow for your employees. To use markup can confuse your employees if you are seeking a 10 percent margin.

The power of this is that all other costs are budgeted as a percentage of revenue. So, as you plan for the coming year, you and your employees will be accurate in marking up work. Good, consistent financial results over the years are a result of disciplined estimating, field work, and financial management, such as using margin instead of markup to add profit to cost.

This is quite simple. To calculate margin:

1. Take the 1 and subtract the percentage desired (1–10)
2. Divide the remainder into the cost (100/.9)

In application, our \$100 cost, divided by .9, is \$111.11. The 11.11 of profit is exactly 10 percent of 111.11.

Even if you don't budget by this markup, some clients restrict your markup to a certain percentage. Margin would be a better way to go because it adds to your compensation for the risk you are undertaking.

Also, for budgeting purposes, it would be beneficial to use this method because it relates profit to a percentage of revenue. All other budget items on your profit and loss statements are expressed as a percentage of revenue. Why shouldn't it be the same with profit?

If you project making 10 percent on revenue, your people cannot achieve that using 10 percent on cost. Knowing your cost and profit is a critical step in any strategic planning.

No windfalls are left in construction, or as a high government official once said, There are "unknown unknowns." Construction contracting doesn't have a lot of uncharted waters. Things are more known here than in other industries. The business is about taking small insights and leveraging them.

We believe contractors are "bleeding from a thousand cuts." There is no major inefficiency. It is the little things that add up to percentage points. In other words, no silver bullet exists for improving your company quickly. There is no secret formula. The closest thing is the discipline to use small advantages, such as using margin instead of markup. These little gains do add up and allow contractors to reach 40 percent or better ROI. This is what they should earn considering all the risk contractors undertake.

After You Win the Job

You win a job at 2 P.M. and you have many new friends at 2:15 P.M. That is what's called the Successful Bidder's Syndrome. You win the work, and then spend the next two days answering phone calls from suppliers, subcontractors, service providers, and other interested parties.

Let me say what others have said. The critical time to pre-job plan is before the job starts, especially the hours after the job has been estimated, bid, and won. As you and I know, estimators are clearest immediately after the bid. They understand the facts, the complexities, and the other parties without any confusion.

After a week, they have gone on to another project to estimate and they start to mix up information in their heads. If you have a download session at this time, the field supervisors and project managers suffer. They don't get the unadulterated facts and, therefore, they don't have complete information about the job. Remember, the estimator is the only one who has slept with this job and who possesses full knowledge of the facts.

When is a great time to have the pre-job planning conference with the office and the field: the afternoon immediately following the bid or the next morning. How do you do this with all the phone calls and visits by your new friends? We minimize access.

A letter must be written by the contractor stating that he politely requests no contact be made with the firm about this project. The contractor will contact them at the appropriate time. The president signs the letter and it is faxed (e-mailed) to all the interested parties. The letter outlines the reasons why the company needs this quiet time. No one should take offense. You will find the letter discourages unnecessary contact with the contractor concerning the recently won work.

As a side note, our experience has been that the suppliers, subcontractors, and others will continue to bid to you. They aren't sensitive to this controlled access after a bid. There is no downside. When you win a job, you will still be popular.

After a few projects, the construction community will learn your culture. You are not to be contacted after winning a project and only an occasional wayward salesperson will call.

What is the result? Your people will enjoy the ability to focus on the project. Your support staff, especially the receptionist, will appreciate the new environment. Additionally, the company has clearly instituted a pre-job planning culture. Those of us in the industry know why:

1. The biggest opportunity to beat the schedule and the budget is in preconstruction planning. If the field and the office don't know the job in great detail, then they will miss significant opportunities in recognizing project changes, scope creep, and other profit impacts.

2. The only opportunity is before the job begins. Once this is missed, it is lost forever. Mobilization day and the days afterward are all-consuming. The quiet time before the start of field work is the only time to study, plan, and think through contingency plans.

3. The best opportunity is just after you win the project. The estimator's memory is fading fast. He is on to the next project and details start being confused from job to job. The download from estimator to project manager to field supervisor is optimum within 48 hours of winning the project.

This is why disciplined processes are valuable. Preconstruction planning is an old concept, however, it does not happen on every job. Those who do execute this process consistently are the ones who are beating other contractors by a nose.

> Superior contractors have their major business processes mapped out in writing and understood by all employees. Resulting in fewer missteps and, thus, they get more done in a day.

Estimating Software

Go to any national convention and you can't miss seeing dozens of software vendors. This is a big business and it is high value for construction firms. The product has made estimating less clerical and more of a management position. In other words, it has made estimating more efficient. Because of its power, counting and measuring are less of a task, taking hours instead of days. For those of us who don't look forward to the job of estimating, computers and software have made it bearable.

I feel that most estimating software is useful for contractors, but I have personally witnessed software purchased one day, and then never used. The salesman did his job. The rub is the time it takes to become proficient. The contractor's busy schedule doesn't allow for training. In several cases I know of, thousands of dollars have been invested with no payoff. The software sits in its shrinkwrap, still unopened.

I am raising a red flag here. Look at all the risk factors in construction—some of it we choose. Buying estimating software (decreasing your cash) and never benefiting from it should not be one of your risk factors.

I recommend looking hard at Microsoft. (See the section "Software" in Chapter 1.) If you use a computer, you can use the

Microsoft Office Suite (90 percent of users do) and, especially, Excel. For anyone just starting to use computers, the advent of the point-and-click system, also known as Windows, makes it all the more easy.

As proof of my conclusion, The American Society of Professional Estimators released a survey in 2005. Here is the background and these are the results:

1. Respondents were asked their satisfaction level with their current estimating software and these are the results:
   - Satisfied: 80 percent
   - Fairly satisfied: 14 percent
   - Dissatisfied/plan to change: 3 percent
   - Other (n/a): 2 percent

2. Respondents were asked if they anticipate change soon (one year or less):
   - No change planned: 93 percent
   - Plan to change soon: 7 percent

3. Respondents were asked the major factor in the purchase of their estimating software:
   - Ease of use: 30 percent
   - Customization: 30 percent
   - Features: 25 percent
   - Price: 4 percent
   - Other (n/a): 11 percent

4. Average time in use
   - 1–5 years: 32 percent
   - 5–10 years: 47 percent
   - 10+ years: 21 percent

5. Respondents were asked the type of software they use for cost estimating:

EXCEL	29 percent
TIMBERLINE	22 percent
OTHER/INHOUSE	14 percent
MS OFFICE/ MS2000	9 percent
MC2	7 percent
PROPRIETARY	3 percent
ACCUBID	3 percent
WINEST	2 percent
QUICKBID	1 percent
HEAVYBID	1 percent
LOTUS	1 percent
ONCENTER	1 percent
PRIMAVERA	1 percent
PROLOG	1 percent
AUTOBID	1 percent
PRECISION	1 percent
CONST LINK	1 percent
BIDTEK	1 percent
MCCORMICK	1 percent

Source: American Society of Professional Estimators, Alexandria, Virginia. Edward B. Walsh, Executive Director—Software Survey

We conclude that Microsoft Excel is clearly the leading solution for cost estimating. Interesting to note that self-created systems are utilized over 50 percent of the time.

Estimating software is a must for any contractor looking to reduce his time bidding work. There are many other benefits, such as more accurate and organized bid proposals. However, like any good idea, understanding its practicality lets you bypass a steep and painful learning curve.

One way to work smarter is to coordinate and schedule backward. That is, work back in time from a milestone and include submittal, manufacturing lead time, and delivery time in planning. This keeps stress and extraordinary costs to a minimum.

Estimating Assemblies

Estimating has gone from an arduous counting and measuring exercise to a less stressful, more global function. The advent of computer technology and software transformed this position in the late 1980s and it continues to change.

Digitizers and estimating software are creations of our country's technology expertise. The construction industry benefits from this every day. Hours of poring over plans are no longer necessary. Our quantity takeoff work can be accomplished in less than an hour (for most specialty contractors).

Has the industry been slow to capitalize on technology's dramatic advances? In a word, yes. Some reasons are compelling. The main reason is accuracy. We agree all contractors should use tools in which we have complete confidence.

Some argue that tools, such as scaled rulers, measuring wheels, and the like, are trusted. We have been successful in the past with these and we should be successful in the future. The construction industry is brutal to those who are careless and inexact.

We would be the first ones to recommend erring on the side of caution. More project problems emanate from bad takeoffs than we care to guess. Suffice it to say that if we count 0 as our quantity then it does not matter what our cost is. Zero times any number is zero. Quantity survey should be an area of caution. The time saving afforded by computerized systems is also compelling, however. In fact, it's more compelling than the possible risk error. Time and money can be saved if you choose to use this approach.

What is the time-saving opportunity? Studies indicate that takeoff and pricing is reduced by four-fifths or 80 percent when you use a digitized takeoff method, cost database, and a calculating summary sheet. Again, you are working at an efficiency improvement of greater than 75 percent. We believe it is significant at the least.

This leaves more time for catching details and giving more thought to the business considerations of the bid. We no longer have to be "stepping and fetching." We can now think through our approach to winning the construction work.

We do not sell software, and therefore, we have no interest in recommending software. So, for practical purposes, there is no software in the market that we must tell you about. They are all brand *X*. Quite frankly, we don't have a dog in this fight.

Part of the power of computerized estimating is assemblies, which are preprogrammed formulas that convert quantities taken off into labor, material, equipment, and other cost units. They can be simple or complex. The assemblies most commonly used are ones that will calculate multiple material quantities from one measurement.

- All assemblies are built with the basic information listed below. Several other factors can be added, but these have to be part of any calculation.
- Length
- Width
- Height
- Each

Surprised? You shouldn't be. Construction is a straightforward business.

From these variables, you should be able to calculate each of the following:

- Lineal feet
- Square feet or square yards
- Cubic feet or cubic yards
- Each (each time the number of parts in the work item)

As an example, a footing length is measured. The assembly converts the following material quantities:

1. Cubic yards of footing excavation
2. Cubic yards of concrete
3. Lineal feet of footing form
4. Lineal feet of reinforcing bar

5. Lineal feet of stem wall

6. Square feet/lifts of footing dirt fill recompaction

7. Lineal feet of slab edge form

8. Number of concrete blocks in wall

9. CY of grout fill

10. CY of cell fill

11. CF of mortar

12. Lineal feet of furring strips

13. Lineal feet of horizontal block reinforcing

14. Number of bricks

15. Number of dove-tail slots

16. Waste/shrinkage factors for all the above

17. Several others depending on the type of construction

We do need to enter in project-specific information in some categories, such as depth of cut and height of wall, but most inputs can be defaulted to code or building customs.

All this comes from a simple, single digitized measurement. Can you now see this is a work smart-practice? It can literally save anyone hundreds of hours.

How do you build an assembly? Quite simply by 1) figuring out the math and 2) creating constants. Let's take the previous example:

We have a footing to dig, form, pour, and so forth. The length of the footing is a constant reference variable. It is 24″ wide by 12″ deep by its length. It will be referred to in your software as continuous footing.

Then, the software should let you select your variables of:

- Width (in feet)
- Height (in feet)

Once the digitizer inputs distances (or you can type in its length), then the computer does its calculation for concrete: continuous footing × width × height/27. Waste is added later.

The variables are unique and to remember them takes some learning, but using this is much easier (and faster) to arrive at quantities. The whole process is not much different than if you used manual means. The computer automates it.

One of the changes that people have to go through is the computer does its calculations in a black box. You input your information into the system and it comes out on a summary sheet. How the system calculated the information, you cannot tell. This leads to some discomfort. If you input wrong quantities, you might not be able to catch an error. However, if you use triangulation, you can certainly catch major errors. That is, if you use any one of the following to double-check the estimate, it will tell you if quantity and costing was reasonable.

Here are some examples:

- SF cost of building to pour concrete
- CY of concrete/SF of floor area ratio
- Total cost of CY concrete installed
- Labor hours per CY to install

Changing to a computerized system of estimating may be uncomfortable for someone who has used a tried-and-true method. It might lead to errors. Nevertheless, the world of estimating is changing. Business considerations have taken over. Clients are less loyal, the cost of putting together an estimate is a consideration, and hit rates have decreased. This all means we have to be faster with our estimates and produce more of them with the same amount of accuracy.

What the Top 25 Percent of All Estimators Do

Here is a list of priorities that all top estimators have. From my experience, these are the areas that they focus on:

1. Know the base bid scope and all alternates.
2. Finish quantity takeoff and labor pricing the day before the bid.

3. Keep your takeoff and pricing organized, and readable for others to build from.

4. Understand the capabilities of all subcontractors and suppliers.

5. Use checklists and markings for all estimates, so nothing is overlooked.

6. Be accurate about cost. Estimating success is not about being low.

7. Create a sense of urgency in all project team members (company team, subcontractors, owner, architect, and consultants). Lead by example.

8. Establish and maintain good communications with field and project management staff. Expect the same of them.

9. Address all gray areas of plans and specifications the day before the bid is due.

10. Use at least two practical double-checks to catch any errors on all bids.

11. Make sure you help the project manager and field manager meet and beat your estimate.

12. Know it is OK to say this project is unusually risky.

13. Promptly hand off the project information to the project manager and field manager. Your memory is fading. Establish a deadline date for this estimate-information turnover meeting.

14. Try to keep all bids with project specifications or have a good business reason why it should vary.

15. Document all verbal agreements or deals. Be upfront about any understandings with your project team. Don't have any undisclosed promises. Get the ugly news out early.

16. Good estimators know their limits and ask for help when it's needed. They are ultimately responsible for accuracy and timeliness. Never assume anything. Confirm and reconfirm.

Excellent contractors require field managers to plan weekly (monthly) in writing. Field managers know the most about a project because they work on it daily. The contractor does review his weekly plan to keep the project at a high level of quality. This also keeps coaching and communication good between the field supervisor and the contractor.

CHAPTER SUMMARY

Getting work means building work. Without this skill, a contractor is just a pricing service.

The estimator's job is more than just counting, costing, and bidding. He is part of the building team more than ever before.

Estimating is more science than art. Here is a list of the steps to show you what I mean:

- Estimates come from counting and price information.
- Costing general conditions involves a checklist of information filled out with project details.
- Overhead application is a formula calculated with the cost of running the construction organization.
- Job sizing is an equation.
- Bid pricing is based on competitor information, as well as your internal company business demands.

All of this is more science than art. The art is woven into the science. Gut feel has to be used about construction methods and how they will impact costs. Can we trust our capability to get the job done in the contract time? What are the uncontrollable issues in this project? Last, what cuts/adds do we need to make as bid time approaches? As you know, we sometimes have to make a guess about extra costs, risk, or opportunity. When negotiating with a client, there is some gut feeling that goes into it. It is unscientific. A word of counsel, be conservative when you do this.

However, estimating begins with science and it should never be a majority of guesses.

Consistently accurate estimating is a process. There are many risk factors and a thoughtful method addresses the controllable ones.

Besides building work efficiently, bidding strategy is the biggest opportunity for the contractor to add profits to the bottom line.

3

The Build Work Process

The next phase of the cycle is the Build Work step, which is better known as project management. *Project management* is critical to the successful operation of any construction firm because it is where you mostly build, manage costs, and then bill the customer. Thus, this the only place you realize profits. Poor performance here negatively affects the other two steps and, even more important, the company.

From a business perspective, Build Work contains two components that can increase its speed (while keeping accuracy high):

1. Executing all the duties of the Build Work Phase
2. Transferring the information to the Keep Track Phase

First, let's look at an overview of project management for construction contractors.

WHAT IS PROJECT MANAGEMENT IN CONSTRUCTION?

Project management is now a term used by many industries. What once was an exclusive term to the construction industry is used by a variety of professionals. The definition has evolved into a less definite one. However, a construction project manager still has clearly defined responsibilities. Also, the process of project management is not ambiguous.

The Right Processes Used By the Right People

Study after study concludes that superior project management is the use of the right processes by the right people. Highly successful companies work smart, that is, they do things that are efficient and effective. Project managers work hard enough. They cannot increase their effort.

Processes Are Critical

Following the correct steps in the proper sequence improves effectiveness. Average project managers (PMs) have improved, not by going back to school, but by following a disciplined approach to managing the construction process.

Construction Is a Business

Positive financial results give companies the fuel to grow. Conversely, negative financial results can kill a company. A business approach to project management differentiates one contractor from his less-profitable brethren.

Two Critical Factors: Financial Management and Schedule Management

Each successful project has two critical factors. Most problem projects result from poor financial management or weak scheduling. The companies that focus on these two areas consistently make higher-than-average profits and enjoy superior client satisfaction.

You Cannot Overcommunicate in Construction

Success often comes in giving everyone the correct information, so they can do their jobs. The PM is a hub who disperses information to suppliers, clients, subcontractors, governmental authorities, and other stakeholders.

Money Is Made in the Field

Without exception, superior PMs support the field. That's where the action is. Keeping the field supplied with the right information to the right person is their credo.

Great People Come from Everywhere

There is no formula. People who like what they do certainly are good at what they do. Additionally, people who believe their company is a fair and interesting place perform conscientiously. Last, those who are trained to succeed perform consistently well.

Follow-up Is a Key to Success

Loose ends end up in someone else's lap, and this could be the client's lap. Tieing up the final pieces gives the project finality and closure to all involved. Persons who appreciate the small details of project management receive high marks from all stakeholders, including clients.

Simplicity Means Speed

This philosophy, which we have observed for several years, is not a sophisticated approach, but a practical one. It covers all areas of construction. Speed (or deadline orientation) is one of the key demands of a project. Two simple processes beat an elegant one every time. This philosophy, coupled with a detailed approach to management, is prevalent in highly respected contracting firms.

Measurement Is Not an Opinion

Measurement seeks facts and verifies results. Good measurement is unbiased, giving executives insight into what is happening. Smart contractors measure events or, in other words, both results (after) and behaviors (before).

Great contractors know that approximately 70 percent of all wasted time is due to material logistics. They understand that most construction stalls when no material is available, when the wrong material is delivered, and so forth.

What Is the Project Management Process?

"A PM is that individual assigned to carry out and be responsible for construction of all or specified portions of a project; also a representative of the owner supervising such work." This definition is according to the *Construction Dictionary*, author: Arizona Chapter #98 of the National Association of Women in Construction, 8th edition.

Project management is like a recent joke about an accountant, an actuary, and an election supervisor. The question to each of them is "What is 2+2?" The punch line from the election supervisor is "What do you want it to be?"

Defining project management varies widely from firm to firm, from specialty contractor (SC) to general contractor (GC), and from commercial to industrial to heavy highway industries. Some forepersons do perform these duties, as well as field management. They are sometimes split between two or more people. In a small firm, the president may be one of the PMs. However, some clear duties, responsibilities, and authorities do emerge.

PMs have two areas of responsibility. One is *discrete,* that is, directly related to a construction job. The other is functional, which translates into the continuous activities that relate more to the business operation. The following outlines discrete activities. Functional activities can be recruiting, continuous improvement, supervising others, and so forth. This section is devoted to the discrete activities.

Project Manager/Estimator?

Let's address the issue of separate or combined PM and estimator responsibilities. We can tell you there is no easy answer. The argument has been going on for centuries and probably started with the Egyptians and the Mayans. It has been their curse on us ever since.

Inherent conflicts exist in the singular PM/estimator role. The first of these is focus. Productive PMs do give their projects great attention. They keep in touch with field supervisors daily and keep the construction process flowing with timely communication, troubleshooting, and other management activities.

Superior estimators have time to put together a thoughtful and detailed bid. They study the plans, specs, and other project documents to make sure of the construction requirements. On bid day, an estimator knows the project well enough to answer questions concerning scope, alternates, addenda, and the like.

Obviously, on small projects, these tasks are not demanding, and a PM can handle them while managing ongoing jobs.

The second conflict is time. The separate duties of estimating and managing make it extremely difficult to give each of these proper attention. What we observed is that bidding is a deadline-oriented activity. A project manager/estimator is always driven by the bidding deadline and will put off a project meeting or the review of an unclear plan detail. But we make money in the field. This is where companies generate revenues and control substantial costs. The project is where most of the risk resides.

In firms that bid and build small projects, combined project management/estimating roles make sense. For projects that are short in duration and have limited detail, any turnover of information would be inefficient. It might even take longer than the job itself.

We have found that construction companies that build large or complex projects use a singular PM. This person can lead the project effectively because they are timelier, and more focused on the project and its progress. One of the talents PMs bring is an understanding of the impact of any changes to the project. They can foresee what effect it has on objectives down the road and can alert others.

The PM is the common link from the construction planning to the closeout stage. This may be the clearest indication of duties. Because of the complex nature of construction, having a single person carry the entire process from planning to completion is extremely important. Successful individuals do understand the interdependency of the chain of events in the construction process and can foresee what impact changes have on three major areas:

1. Cost
2. Schedule
3. Quality

Cost PMs are concerned with the cost of the project that translates into profits for the company. Whether changes impact the original estimated costs or COs, PMs clearly must be concerned with keeping costs in line and/or collecting for any COs on the project.

Schedule PMs must be observant of the schedule. Certainly in the last few years, the words "fast track" have lost their impact—every project is on a fast track. In our instant society, the appreciation for proper coordination has declined. The perception is construction jobs are supposed to be manufactured, even though new parties are involved on a unique design in a place where no one has built before. This sounds unfair and it is, but this is what is expected.

Quality Clearly, from the people we talked to and worked with, quality is nonnegotiable. Contractors do not see this as something that can be scrimped on or circumvented and that is a compliment to the industry. We take pride in what we do, and we continue to see our projects as an extension of our personal integrity.

PMs do not perform clerical tasks. To have a PM making copies, typing transmittals, and doing general office duties is not the best use of their time. To restate, the PM should focus on cost, schedule, and quality. Someone who is tasked with clerical duties should handle other less project-specific duties, such as (1) copying of submittals, (2) typing correspondence, (3) applying for payment and performance bonds. The administrative staff should handle these duties, while the PM focuses on leading the project.

The PM is the first to plan the construction of the project. Of the three stages of planning, building, and closing out a project, planning is the most critical. I have personally experienced and observed that when a job is well-set up, and the information is flowing early from the client to us, and vice versa, those projects do well. It is common knowledge that a construction firm's largest opportunity is to affect the outcome of a project. If this is missed, that opportunity is missed forever.

The major duties a PM should undertake in this planning stage are:

- **RFI documentation and submission.** The submission process should be started in the early stages of the pre-job process. The earlier we start uncovering the unclear areas of the project plans and specifications, the better. The field manager can better plan and coordinate this work with this information.

- **Turnover meeting.** This is a key meeting in the life of the project. Sitting down with the estimator and going through the estimate, project documents, and bid file has to happen. The earlier this occurs, the better. Remember, the estimator's memory fades with each passing day. Day 1 after the bid is significantly better than day 20.

- **Know the client** or the client's decision-maker. Do you have a construction-savvy client? It's important for you to know this before you start building. Otherwise, a loss of dollars and mounting frustration can occur. Certainly, having senior management involved early with a difficult customer can make the best of a poor situation.

- **Scheduling.** Placing the building sequence in a documented form is another important task in a successful construction project. On some projects, this can be ominous and complicated. But, the more project parties, such as field supervision and subcontractors, can come together to create and review the schedule as well as the higher buy-in, the more practical it can be.

- **Preconstruction meeting.** Before the building process begins, the PM must fully educate your field supervisor, as well as other employees. This meeting should be a well-organized and well-documented event. Some typical items to discuss and share are the status of submittals, project schedule, outstanding

RFIs, your contract's scope, and so forth. Without this information, your project team is flying without radar and will inevitably make mistakes. This can cost you in many ways—both tangible and intangible.

- **Confirmation of estimated quantities.** My observation has been that this is sometimes an overlooked step that can lead to a high amount of returns, lost time, and waste. I have seen firms experience as much as 20 percent overordering due to this factor. Using the estimated quantities as the order quantity is a problem in an effective purchasing process. The estimate is just that—an estimate. And, the estimate was usually performed with a myriad of interruptions and the use of overage factors. Additionally, the field supervisor's approach to the building process is invariably different than the estimator's approach. Smart project managers retake off job quantities to make sure they order the correct amounts. Estimators cannot be held to exact counts as jobsite conditions are apt to change.

- **Material buyout.** Right after winning the bid, you must make buyout decisions. The material buyout decision is the first of many steps to the eventual installation. Submittals, shipment release, delivery, and material staging are all necessary, but cannot happen with the purchase decision being made. Our research has shown that up to 70 percent of recoverable lost time is due to material problems. The PM leads and administrates the construction project in the following ways:

1. **Client relations.** Whether you have a hard bid or a negotiated client, this relationship is key. Good relationships mean that contractors can have thoughtful exchanges with the customer on satisfying the schedule, cost, and quality issues inherent in every project. Bad relationships mean the conversation never occurs and frustration by both parties tends to follow.

2. **Financial performance.** Every PM has a fiduciary responsibility to their firm. This is the financial management of their construction project(s). Money is the key ingredient in all

construction firms. Without money, the company (and their employment) will cease to exist. Knowing where the project is in terms of costs versus physical progress must be clearly understood. If a project is in trouble, they should communicate this to senior management. We have observed that repeated profit fade on a PM's jobs does indicate a weakness in several areas, including financial management.

3. **Change order management.** Certainly, this can be key to a successful completion of every project. Large, uncollected dollars in COs can devastate the financial picture. Identifying, documenting, communicating, submitting, and collecting these deserved revenues cannot be ignored. However, sometimes it is important to trade out for other considerations on a project. This certainly makes sense in certain circumstances. The thrust, though, is to make sure we manage the contract we agreed to and to make certain that any changes to the project are communicated to the appropriate parties.

4. **Major material expediting.** Material in construction is almost like oxygen: without it, there is no life. And, without material, this is no construction process. Major items such as structural steel, chillers, transformers, and so forth are critical to meeting project milestones and, typically, affect the critical path schedule of the project. Critical paths are defined as having little or no *float*—which means a delay here can significantly impact project costs and schedule.

5. **Billing/accounts payable.** The financial responsibility for the job resides with the PM. They are running a small business (a construction project) and must look after the costs and the revenues. Their in-depth knowledge of what has already been done and what must be done makes them the appropriate person to perform this task.

6. **Troubleshooting.** This is a talent and a skill. Some of it is innate (talent) and some is learned (skill). Effective PMs know where problems lie and can see them in terms of small pieces. From there, their field and management experience can produce several alternatives or scenarios. Working with the project partners can forge a solution all can live by.

The PM supervises the closeout process of the project. Some typical areas are:

- **Closeout documentation.** Warranty letter, maintenance bond, as-built plans, specs, and so forth are part of the information for the owner to operate the building efficiently. This closeout documentation has to be collected and submitted in a timely fashion if you are to collect your final check.

- **Closeout outstanding COs.** Languishing COs should be handled before the end of the job. In different parts of the country, some COs are always paid at the end of the job, regardless of the project schedule. However, it is still risky to leave this revenue uncollected after the firm has incurred the payroll, material costs, overhead, and so forth for the work. Add the cost of interest to that and the risk is increased.

- **Postproject review.** PMs must be leaders in this area. The information they capture can be both invaluable and a leverage point. Mistakes made twice have no place in this industry: the business is unforgiving. Construction firms should know what went right (people, techniques, and materials) and should repeat this. They should also know what things went poorly, so they do not repeat them.

- **Submit final billing and collect the final check.** In the construction business, your net profits reside in retention. Collecting them is paramount and they should be given to the PM, who knows the history of the job. The PM can quickly fix any deficiencies the client might be concerned about before the final payment is made.

PMs are the single human link in all phases of construction, making them a key employee in ensuring project success. Overwhelming PMs with duties that limit their time and focus can lead to lower margins, schedule difficulties, and quality problems. Contrarily, giving them clear guidelines and expecting excellence can produce greater results. Focusing on the PM's "highest and best use" in relation to duties is paramount because then you can expect them to perform those duties. See Figure 3-1.

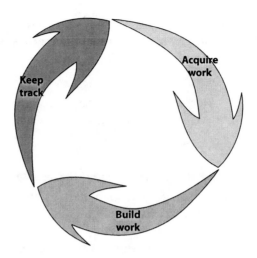

FIGURE 3-1
The build work or project management phase must be defined. Everyone learns a different method causing miscommunication and other problems. Keeping the process consistent leads to faster building and less labor expense. These are two key components of a successful construction project.

Require specific labeling and/or packaging to keep labor productivity high. Labor overruns are a great risk on a construction project. This is one way to keep labor as productive as possible.

Preconstruction

During the preconstruction phase, the PM's responsibility is to plan and execute preliminary activities. As you look at any construction segment, every specialty or GC performs better when they accomplish these preliminary activities immediately after the project is awarded.

An important preconstruction task is to review the contract documents by the PM and superintendent. To understand the contract is to protect the budget. Also, the mobilization plan must be developed by both these managers. The PM is responsible for creating a construction schedule, a schedule of values, the project files, and the job logs. They must facilitate setting up the project in the company's project management system (paper-based, Expedition, Prolog, ConstructWare, and so forth).

Require the field manager (foreman, superintendent, leadman, and so forth) to know the weekly weather forecast for their projects.

Key Responsibilities of the PM

Superior project managers focus on just a few critical areas. Below is a typical list:

- Review and know the contract documents
- Create a plan to beat the schedule and budget
- Develop the CPM schedule
- Create a schedule of values
- Review the preconstruction survey
- Set up the project in the company's PM system
- Assist in developing a mobilization plan
- Buy out the critical path items first, and then the other needs
- Delegate the proper tasks to those who can accomplish them best
- Define and pursue regulatory requirements

Understanding the Contract

Examine and carefully read these items in the contract documents, subcontracts, and any purchase orders. Make sure you understand the implications of these items. If you are unsure, ask your superior for assistance.

1. The particular type of contract-delivery mechanism, such as CM-at-risk, fixed fee, and so forth
2. Payment process, terms and conditions, including retainage, lien waivers, and requisition backup requirements

3. Time limits for submission of documents

4. Unit prices/alternates/allowances

5. Liquidated damages or other penalties

6. Estimating and bidding assumptions affecting the work

7. Purchasing requirements, including owner-furnished material

8. Minority participation goals

9. Project labor agreements or special union issues

10. Closeout requirements

11. Schedule and project milestone requirements

12. Delay notification and changed conditions requirements

13. Insurance, Workers' Compensation, payroll, and bonding requirements

14. Exculpatory language that is unreasonable toward your company

The PM and field manager must be familiar with every aspect of the contract documents. To do so can make or save time and money. They must identify where errors and omissions are present, and point them out to the responsible parties. Communicate by issuing Request For Information (RFIs) as needed to clarify details. Taking time during preconstruction can save both frustration and potential embarrassment, both of which can lead to poor business relationships in the future. See Figure 3-2.

> **Proceed on changed work only after written acknowledgement from the client. Do not rely on verbal communication. This keeps a more clear and enforceable claim on time and money.**

Turnover Meeting

The purpose of the turnover meeting is to communicate critical information to the PM and the field manager from the estimator. These meetings must happen sooner rather than later because the estimator's memory is fading or becoming clouded with the next project to bid.

ABC contracting									
President									
Project manager									Holds turnover meeting and follows agenda
Foreman									
Estimator		Receives job award notification and enters budget into system		Estimator calls for job turnover meeting with 24 hours		Sends to project manager plans, bid, etc. before meeting		Attends turnover meeting and follows agenda	
Estimating group									
Purchasing manager									Attends turnover meeting and follows agenda
Accounting manager									

FIGURE 3-2

This example is part of the process approach we recommend. Contractors benefit greatly when they define major processes and monitor the compliance of the steps involved. Because this is electronic, it is low maintenance, it updates instantly, and there's no need for paper.

The following are what should be discussed at a turnover meeting:

1. The estimate and the strategy for beating (not meeting) the projected cost
2. Critical material and buyout issues

3. Long lead-time delivery items and the schedule impact of those items

4. Key subcontractors, suppliers, and other involved third parties

5. General conditions and unit productivity budget review

6. Union issues (if applicable)

The PM has certain responsibilities arising from this meeting which are critical to getting the job started correctly. First, he should develop a premobilization schedule. This schedule should include all the things that must be accomplished before mobilizing the job site. Some examples are as follows:

1. Building permit

2. Fencing around job site

3. Trailer setup

4. Traffic management plan

5. Regulatory requirements

Summary

Many contractors should add a detailed summary of the scope of work that is required for each subcontractor to meet the plans and specifications. This addendum supports the subcontract, but it does not replace it. It simply identifies those items that may be unique or special requirements of that particular subcontractor. This document is legally binding when attached to the subcontract. Don't forget to always include this scope document in the start-up package to the field supervisor.

Delineating the scope overlaps that often occur between different trades can help. This also clearly defines the commitment made by a subcontractor and helps the PM insist that a subcontractor perform those tasks described in the scope of work summary.

When you start a project is not as important as when you finish in construction. Liquidated damages are levied at the end of a job. Savvy contractors will delay the start of a project by a day or two, so they can start organized and be productive.

Start-Up Schedule

Everyone knows how critical it is to "get out of the ground" quickly. The first 30 to 90 days on a job can make or break a project. The PM should put together a schedule of early construction activities, as well as critical supplier and subcontractor buyouts and submittals, while the working schedule is being developed. Typically, this schedule is built with significant input from the project superintendent and major subcontractors. This information eventually goes into the creation of the baseline logic schedule. The goal is to anticipate all the important items that must be done prior to, and early within, the construction phase of the project.

The schedule should include such items as:

- Early major milestones
- Permits to obtain
- Expected problems and the approach to minimize them
- Critical decisions required by the client or architect
- Critical procurement tasks for major buyout items
- Phasing requirements for construction
- Sequencing and duration for the major phases of work

Turnover meetings must be quality affairs. They must be done with the idea of a complete transfer of information to the PM and field supervisor. Notes should be taken and follow up for any unresolved questions must be done. The momentum created by the meeting can't be lost. The contractor's leadership must assure this momentum is continued.

The biggest opportunity to reduce cost and increase speed is at the beginning of the project. Once this is missed, it cannot be recovered.

Contract Types

The contractor's working relationship with the client is greatly influenced by the contract. Certain types of agreements encourage more openness and patience, while others do not. Understanding these contracts, the rights and responsibilities they afford, and the potential consequences cannot be overstated.

Here are the basic types of contract agreements:

Fixed Price/Lump Sum   This contract stipulates that the contractor must build the project for a fixed price. In theory, this type of contract minimizes the owner's financial risk.

Cost Plus Fee   Most owners do not use this type of contract except where the scope of work is either small or unknown, such as renovation or retrofit projects. This type of contract creates significant risk for the owner and minimal risk for the contractor. Generally, when this type of contract is used, it also contains a Guaranteed Maximum Price (GMP) to limit the owner's risk.

Negotiated Contract   Price is negotiated on the premise that the owner will receive better service and performance as a result. Generally, the owner also has more say in the performance criteria in this type of contractual arrangement. This also allows contractors to differentiate the value of their services on something other than price.

Competitive Bid   Often used in the public environment, this type of contract is awarded to the lowest responsible bidder. The primary concern here is price. Although its use has declined somewhat over time, the competitive bid is still frequently used. Competitive bids can be made through either an open or a closed process. Closed-bid procedures allow owners to be more selective in whom they invite to bid.

Delivery Method of Competitive Bid

This is the traditional process that most contractors grew up with. It is straightforward and well used over the last decades.

General Contractor With this type of delivery method, the owner hires an architect who designs the project. The design documents are used to solicit bids or to negotiate a price for the construction of the project. The architect monitors the contractor and ensures that the plans and specs are followed as directed. Any deviations from the documents must be approved by the architect. Typically, these jobs have a longer duration than other delivery methods.

Construction Manager Owners often hire a representative who is knowledgeable of the construction process to manage the construction of their projects. The contract methods of construction managers (CMs) come in two types. The first type is *CM Agency,* which is when a firm is hired to represent the owner, but holds no subcontracts and is not legally responsible for the final cost or schedule of the project (in this case, risk is negligible). The second type is *CM at Risk,* which causes the contractor to take responsibility for managing the subcontractors, as well as stipulating a final price and schedule to the owner. Although CM at Risk has more risk for the contractor, it also allows for opportunities to generate cost savings and to share those with the owner. This method also allows the contractor to be involved earlier in the preconstruction phase and create cost-saving opportunities for the owner.

Design-Build With the *Design-Build* method, the owner has only one contract, which is for both the design and the construction of the project. More and more owners are requesting this form of contracting and many are negotiated fixed-fee arrangements. Design-Build has an increase in risk for the contractor because the entire team is now responsible for both the design and the construction of the building.

Understanding the different types of contracts and their unique characteristics influence how projects are built and your contractual relationships with other parties on the project. These relationships are important in that they may dictate the amount of leverage you have in managing the construction of the project and your company's overall performance.

Use group-mapping process, such as our Interactive Mapping and Planning Methodology (IMPM) to create schedules or define critical business processes. This creates buy-in and assures compliance.

Project Budgeting—Setting the Financial Stage

The proper management of a project involves more than just getting the project built. Financial management is a critical part of the overall project management process. If a project is managed well financially, it is far more likely to be successful and profitable. If your organization has the appropriate resources—reports, documents, and checks and balances—you should have no surprises. Remember to use all your available resources to help manage the financial aspects of your project. A well-built quality project that loses money is still a losing situation.

Project Budget

Generally, a job budget is created during the estimating phase of a project. Cost codes are set up to the appropriate items and the values are entered as the estimate is developed. This original estimate is handed over to the PM during the turnover meeting. In many cases, the PM may add additional items or expand on the cost codes used by the estimator to more accurately reflect how the job will be built. In other words, a reestimating process occurs to create the baseline budget. For example, every subcontractor and vendor should have one specific cost code assigned for their specific work. Actual buyout changes are also included in the baseline budget. The *baseline budget* is the benchmark from which the financial performance of the project is measured.

It is essential for the PM to have a thorough knowledge of the scope of work and the detailed budget if he is to manage his project effectively. He should review that budget regularly and make necessary changes on a monthly basis for management approval. Your company should conduct regular monthly (at least) budget reviews of all projects in which the budget is updated for changes that have occurred or are anticipated. This becomes the *revised budget*. These changes must be based on an analysis of what is needed to complete the project and meet the required schedule for completion. No COs should be included in the revised budget until they have been approved and signed by the correct person at the client's firm. In fact, all COs should be separated on jobs for easier tracking. Good project management means using the budget to manage the job, not for the job to follow the costs.

From these baseline and revised budget figures, various reports will be generated for periodic analysis. Some examples follow:

- Job Cost Analysis Summary Report
- Job Cost Analysis Detail Report
- Percentage of Completion Comparison and Projection Report
- Subcontractor Status Report (if appropriate)

Your ability to manage risk on a project is in large part due to your ability to manage your costs. When the original estimate becomes the revised budget with its assumptions about productivity, that is in itself what defines the risk components you must manage.

> Teach your foremen to have eight hours of material to install at least ten feet away from crews. Along with a steady flow of information, this keeps crews as productive as possible.

The PM Must Be Labor-Sensitive

As we said previously, labor is where the risk is and the reward is. We believe this is true for the labor-intensive contractor and for the GC, regardless of whether or not they self-perform:

Look at the following example. This is a simplified profit and loss statement from a small SC. Perform the following calculations:

- Labor was inefficient by 10 percent
- Labor was more efficient by 10 percent

Based on these numbers, the answers are as follows:

- 10 percent less-efficient labor equates to breakeven or zero profit
- 10 percent more efficient labor equates to a doubling of profit

Specialty and labor-intensive contractors understand this. They live or die by working with organized GCs and owners.

The quality of a GC is largely determined by the quality of the subcontractors with whom they work. If you are costing your subcontractors efficiency and, therefore, profits, quality subcontractors will not continue to work with you. See Figure 3-3.

As evidence, we know several SCs who give out different prices to different GCs for the same job. The reason is the ability to plan, coordinate, and schedule with each GC.

Let's say you are targeting a productivity gain on your jobs. Surely, your field managers and crews must be involved because they will be the focus on the effort. Some of the best contractors I have worked with keep the message simple and clear.

Based on the previous profit and loss statement, working just 20 more minutes a day per person (cutting 20 minutes of wasted time), translates into a 40 percent gain in profitability. See Figure 3-4.

Scheduling

How does a superintendent begin the planning and scheduling of a new project? For planning, it is wise to use paper, pencil, and a cell phone. For CPM scheduling, software running on a computer is needed. Field supervisors do not typically have laptops at their side and, without a computer, they cannot run scheduling software. So, the question becomes how do they create a rough draft of the beginning CPM schedule to see if they can build the project in normal time?

For average and smaller contractors who need to work smart, several techniques can help you quickly produce needed project information (e-mail us at mstevens@stevensci.com for this information). We offer a scheduling computation form that assists contractors to determine basic schedule information before they pull out their laptops and P3s.

Job management checklist

Job name:	Date:
General contractor:	Job number:

Responsible parties
Estimator _____
Project manager _____
Superintendent _____
Safety director _____
Other _____

Architect _____
Engineer _____
General contractor _____
General contractor's superintendent _____

Job information
Building permit number _____
Job start date _____
Job completion date _____
Job plans dated _____
With revisions dated _____
Addenda numbers/dated _____

Specifications dated _____
Warranty date _____

Comp.	Activity	Resp	Date	Remarks
1	Win job/communicate internally	PE		
2	Turnover meeting/estimator and PM	PM		
3	Verification of quantities	PM		
4	Name field and office staff	PE		
5	Pre subcontractor review	PM		
6	Critical lead time review	PM		
7	Determine subcontract parts	PM		
8	Contract checklist	PM		
9	Review/approve contract	PE		
10	Performance payment bond	PE		
11	Insurance certificates	OM		

FIGURE 3-3
Simple goals give people more confidence that they can succeed. Also, an organized client can help improve a contractor's profitability.

Sales	$500,000	100.00%
Direct costs		
Labor	**200,000**	**40.00**
Materials	200,000	40.00
Equipment	17,500	3.50
Subcontractors	12,500	2.50
Total direct costs	$430,000	86.00
Gross profit	$70,000	14.00
Overhead	$50,000	10.00
Net profit (before taxes)	**$20,000**	**4.00%**

FIGURE 3-4
This is a simple profit and loss statement for a specialty contractor. Notice the amount of labor cost.

> Have a culture that the home office's purpose is to make sure the right information and the right material goes to the right field person at the right time and the right place. That is Job 1.

Creating a Real-world CPM Schedule

A practical and constructible schedule is uncommon in the construction industry. Even with all the software and training on CPM scheduling, we still have those who build and those who schedule. For the most part, they are two different individuals, which is to be expected. However, the superintendent should be creating the schedule and the scheduler should facilitate the process. Here is one way to put the field approach back into a CPM schedule.

This scheduling process was created with practicality in mind. The process includes field, office, and subcontractor management (and, in some cases, supplier management)—the group that builds the project. This method results in both a higher buy-in from the stakeholders of the project and better communication. It produces more detailed and work smart thinking. The end product is that your project is built on paper before it is built in the field.

Planning must occur before scheduling. In recent times, contractors have tended to do little or no planning before the schedule was produced. Getting the schedule created and printed has been a checklist item to be crossed off, instead of an opportunity to better plan, coordinate, and beat the contract deadline. Some young, certified smart PM has been tasked with producing the "pretty picture" of the CPM schedule, and its production satisfies the owner's requirements. The planning is done later by the superintendent. He is essentially building the project with two sets of books: the CPM schedule for the owner and the "mud on the boots" process the superintendent uses. Never the twain shall meet.

This process forces that planning is done and the schedule is built. In addition, it forces communication between the field and the scheduler. As a result, the project is better coordinated, produces less conflict, and creates higher satisfaction all around. The following process is a form of the Interactive Mapping and Planning Methodology (IMPM) we use in consulting.

> Use the punch-as-you-go methodology to keep punchout work to a minimum at the end of the job.

Steps to Interactive CPM Scheduling

> **Step 1:** Determine the time, date, place, and participants for the scheduling process. You will need a room with a large wall(s), an ample supply of 5×8 index cards, colored markers, and tape.
>
> **Step 2:** Have your assistant lay out preliminary cards containing the project milestones on the wall before the meeting. Remember to establish shorthand labels for the schedule components, if this has not already been done. Both of these will save time.

Make sure everyone involved in this scheduling meeting has a complete and detailed understanding of the project demands and resources available. Determining manpower, material, methods, money, machinery, and time needed (five Ms + T) are crucial to creating a viable schedule.

Before you start the meeting, place the project milestones on your wall. Again, this saves time and lets the group focus on the details of the job. Some standard milestones might be:

- Mobilization
- Set forms for foundation
- Top out
- Dry in
- Start drywall
- Completion

Require each person attending to have made-up cards that contain activities (one activity per card) with their estimated time. Make a minimum number for them to bring, say, 25, with no one activity spanning more than 10 working days. This will keep the schedule specific and, thus, measurable.

> **Step 3:** Hold a scheduling meeting. On the wall, complete the posting of the cards that note the activities. Include items such as submittal and material lead-times.
>
> **Step 4:** With the group assembled, establish logic— predecessors, successors, and constraints—such as excavate building pad, dig footings, form footings, run in electrical, run in plumbing systems, owner-furnished equipment, and so forth.
>
> **Step 5:** Set time durations for each work activity. Use normal crew sizes and normal production rates.
>
> **Step 6:** Review to ensure the same time units are used throughout—shift, hours, days, weeks, and so forth.
>
> **Step 7:** Add time durations, crew sizes, and hours to schedule activities.

Add the days to find the project duration of the job you just created. If days need to be trimmed from the schedule, start the subroutine of schedule compression in the following order:

1. Overlap activities with others
2. Run activities in parallel with others
3. Shorten activity durations
4. Increase the amount of equipment used
5. Increase the size/number of crews
6. Increase the number of hours worked

As you can see, number 1 has a limited negative impact on safety, quality, and cost. As the numbers increase, a higher chance occurs of lost-time accidents, quality deficiencies, and cost overruns.

> **Step 9:** Agree on the schedule, the logic, duration, milestones, and so forth. Number those cards, so you can reconstruct them when you input them into the computer. Then, input them into your software.

Here are two tips from the school of hard knocks:

1. Number the schedule activities by increments of 100 (not 10). This lets you accommodate changes to the project and reflect them in detail in your schedule.
2. Save your original schedule under its project name, and then save it again as "what-if". The what-if is for trying different scenarios. This can help you keep your experimentation from corrupting the original work and possibly losing it.

> **Step 10:** Run both forward and backward passes to uncover your earliest start times, earliest finish times, latest start times, and latest finish times for each activity. Consider normal rainfall, historical snow days, holidays, general delays, and so forth. Make a backward pass to uncover the critical path.

> **Step 11:** Establish calendar dates at the bottom of schedule for mobilization, work starts, milestones, and work completion.

Step 12: Load with costs and billings (cash flow).

Step 13: Publish, review, and edit. Return to steps 10–13 until a satisfactory schedule is created.

Words of caution: do *not* have multiple schedules. Certainly, the temptation is there, but you will find yourself better served professionally, personally, and legally if you keep only one schedule. The major reason is the administration of such a schedule will be easier and clearer to all parties concerned. If your schedule must be very detailed, then so be it.

Remember, scheduling is not about software. Software is just a tool we use to make the publishing and administration of the schedule easier. Schedule creation still is about field experience, market conditions, resource management, and project knowledge. A high-level schedule takes all of these into consideration.

> Use change-order language that reserves the right to pursue additional costs if the client changes the work instruction again or if others interfere while change-order work is being installed. (See change-order release the form later in this chapter.)

Baseline Schedule

As the old saying goes, "Time is money." Nowhere is this more evident than on a construction project. In the world of the PM, the schedule is your tool for controlling time, resources, and money.

The following is what you need to have on your schedule:

- All the required sequences for the construction of the project, (your schedule is also a document for recording and reporting progress)
- A timeline for reasonably projecting the amount of overall time to complete the project and the various timeframes for reaching milestones
- Calendar dates for the beginning and ending dates of construction tasks or activities

- Identification of high-priority activities (critical path activities)
- A guide to manage the project in a shorter length of time, if required
- A plan for scheduling subcontractors and vendor deliveries
- A mechanism for evaluating alternative construction techniques or methods
- A document for evaluating the impact of delays and changes

Components of a Baseline Schedule

Here are some hints in creating a baseline schedule. Each of these will help make your task easier.

1. Include graphics that are easy to read and timescaled for easy understanding.
2. Include a schedule summary for executives who will not want to see every subcomponent detail of each phase of construction.
3. Outline only key milestones.
4. Review your assumptions that impact the schedule completion date.
5. Define your means and methods that are critical to the accomplishment of your schedule, but be prepared to discuss alternatives, if required.

Resource Loading

Make sure you construct your schedule with all the appropriate input and that all parties agree the logic is well-thought-out before you begin resource loading. The logical building sequence must take place first before you can begin loading manpower and cost information. Once that is done, the schedule can be used to do the following:

- Set projected production rates
- Manage manpower requirements
- Calculate equipment and material needs

- Maximize utilization of float time for a more efficient completion target
- Create monthly payment justification in situations where payment requisitions are based on (cost loaded) documented schedule updates of physical progress

The purpose of a schedule is to enable the PM to run his job most effectively, not to create several reams of accounting reports or legal documentation. However, the schedule will be one of the most important pieces of evidence if a claim is filed or if litigation occurs.

> **Update as-built drawings weekly, which keeps them timely at the end of the job. The habit of the industry is to update them at the end of the project, relying on memory and notes. This leads to some misinformation. Owners place a value on accurate as-built drawings.**

Critical Path Scheduling

In layman's terms, *critical-path scheduling* is planning, measuring, and control. This describes one of the essential tools of project management: the project schedule and this is what most people think of when they hear the term "project management." This is a dedicated course in any construction management curriculum; it is the basis for a majority of construction claims. And, last, it is the only way to show the complicated relationship among tasks, time, manpower, equipment production, material delivery, delay, weather, and all the other inputs of a construction project. The *project schedule* is a large calculation that is displayed in graphic and numerical form. For these reasons, it is important to put scheduling techniques in the proper context of the essential roles of project control wherever it occurs.

Typically, planning and controlling are performed by the PM. Because measuring is done by others, our discussion will not include it.

When related to construction processes, the responsibility for directing the project occurs at several levels, is performed at various times, and is typically the responsibility of multiple entities throughout the life cycle of a project. However, regardless of whether we are discussing the subject with a construction management firm, a GC, or a subcontractor, a commonality in the methods and practices is used by each of these organizations in contracting.

This common function is a key duty of project management. The challenge is to take an idea committed to paper and funded by money and, subsequently, placing it into physical form. Each previously mentioned entity assigns an individual—typically a PM, who, many times, also carries another title—to represent their interests during the construction process. Each of these PMs is responsible for organizing, directing, and controlling the limited resources needed to complete the project. They do this many times in concert with the project superintendent. The project consists of a defined set of work activities performed in a limited duration. And, the entire project is treated as a separate profit center.

When the physical work of constructing occurs, the nature of the process becomes complex enough to demand a team approach to project management. While one individual may carry the title of PM, in reality, a group consisting of PM, superintendent, project engineer, and supervisors from the subcontractors are essential to the successful completion of the project.

Ultimately, the PM is responsible for the use of resources. The three resources defined in any construction contract include cost, time, and quality. Almost all of a PM's time is spent either planning or controlling these three items.

In our discussions of scheduling techniques, we address these critical factors. However, this discussion must include both the planning and control of this valuable resource. In addition, it must include the relationship between time and the other responsibilities of the contractor for the cost and quality of workmanship.

According to the Project Management Institute's *Project Management Body of Knowledge,* project management is defined as:

". . . the application of knowledge, skills, tools, and techniques to project activities in order to meet or exceed stakeholder needs and expectations from a project. Meeting or exceeding stakeholder needs invariably involves balancing competing demands among:

- Scope, time, cost, and quality
- Stakeholders with differing needs and expectations
- Identified requirements (needs) and unidentified requirements (expectations)."

Excellent contractors start their laborers earlier than journeymen and operators each day. This allows the entire crew to start fast on a daily basis.

Schedules as Planning and Control Tools

While this might be a theoretical way to introduce the topic of construction scheduling, it is necessary to see where scheduling "fits in" with the overall process of planning, communicating, and measuring construction. Scheduling is not the same as managing projects, but it is one of the key success factors to successfully manage a project.

Whether or not a formal schedule is produced, every project is "scheduled" (date commitments are made, deliveries are arranged, and so forth). What we present here are some tools and techniques to help make the job of scheduling more effective and easier. Scheduling techniques should be considered as "just another toolbox" filled with a variety of options that can be used to develop the initial schedule, to represent it effectively in various ways, and to use it to control one of the most valuable resources available to the project management team: time.

The use of time during a construction project is related to the cost of the project and to the level of quality that can be achieved. In other words, cost control, schedule control (time), and quality control are closely related processes. The following well-developed cost accounting model can also be closely related to the processes of schedule planning and control.

Schedule Creation: Steps in Schedule Development

There is no hard and fast rule for the number and order of steps required to create a CPM schedule. The process might be divided into four phases: data collection, initial schedule development, schedule adjustment, and schedule publishing. More specifically, this process could be broken down as follows:

1. Data Collection

    A. Determine work activities.

    B. Understand/decide the logical sequence of those activities.

    C. Determine the crew production and, thus, the time to complete the tasks.

2. Initial Schedule Development

    A. Determine the logical sequence of activities and relationships (start-to-start and finish-to-start) among the activities.

    B. Estimate the activity duration.

    C. Compute the network of activities via computer software.

    D. Compute the early and late dates, and the float for each activity.

    E. Assign the resources (manpower, money, machinery, and so forth) required for each activity.

3. Schedule Adjustment

    If days need to be trimmed from the schedule, start the sub-routine of schedule compression in the following order:

    A. Overlap activities with others.

    B. Run activities in parallel with others.

    C. Shorten activity durations.

    D. Increase the amount of equipment used.

    E. Increase the size/number of crews (this is costly to contractors because inefficiency will rise).

     F.   Increase the number of hours worked (this is the last resort because safety is compromised).

     G. Adjust the scheduled start dates of activities to avoid the overuse of limited resources assigned to activities.

4. Schedule Representation

     A. Consider the audiences that require schedule information and determine the appropriate schedule representation for each.

     B. Print and distribute schedules.

Required Inputs

Clearly, scheduling is not the first process to be accomplished during the preconstruction phase of a project. Several other processes must be completed first to provide input into the scheduling process. Planning must always be completed beforehand because it provides the strategy to build the project, and thus, the general direction of the construction process. The schedule has to follow. Similarly, once the schedule is completed, it provides important input for other phases of the management cycle. Generally, the following items must be completed to generate a complete schedule:

- Detailed work scope description
- Contractor's estimate, appropriate crew size, numbers of crews, and crew productivity rates
- Subcontractors' input on phasing and the duration of subcontractors' activities
- Creditable sources of field information (generally, the subcontractor field managers and GC's superintendent) regarding organization of job site, relationship among subcontractors, and the impact of expected job site conditions on crew productivity
- Plan to meet or beat the estimate and project schedule

Once this input is provided, the best approach to plan an effective schedule is to work in a team environment, which may include the superintendent, PM, key subcontractors, project engineer, estimator, and computer scheduling specialist.

> Specialty contractors know that CPM scheduling is of limited value to their operations. What they need most is resource-coordination software. For subcontractors, prime contractors make the schedule and they can change it when they want to. They have a contract that will enforce these changed time horizons. A better approach is to stay ahead week to week and coordinate your resources efficiently. In any event, working with a well-coordinated prime contractor is a must.

Task Identification and Sequencing

The Work Breakdown Structure (WBS) is an important tool used to subdivide a large or complex project into small, manageable pieces. Some of the tools used to generate the WBS are standardized templates (usually paralleling an existing chart of accounts) to assure that items of work are not missed. WBS templates can also be adapted from a previous WBS used on a past project or from standardized industry formats.

WBS is composed of several levels of detail until the entire project is broken down into small enough packages so they can be:

- Accurately priced
- Confidently scheduled
- Assigned to an individual company or person
- Expected to result in a specific outcome or deliverable

WBS is not finished until each of the previous can be accomplished. This breakdown process is called *decomposition*:

- Overall project (historical landmark redevelopment)
- Project phases (demolition, remodel, new building)

- Major parts of the project, that is, foundation, structure, finishes
- Identifiable elements of the project "work packages"

Each step in the decomposition process might be used in the generation of a specific item, an alphanumeric code that identifies the unique combination of the project, a phase, the major parts, and a constituent element of every work item on the project. The *cost code* or work package label can be used for estimating, scheduling, procurement, tracking, and performing key elements of the project. Because each digit in the code relates to a different level of the WBS, most software packages can wrap-up cost and schedule information to the next higher level to summarize both plan and performance by major element or by phase. If this project is part of a larger program, tracking information can also be summarized at the program level (across all projects).

Use monthly schedule narratives as a way to further document project issues, delays, and other events. This is similar to the field supervisor's daily report, but it is done each month by the PM.

Task Sequencing

To schedule a project, you need to break the project down into levels of activity that, at a minimum, let you clarify the types of activity, expected intermediate outcomes, and relationships among activities. In this case, relationships refer to the dependencies of one activity on another. Most activities in a project will require some, if not all, of another activity to be completed before it can begin. The terminology used to describe these relationships is "predecessor" and "successor." These terms are used to describe the relative relationship between one task and the tasks it is linked to. Events that must be completed prior to the start of the activity you are looking at are called *predecessors*. Activities that are dependent on the task you are looking at are called *successors*. *Partial dependencies* may also exist, where a portion of a predecessor task must be complete, but not the entire task, before the current task may begin.

If you used the alternative technique previously described as "backward scheduling" for identifying the various tasks of the project, you would already know the dependencies or sequence of the tasks. If, on the other hand, you used a WBS approach to identify individual tasks, you would need to determine the logical relationships between one task and another. Think in terms of inputs needed to support the current activity and their sources as opposed to organizational divisions. For this reason, the dependencies between tasks often jump the organizational boundaries frequently used in the development of the WBS.

In either case, the logic of the relationships might be expressed through descriptive statements and/or by diagrams. The following activity requires you to convert written logic describing the relationships among tasks into a flow diagram depicting the relationships.

> Profitable contractors keep change-order cost separate from the base contract on their cost reports. In case of disputes, this lets the contractor know and present change-order costs to the client. Also, this allows better understanding of productivity and CO costs.

Understanding the Critical Path and Determination of the Project Completion Date

One of the first questions the scheduler must answer is "When can this project be completed?" Obviously, this question cannot be answered until the activities are identified and the relationships among the activities are determined. Several methods of identifying these activities and relationships were discussed in the previous section. Ultimately, however, the network of activities—showing the tasks that need to be completed and the order in which they must be done—must be carefully planned by people with extensive knowledge of field operations. In most companies, sketching this network is the responsibility of general superintendents, superintendents, and field managers. Just completing the network, however, is not enough to determine when the project will be completed. The length or *duration* of each activity must also be determined, either by experience or through calculations. This process is described in detail in the next section, but it is necessary to introduce the topic now, so you understand the concept of the term "critical path." Each route through the network of interconnected activities forms a path from the beginning of the project to the end. Some paths that connect related activities may be assigned to a single subcontractor or monitored by a single field engineer, but normally the relationships are more complex than that.

If you follow all the possible paths through the project and add up the duration of each activity along each path, one path will be found to be the longest. This is called the *critical path*. This is the textbook definition of critical path. In practical terms, this represents the shortest possible time in which the project can be completed. If any activity along the critical path is delayed by even one day, the entire project is delayed. This is why activities along the critical path require the most attention by all members of the management team. However, care must be exercised to track the progress on all paths through the schedule. Delays on paths that were nearly as long as the original critical path could easily create multiple critical paths or cause a seemingly unimportant activity to delay an entire project.

Task Duration Estimating: Calculations of Durations Using Production Rates

After tasks or activities are identified and some fundamental sequencing is determined, the expected duration of each activity must be determined. These durations are frequently estimated using the experienced judgment of the field supervisor or another member of the project management team. That experience with normal production is critical to the scheduling process but, sometimes, it is necessary to determine durations more precisely. Certain activities have standard estimates of duration based on common practices. For instance, because of drying times, taping and finishing drywall in one section of a building is almost always a four-day activity, reflecting one day each to tape, block, skim, and sand. While the process can be shortened by using accelerators or lengthened due to inadequate labor resources, typically, you do not have to calculate production rates for this activity to allot four days to it in a schedule. Many similar insights also exist.

But what happens when that inside knowledge doesn't exist or you have to find ways around typical practices to accelerate the completion of a project? How can you justify extensions to the schedule due to a CO work ordered by the owner? In these and many other cases, the duration of activities must be precisely calculated from production rates. These production rates are readily available from either the estimate for the project or from standard estimating guides, such as Walker's costing service, Craftsman, or RS Means costing service.

The formula for determining the activity duration is straightforward:

Work Quantity/Production Rate

This formula should make intuitive sense. If you have 10,000 square feet of carpet to lay and you know from past experience that you can set up, lay, and stretch 500 square feet of floor carpet in an hour, then you are looking at 20 to 21 hours of work. If you are working alone, you would estimate this project would take about three days. Another way to look at this is to say that you average 0.002 hours per square feet of carpet to be laid (1 hour/500 square feet per hour). Multiplying 0.002 times 10,000 square feet yields an estimated table duration of 22.4 hours.

This calculation of activity durations can be standardized by using the upcoming simple table. The activity number and description come from the work breakdown structure or another template of work activities for a project. The budget reference might be from the project estimate recap sheets, company cost codes, or an estimating reference text, such as *Means*. Work quantities for each activity come from the project estimate or from your own quantity takeoffs. Production rates must be consistently stated in terms of the same unit of time, such as daily output (quantity of units per day), and all assumptions about crew and equipment balance must be carefully considered in selecting this rate. Estimated activity duration is simply the work quantity divided by the production rate. This form could easily be created in a simple spreadsheet to automate the process of determining duration estimates. While, for most projects, you might not want to complete this form for every activity in the schedule, it may be appropriate to use this method to check the initial estimates of duration for all critical activities.

Accuracy of Estimates of Duration

The duration of a task represents an estimate of the amount of time required to accomplish the task. This estimate may be based on a number of sources including, but not limited to, past experience, standard databases, and comparisons to similar events. The estimate is also based on a number of assumptions, such as skill level, conditions, number of resources, reliability of suppliers, and so forth. The combination of these inputs means that the output of the estimating process—a specific value of time—represents a point along some distribution of possible times.

The point we identify as the range of possible times is influenced by the various inputs previously identified. For example, if we believe a task takes approximately 10 days, and we consider only the actual time to perform the task and feel relatively confident in the abilities of the resources being used, we would probably provide an estimate of 10 or 11 days. If, on the other hand, we were concerned about the production of a crew and knew we would be held to the duration given, we might give an estimate of 15 to 20 days. There is no difference in the actual work to be performed in either case: the difference in the estimate is based on other factors, including human behavior.

Understanding Schedule Logic: Required Inputs for CPM Schedules

The first steps in creating any schedule are to do the following:

- Identify a list of activities to be scheduled
- Determine the logical sequence of activities or the relationship among the activities
- Estimate the duration of each of the activities

These preliminary steps can be accomplished by any of the means outlined in the previous sections and might be summarized in a note card similar to the one in Figure 3-5.

Activity number
Activity description
Estimated duration
Predecessor(s)
Successor(s)

FIGURE 3-5
This is the basic building block of a CPM schedule.

Once these preliminary steps are completed and recorded in some type of an organized format, the next step is to start to construct the network itself. Computers now do most of the work.

> Contractors must document COs in great detail. This gives them the greatest chance to collect all costs and time extensions.

Schedule Compression: Using CPM Schedules to Deal with Schedule Crashing

A contractor seldom has the opportunity to dictate the overall duration of a project. Project completion dates are more likely determined by owner move-in or start-up requirements as specified in the contract documents. Almost always, at least in today's market, the contractor would prefer to have more time to complete the project. Perhaps this is why most schedules, when they are first produced, exceed the time limits allowed by contract and must be reworked to meet contract deadlines. This shortening of the overall schedule is known as *schedule compression*, which also occurs when a project is running behind schedule and must be accelerated—or *crashed*—to meet the original completion date.

Every construction activity has a cost associated with accelerating that process. For example, completing a 10-day activity in 6 days may require overtime, inefficient crew combinations, extra supervision, different materials, and/or expedited deliveries. Each of these has a cost associated with it. It has been said that anyone can compress a schedule, as long as you give them an unlimited budget!

In reality, though, the goal is to reduce the length of the schedule for the lowest possible cost. The basic process for accomplishing this is as follows:

1. Reexamine the logic of the schedule to see if changing the relationship among activities will impact the schedule completion. For instance, changing a "finish-to-start" relationship to a "start-to-start with a lag" might shorten a schedule with no cost and/or little impact on operations in the field.

2. Consider splitting long activities into two or more shorter ones. You may find that later activities are dependent on only part of a long activity, not the whole thing. This will shorten the schedule.

3. When no more changes can be made to the schedule logic or to the activities themselves, start by shortening the activity on the critical path with the lowest cost to accelerate. There is no reason to shorten a noncritical activity because this will have no impact on the overall schedule.

4. After shortening each activity, recalculate the early and late dates and the float for all activities to see if the critical path has changed.

5. Continue to repeat steps 3 and 4 until the project length is reduced to comply with contract requirements or the cost to compress the schedule has become excessive. Generally, the result of compressing a schedule to its maximum amount is you have multiple critical paths. In some cases, nearly all activities will become critical, which introduces a high level of risk, and this requires intense management of the schedule.

In a situation where the owner has ordered or is considering schedule acceleration, it is sometimes helpful to graph the cost of acceleration against the number of days saved. In this way, you can clearly demonstrate the impact of this compression and you can justify the cost of this change to the contract. This process is demonstrated in an upcoming example. At the same time you are justifying the cost of acceleration, you are creating a plan for how to accomplish the acceleration if the owner decides to go forward.

Completing a schedule compression exercise for a large or complicated schedule can be difficult. Forgetting "where you are" becomes easy, that is, knowing what things you already changed and what costs you already committed. Using some type of running log to keep track of the potential changes to the schedule is helpful.

> Excellent contractors confront problems promptly. They have a proactive approach and look for "rocks in the road." This keeps problems from festering or from turning into major issues and battles.

Schedule Compression Cost

The construction industry used the term "fast track" in the 1980s to describe a pace in building a project. That term has not been used in a while: now it is state of mind. The assumption is that all construction will be done quickly. In other words, it will be done quicker than construction work was done in the 1970s . . . or the 1980s or the 1990s.

The new term is "flash track." To be clear, this is not the term being used, but it is the attitude on a majority of job sites. Craftsmanship and safety are considered constant. In the owner's eyes, speed has no effect on the level of quality or safe working conditions and habits. This is a dangerous and foolish assumption.

As contractors continue to battle this expectation by owners, we offer a simple calculation form to derive the extra cost of schedule compression (see Figure 3-6). This rudimentary sheet is offered as a help to those construction leaders who are aware of the dangerous path the industry is on. The contractor's construction service (which is linked to his professional reputation) is in danger of losing its quality. Additionally, his safety focus might be less and, therefore, lives could be lost in the owner's drive to be quicker to market.

The form is simple to use. From the left on the form, you'll see:

Compression Activities These are the activities that are our focus, the activities that should be on the critical path. Typically, for

Compression activities	Daily cost to compress	Reduction in days	New schedule duration	Increase in cost	New project cost

FIGURE 3-6
This form helps calculate the total cost of schedule compression.

a building project, in the stream of earthwork, these activities are foundation, structure, roof, building skin, interior framing, building systems, ADA, and finishes. Other activities can be pursued at convenient times.

Daily Cost to Compress   Calculate the additional activities you will undertake to gain speed. The amount of lost time due to material logistics is 70 percent. Make sure you have the material staged well before adding labor and equipment. Additionally, give your subcontractors some room to operate. They will be more productive without the interference of other trades.

Reduction in Days   Estimate when the physical completion of work tasks will occur and compare it to your most recent, updated schedule. The difference is the reduction in days to schedule. Be conservative: construction is a detail-oriented business. The more careful you are now, the less schedule revisions you will need later. This helps make your creditability grow.

New Schedule Duration   Simple math. Subtract the reduction in days from the most recent, updated schedule. This will show target days to complete the work task.

Increase in Cost   Take the daily cost to compress and multiply it by the total days of the work task left (or to perform). Do not include the original estimated cost.

New Project Cost   Add the cost to date for the task from your cost report to the Increase in Cost section for the task. This is your total cost upon completion. See Figure 3-6.

When you add all the columns, you will know the bottom-line impact to you in cost and time. What this form does not calculate are the potential problems with quality and business relationships. All contracting businesses rely on these two by reputation, so caution and introspection are also needed before you pursue an aggressive schedule compression.

Hold daily project team meetings to force communication and planning on the job. Not only is this an operational method, but it trains people at the crew level to think like managers. When they become managers, they will be further along in their communication and planning skills.

Appropriate Level of Detail on Schedules

There is no easy answer to the question "How detailed should the schedule be?" The safest answer may be "It depends!" It depends on many variables, some of which include the following:

- Superintendent and PM preferences
- Company policies
- Owner requirements
- Group preference to use or review
- The amount of time before a scheduled activity is to be performed
- Whether the contractor uses his own labor or a subcontractor
- Task complexity

In short, the level of detail displayed on a schedule should depend on whom the schedule is intended for and the time for the planning horizon. The following sections describe (1) the scheduling tools available to vary the level of detail within a single schedule, and (2) an approach to vary the level of detail as the time for an activity approaches.

Superior contractors extend personal courtesies to clients, subcontractors, suppliers, and others. This keeps the relationship civil, even though difficult project problems may occur. They know this keeps most customers and partners actively working with them.

Level of Schedule Detail and the Planning Horizon

One of the necessary considerations related to schedule detail is the length of time until an activity is to take place. It makes intuitive sense that, early in the planning for a project, you may need nothing more than a general idea of when each phase of the project will occur. However, when an activity is to begin next week, a much more detailed plan is necessary to ensure everything will be completed without a hitch. Many companies address this varying need for scheduling detail with a multistage approach known as SHPS (Short Horizon Planning and Scheduling).

A *SHPS* program starts with a general schedule for the entire project, which identifies project start and finish dates, as well as completion milestones for each phase of the project. Depending on the complexity of the project, a more detailed schedule may be produced for the first 90 days of the project. Next, a very detailed three-week look-ahead schedule is created, addressing everything from field work to submittals and deliveries. This look-ahead schedule is updated weekly, which means each week is planned three times as the activity comes closer to its scheduled start date. During a weekly subcontractor coordination meeting, all activities scheduled for the coming week are reviewed in detail to make sure all support activities (material, tools, manpower, and approvals) were achieved to ensure that each of these activities can be completed. Finally, a quick daily huddle is held to confirm that all parties are still on track and that nothing has occurred that would require a last-minute change in plans.

Various simple forms can be developed to meet the needs of individual companies to improve this multistage planning process. The key is not to waste too much time upfront on detailed schedules, but to constantly increase the level of detailed planning as the work progresses. This detailed planning should concentrate not only on activities in the field, but on all the supporting tasks, such as submittals, deliveries, approvals, inspections, and so forth. As the planning horizon draws closer and it is clear exactly when on-site tasks will occur, the schedule process should start to break general activities down into more detail to ensure the plan is executed. A systematic approach is needed to manage this process of increasing levels of detail.

Other Aspects of Scheduling

Complication in the world of construction continues to mount. As in society, we have more chaos. In essence, more people, different material, and countries of manufacture are involved. No doubt, an average project has more obstacles to overcome than a decade ago.

To address this, I must tell you my experience as I work with contractors. The industry has changed to say the least. No longer is the name of the game to build the project. These days, the name is read the plans and specifications, know the contract, and address the issues one at a time. In other words, we must balance our contracting risk with the potential for gain.

How do contractors dependably coordinate these demands, and then communicate their direction in an efficient and effective manner? We do this through a CPM schedule and this picture is worth more than a thousand words.

To be clear, every PM should focus on schedule management and financial management. These two areas, done well or poorly, decide a project's fate.

Excellent scheduling processes and techniques have value to the contractor. They graphically and numerically display a complicated process. From these data sets, an outsider can understand the process of building work. They give the owner a road map and a path to take in building a project. However, a construction schedule is a double-edged sword.

1. They protect the contractor from being adversely affected by owner delays and construction changes, latent or otherwise.
2. They give the owner a tool to adequately monitor the contractor's performance.

Owner Approval of the Schedule

Owner approval of the schedule is a critical step in project management. Some confusion typically revolves around contract clauses that specify the owner's approval of construction schedule. The following points can help give you some clarification.

1. The contractor's schedule must meet all the contract requirements.

2. The contractor's schedule must provide enough information so the owner can create other project-related schedules. Owners must be given enough detail to be able to monitor construction progress and be given the tools to explore alternatives to mitigating delays.

3. The contractor's schedule must provide the owner with enough information to independently evaluate proposed changes and potential delays.

> Send maps of project locations to suppliers and others to keep late deliveries and "I'm lost" phone calls minimized.

Right to Finish Early

On some projects, contractors will choose to finish early. Although accelerated schedules may cost the contractor, reasons do exist for finishing significantly earlier than the contract specifies. Some of the reasons may include (1) complete the project earlier due to the rainy season or winter beginning, (2) the contractor may want to free up some equipment for his backlog, (3) simple overhead reduction.

Most owners welcome an accelerated schedule. They can occupy a building earlier and, thus, enjoy its benefits, such as revenue or technology, sooner. But, some owners may find an accelerated schedule problematic. Careful plans may be disrupted, such as a building that cannot be occupied before a certain date. Borrowing may be accelerated. More often than not, owners have to rethink and replan their logistics for project use.

Court decisions have been largely in favor of contractor finishing early. Furthermore, owners have been liable for actions that have delayed contractors from completing the project in accordance with an early completion schedule. In other words, the owner cannot delay the start of the project or hinder the contractor's progress once construction starts.

A delay claim that is identified and documented can later be abandoned if no serious impact results. However, a claim that is never identified and, thus, never documented is almost always lost. In construction, being successful in court is closely related to being well-documented.

Work Breakdown Structure (WBS) and Its Effective Use

I'm amazed at how often people ask questions like "How many tasks should this project have?" or "How much detail should I have in the project plan?" WBS codes or project cost codes should be used for the following:

- Estimating task scheduling numbers
- Cost accounting; budgeting/budgeting control
- Job cost reports; labor/equipment time cards
- Purchase orders; project filing systems
- Contracts/subcontracts submittal control
- Senior management reports; daily field reports
- Material monitoring; task identification

Projects are comprised of a multitude of individual tasks. To understand the project as a whole, you need to break it down into small enough pieces, or tasks, to let you clearly identify outcomes at a level assignable to individual resources. The WBS approach is one technique that facilitates this effort, but one drawback of the WBS is it fails to identify the relationships and dependencies among many tasks.

(Go to www.stevensci.com, click on "free forms", for a WBS listing)

A complete WBS is essential as an input to numerous other processes, such as:

- Activity definition
- Resource planning
- Cost estimating
- Cost budgeting
- Progress scheduling
- Performance reporting (cost, quality, and schedule control)
- Purchasing

This multilayered process has several advantages to the singular WBS approach in that tasks are defined in terms of the needed deliverables as they are developed, and their relationship to other activities is already clarified and documented. It also tends to break activity down into smaller pieces, allowing for earlier handoff of deliverables and, therefore, earlier start of successor activities. A disadvantage is the lack of a consistent organizational structure present in the WBS, which facilitates assignment of cost and tracking codes for management and reporting purposes.

The usual mistake PMs make is to lay out too many tasks; subdividing the major achievements into smaller and smaller subtasks, until the WBS is a to-do list of one-hour chores. Getting caught up in the idea that a project plan should detail everything that everyone is going to do on the project is easy. This springs from the college graduate's perspective that a PM's job is to walk around with a checklist of 6,734 items and tick each item off as people complete them. This view is usually linked with another fallacy. Namely, that the project plan should be a step-by-step procedure for doing everything in the project, just in case you have to do it again. If the PM is managing the wrong things, you can certainly find the fault in a written form, but that shouldn't be the reason for this minutely detailed approach.

The problem is this: we have only 24 hours in a day to manage the project.

There is no time to spend managing details. That is, because a project has surprises and problems, the managers need to be squarely focused on resolving, not chasing, inconsequential detail. This is also known as *managing by exception.*

Owners encourage these fallacies by marveling at monstrous project plans because they make it seem the PM has thought of everything. Unfortunately, on significant cross-functional projects, there is absolutely no chance the PM will think of everything. The subject matter experts and the specialists are the ones we must hold accountable for that.

The result of these fallacies is that PMs produce project plans with hundreds or even thousands of tasks. Many of them have a duration of a few hours or a few days. Does this level of detail give us better control and lead to successful projects? In my view, a to-do list approach does not give effective control, and it interferes with the achievement of a successful end result.

First, the laundry list approach leads to, and even encourages, micromanagement of the people working on the project. Micromanagement is appropriate when you have culls from other parts of the world working for you, but few project teams are composed entirely of these transient people. The majority of your project team members will not thrive under micromanagement, just as you would not. This style tends to encourage dependency on the PM, rather than independence where people are held responsible for their results.

Second, PMs are more effective leaders when they hold subordinates accountable for reaching milestones, rather than completing a list of tasks. How often does it happen that people complete a list of tasks and achieve nothing? When we base our assignments and monitoring on well-conceived and measurable achievements, no one loses sight of the desired end result.

Third, the laundry list approach is hard to maintain. People have to report on many tasks, which decreases the odds of receiving accurate and timely status reports. The loss in productive time approaches 5 percent just for the report and filing needed. And, don't forget the loss of focus. It takes 20 minutes on average to get to a point of deep concentration. Disrupt this concentration and you have lost deep focus. The PM, with or without clerical support, has a great deal of data entry to do to input all this status data.

Amid the pressure of ongoing, multiple projects, tracking can fall behind. It may even be dropped because the amount of effort is too large. This might sound like a stupid and improbable solution, but it happens with alarming frequency, even on large and important projects. The logic is, "No one is looking at all that detail anyway, so why spend all that time to catch up?"

As a rule, we like to see the majority of assignments in a project plan have durations that are 10 days in length or shorter. Coupled with this, we advocate weekly status reporting of hours worked, percentage completed, and an estimate of the hours of work remaining to complete the assignment. This combination allows the PM to maintain good control, while placing the responsibility for achievements on the team members.

> Good construction firms make sure each manager is responsible to only one executive. They also have an up-to-date organizational chart. This keeps chain of command confusion (and politics) to a minimum.

Most Contractors Need a Coordination Process (Not a CPM Schedule)

Only one contractor (the GC) on each job creates, publishes, and controls the CPM schedule. All others (SCs) are held to it.

The contracts are thicker and more daunting, written by increasingly smart lawyers. Once signed, there is little wiggle room.

Claims consultants are expensive. As a general rule, a serious claim is not worth pursuing if it is less than $500,000. Given that most claims don't make legal and financial sense to pursue, the large attention given to CPM scheduling by SCs doesn't make sense.

What do SCs need to pay attention to? They need to pay attention to the coordination for all their jobs, that is, once we commit to contract a job. The question is not if we are going to build the work, but when.

The approach to coordinating work varies from construction firm to construction firm. There is not a standard practice. Just as construction is a fragmented business, so are the practices.

To coordinate work effectively, these basic elements should be covered:

- A client-contact system
- A look-ahead system
- A communication system to most levels of a construction company

A *client-contact system* can be as simple as a cell phone and a weekly job site visit. You need to communicate with these customers to let them know you are meeting their schedule, but, rarely are things this simple. Most clients are actively monitoring your progress and they don't wait for your phone call for an update.

Construction firms rely on field management to update them daily on the latest concerns or demands of the client. Some contracts require a formal monthly meeting with documented updates. Clearly, in a subcontractor-to-GC relationship, you cannot wait for the monthly meeting to see if the client is satisfied. To stay ahead, this is a weekly requirement.

A *look-ahead system* must be written because it shows the demands of your contracted work. Superior look-ahead systems project more than a week. Some go out a month and seek to force everyone to plan. Monthly look-ahead systems are effective. They have fewer surprises than weekly ones.

Contractors will require field mangers to submit their written plans in detail to the executives. From these job plans, an overall company-wide coordination schedule is produced.

Remember, the farther out you plan, the more uncertainty increases. And, the closer in you stay, the more certain things are. Time and energy should be spent more on next week's details, rather than the details for next month. However, do spend some time on next month, or you will be rudely surprised.

It is much better to know you have a spike in demand for labor hours next month than next week. The same goes for equipment. That is a difference of three weeks, which is a world of time to solve such a major problem.

A *communication system* gives people the information they need to manage. If you hired robots, you don't need this. Seriously, you and your managers—field and project—need to know about problems at the earliest possible moment. Your communication system should deliver that. Some contractors use white erase boards, others use computers, and still others use paper. Whatever is most effective for you is the best system.

> Do not allow internal conflicts. Make sure all departments (estimating, field, and accounting) work well together and share vital information.

Better Coordination Through Resource Forecasting: A Practical Approach

Day in and day out, contractors constantly put out fires. They are good at it, but this reactive type of management is neither profitable nor healthy. Watching a construction company owner keep dozens of balls in the air is something to behold. No other business has such a constantly changing set of challenges.

A common contractor's complaint is the lack of coordination inside and outside of his office. This issue revolves around the fact that labor and equipment are always at the wrong place each day.

Part of this problem may be that field management takes and hordes these resources, causing a shortage on other jobs. Other days, it may be that your PMs are not communicating well with the field. Everyone is trying to do a good job, so what is the problem? The problem is the process.

In other areas, does it seem there is too much to bid everyday? Are you taking on more work from your clients when you should have said no? Contractors are some of the best entrepreneurs in taking a challenge and making it work. In the back of your mind you think, "I will figure out a way to get it done. I always have."

One of the hardest words for contractors to say is no. Saying no is not in their character. Contractors remember when work was not plentiful and it was hard just to sell a job, but these days are far different from the early 1990s. Construction companies that are selective in their work are reporting excellent net profits before taxes. Executives comment that they did not believe these margins were attainable until the last 10 years. Yes, these are outstanding times in most parts of the country.

Part of the process that companies attribute these higher margins to is the aggressive management of resources. Sometimes, companies have a point person, such as a production manager, who is focused solely on labor. The production manager places the right people on the jobs where they can be the most productive, while balancing the demands of the customer who would like as many people staffed on his project as possible. The production manager negotiates with the customer and resolves any scheduling problems. Interestingly, this manager may keep the information in his or her head or on a ledger, but this is the person who schedules a complex challenge. This skill is not easily assimilated if the production manager leaves the company.

Other companies use a scheduling board, which is posted in a visible place. Production coordinators (as they are sometimes called) do much the same thing, however, they balance the demands of the field foreman for people with a limited supply of good people. The foreman interacts with the client and determines the number of people he needs to build the job while meeting the schedule. This can be a difficult decision for the production manager. As with most professions, playing catch-up is not a desired position. No one wants to be behind the curve on this.

Both of these examples are reactive approaches to scheduling. They operate on the principle that, if there is no complaint, there is no problem. If a customer or foreman has a need, then it is time to act. This type of process leads to stops and starts. For example, people or equipment being pulled off jobs to soothe a client's grumbling. As we've learned, people do become more productive as they continuously work on a project (up to a point). If they have to come back, it is a disruption. Time is lost as they relearn the project plans, get reacquainted with the people, and relearn the multiple variables of the job.

Stevens Construction Institute has taken the time to study forecasting and scheduling, and it has made a concerted effort to make its approach simple and effective. Some of the principles used make for a long-term solution to an age-old problem.

The following principles are central to effective forecasting:

- Principle 1—Contractors who constantly focus on managing scarce resources will outproduce their competitors who do not. Only through a structured process can consistent results be achieved.

- Principle 2—The use of common software leads to faster training and less expense than specialized software. (Contractors make money by what software does, not by owning and operating it.)

- Principle 3—Production forecasting is effective when people closest to each component perform the projection. That is, (A) production people project current work demands, (B) estimators project probabilities of winning jobs, and (C) other managers schedule planned outages, for example, vacations and equipment overhaul.

- Principle 4—A structured process is needed to free up people to think clearly, not just do the act of scheduling and forecasting.

You will find these principles can aid you in creating an effective system. They are common in all the ones we have studied and worked with.

Now, let's go into some detail in a typical system. As part of the explanation, some terms should be defined first.

- *Resource*—any key ingredient in the construction process. Typical resources are skilled people, key management, heavy equipment, material on allocation, and specialized tools.

- *Scheduling*—the activity that determines where a resource should be on a given date and time. This involves many considerations, such as logistics (where the resource needs to come from), demands of the customer, congruence with the needs of the job, and cost consequences.

- *Forecasting*—the activity that projects need over an extended period. Forecasting is an educated guess based on many factors: projected completion and start dates of jobs, current backlog of work, current outstanding bids, and projected construction activity of market. This is the same process an estimator goes through in his work; again, it's an educated guess gleaned from various information sources. However, an effective forecasting of needs helps construction companies keep from having an extremely high- or low-work volume. It keeps them moving right along at a steady, more efficient pace.

When we look at resource forecasting, we break it down into four distinct areas:

1. **Work in hand.** Current work committed by contract, letter of intent, or verbal notification to mobilize and man the job.

2. **Outstanding bids.** These are proposals not yet rejected or accepted by the customer. This is also known as bids still in play.

3. **Outages.** Special demands of the resources, such as the planned rebuild of equipment, vacation, or other leave of key personnel and material on allocation and, therefore, scarce.

4. **Summary forecast.** The resource demands are added together here to give a picture of what the next weeks or months look like. Do we have enough people? Should we start inquiring about renting equipment? Is it time to start prefabricating extra material for an impending rush of work? In this example system, we have to use the following subcomponents to arrive at the best information.

The following example can give you some idea about how this forecasting system might work.

- Monthly work projection—This reflects the work-in-hand and projects the demands for the scarce resource. The PMs forecast their jobs and they are the best people to do this. They input the number needed for the resource, such as a Caterpillar D-9 or for lathers and plasterers. See Figure 3-7.

ABC construction company
Monthly equipment projection

Project manager:_____ James Duff   Date:
Job name:_____ Young cars sales center

Equipment: ⇩	Next week	Week 2	Week 3	Week 4	Week 5	Week 6	Comments
D-3							
D-5							
D-8							
D5 H/D6 M							
D-9							
631							
621							
613							
< 30 M. Ton							
30–50 M. Ton							
> 50 M. Ton							
Rock							
Articulated							
815							
Vibratory smooth							
Vibratory pad foot							
Vibratory trench							
Water wagon							
Motorgrader							
IT loader							
416							
Fuel tanker							

FIGURE 3-7
PMs must update their needs weekly. In this example, the PM places his equipment counts on this template each week. This uploads into a master for review and planning action by executives.

- Monthly bid projection—This requires the estimating group to list each project bid, load with critical resources needed, and the probability of winning the job. All open projects (this is where the company is still being considered) are updated periodically. Resource allocation should not change; however, the probability of winning might. See Figure 3-8.

- Outage sheet—The shop manager or the Human Resources manager updates an Outage Sheet (engine rebuilds, vacation schedules, and prefabricated material production demands). This information can help determine how the field schedules will be affected. See Figure 3-9.

The Executive Forecast Sheet gives senior management a street-smart view of the future. Note that bid projections (B) are separate from actual demands (A). This keeps executives from overreacting to aggressive bidding. See Figure 3-10.

Some contractors can do this in their heads. This is an amazing talent. The rest of us need a process. Remember, this kind of structured approach adds value to the contracting firm when it is sold.

In this example, these input sheets and the summary page are accessible via the company intranet. We have used spreadsheet software with macros, which allows real-time information for senior management. As soon as input is placed, the system recalculates a new output.

The next step to adopting this approach is to implement the process.

- As in all improvements, people need training to assimilate the new process. This gives them the knowledge to use it and the confidence to start using it.

- Care must be taken to test the process in your company. Typically, successful tests are performed on a small basis with some of your best people.

- Meetings must be held on a periodic basis to review forecasting results. Further discussions are needed to refine overall demands predicted by the template. Questions you might hear are "How can we satisfy demand?" and "Can we move a start either earlier or later to take out the overcommitment?"

ABC construction company
Monthly equipment bid projection

Estimator: _____

Job name: _____   Date: _____

Equipment:	Current week	Week 2	Week 3	Week 4	Week 5	Week 6	Probability
D-3							
D-5							
D-8							
D5 H/D6 M							
D-9							
631							
621							
613							
< 30 M. Ton							
30–50 M. Ton							
> 50 M. Ton							
Rock							
Articulated							
815							
Vibratory smooth							
Vibratory pad foot							
Vibratory trench							
Water wagon							
Motorgrader							
IT loader							
416							
Fuel tanker							
Fuel buggy							

FIGURE 3-8
Bid projections are important to keep surprises to a minimum. As clients want longer to buy out a project, contractors have less planning time. A good forecast can give an executive a heads-up about a job that might start next week.

ABC construction company
Re-build sheet

Date: _____

Equipment: ⇩	Current week	Week 2	Week 3	Week 4	Week 5	Week 6
D-3						
D-5						
D-8						
D5 H/D6 M						
D-9						
631						
621						
613						
< 30 M. Ton						
30–50 M. Ton						
> 50 M. Ton						
Rock						
Articulated						
815						
Vibratory smooth						
Vibratory pad foot						
Vibratory trench						
Water wagon						
Motorgrader						
IT loader						
416						
Fuel tanker						
Fuel buggy						

FIGURE 3-9
This rebuild sheet is a crucial sheet for equipment. This can be adapted to human resources. The executives must know the amount of their resource. If the machine or the man is out, this can limit your capability and client satisfaction, especially during the vacation season.

ABC construction company
Executive equipment forecast summary

Date:_____

Equipment:	# of pieces	Current week		Week 2		Week 3		Week 4		Week 5		Week 6	
		Actual	Bid	Actual	Bid	Actual	Bid	Actual	Bid	Actual	Bid	Actual	Bid
D9													
D8													
D7													
D5 H/D6 M													
D3													
		Actual	Bid	Actual	Bid	Actual	Bid	Actual	Bid	Actual	Bid	Actual	Bid
631													
621													
613													
		Actual	Bid	Actual	Bid	Actual	Bid	Actual	Bid	Actual	Bid	Actual	Bid
< 30 M. Ton													
30–50 M. Ton													
> 50 M. Ton													
		Actual	Bid	Actual	Bid	Actual	Bid	Actual	Bid	Actual	Bid	Actual	Bid
Rock													
Articulated													
		Actual	Bid	Actual	Bid	Actual	Bid	Actual	Bid	Actual	Bid	Actual	Bid
815													
Vibratory smooth													
Vibratory pad foot													
Vibratory trench													
		Actual	Bid	Actual	Bid	Actual	Bid	Actual	Bid	Actual	Bid	Actual	Bid
Water wagon													
Motorgrader													
IT loader													
416													
Fuel tanker													
Fuel buggy													

FIGURE 3-10
What you see is the summary of the previous three sheets. It alerts the contractor to a spike in demand and, conversely, any slow periods.

Why would a company undertake such a change in its operation? There must be compelling and lasting benefits. From our experience, we have found the following:

- This process forces communication about resource allocation, thereby decreasing outages and work-arounds. As a result, utilization and productivity increase.

- Forecasting should occur in an open environment, therefore, everyone will think and learn more about it. Remember, charging one person to do it will become a serious operational problem when that person leaves.

- You will have fewer surprises and, therefore, more steady and efficient use of resources on each project. Less firefighting translates into more time for planning and scheduling.

- Bidding is treated as a pipeline, and so it will be better managed.

In summary, contractors struggle with the feast or famine cycle of construction. Companies that target larger work have intimate knowledge of this. The swings are enormous, sometimes on the order of hundreds of craftspeople and equipment pieces. Firms that focus on smaller work feel it also, but they feel it less.

These swings never go away. But, taking a forecasting approach that gives you proactive information can minimize them. With this information, an executive can then move projects around to minimize disruptions. Sometimes, this involves prompting the client to start and mobilize earlier. Other times, contractors must start the prefabrication of material, storing on site, and installing it later.

Expert resource forecasting does accomplish a fundamental function: it keeps resources working in a steady, efficient manner. Accomplishing this is the key to higher profits. Years ago, the battle was winning work. These days, the question is winning the productivity battle on jobs. Only through a thoughtful, structured process can this battle be won.

Savvy contractors create job-cost reports that project best and worst cases at completion. They know it takes four average jobs to make up for one bad job. They believe strongly that any hint of a bad job must be caught at the earliest stage.

Managing Construction Meetings

An old construction saying states "meetings will continue until productivity increases." We know and have lived by this saying. Meetings can be time wasters. However, done correctly and with discipline, meetings are the only way to gather and disperse information between two or more persons. Additionally, they force people to give nonverbal hints as to what they think. More is communicated in person than in an e-mail.

Most Construction People Hate Meetings

Construction people would rather be building something than talking about it. This is a problem disguised as an opportunity for you. The opportunity is being good about the time and subject discipline of meetings which will make you more popular with others. Hence, your professional reputation will grow.

Meetings Are Important in the Responsibilities of Every Manager and Executive

Meetings are often the vehicles used to communicate information and make important decisions. Obviously, productive meetings are critical to a project's success. Poorly run meetings reflect on you and your company, regarding how organized the project seems and the degree of importance placed on it. As the primary facilitator, you are responsible for providing leadership and direction in the meeting. The following are some guidelines for running effective meetings:

Guidelines

Leading above average meetings is part art and part science. Here is a list of tactics to keep meetings organized and informative.

1. Every meeting must have an agenda. This agenda will guide attendees on the purpose and objectives for the meeting. Adding time segments gives you a ready excuse to move on to the next subject.

2. Communicate the agenda at least 24 hours before the meeting. This allows people adequate time to prepare.

3. Invite only those who need to be there and who can make decisions. Any others will feel the need to talk to justify why they are there and waste valuable time.

4. Use the agenda as your guide in running the meeting efficiently. Take minutes or, better yet, have someone else take minutes. This lets you concentrate on managing the meeting.

5. If there are assignments made during the meeting for follow-up, ensure that each person knows what they are responsible for and when it is to be completed.

6. Discipline your meetings. Many clever techniques have been created over the years by frustrated contractors. Here are a few:

   - Start your meetings on time and announce "We start on time to reward people who come early and penalize those who are late."

   - The last person in the door takes the notes and has to distribute them. Most people did not enter the construction profession to become a secretary. This keeps attendance prompt.

   - Stand-up meetings keep people from getting comfortable in chairs. In my experience, this works nicely.

7. Determine which items to discuss at future meetings. This may include items in which you do not currently have adequate information to make a decision.

8. Tell visiting speakers to keep their comments to a certain time limit. Some people who are not part of the regular group may try to "sell" themselves with needless information.

Types of Meetings

In the construction process, there are meetings that are held to keep the project moving forward. These gatherings help keep coordination at a high level. Here are some typical ones:

Project Turnover Meetings   Estimating may run this particular meeting. This is one of the most important meetings in the entire life of a project. All project team members should be present.

Project Coordination Meetings   Meet weekly with subcontractors and major suppliers to encourage them to work together and also develop a set of fully coordinated shop drawings, which are eventually approved by the engineer. Discussion in this meeting should include the priority of construction space and possible conflicts that may exist. On larger or more complex jobs, some companies may employ a MEP coordinator to assist with this process.

Project Review Meetings   The project will typically run weekly or biweekly project review meetings. The purpose is to update management on the progress of the job and draw on the experience of other managers in the company for assistance. The PM prepares the project review meeting package for the meeting, which should include the following items:

- "Hot" issues list
- Budget review
- Buyout status
- Project schedule
- Subcontractor/supplier status report
- Change order log
- RFI log
- Shop drawing log
- Delivery schedule and procurement issues

Weekly Subcontractor/Supplier Meetings   The PM facilitates meetings with representatives of major subcontractors who can commit resources (manpower and money) for their companies. The PM should generate minutes and distribute them within a reasonable time limit (two days) of the meeting. The meeting covers the following topics:

- Manpower
- Delivery of materials and equipment
- Change order pricing and requisitions
- Project schedule
- Submittal status
- Coordination between trades
- Action items to be accomplished by next meeting

Set the right example by starting these meetings on time and use your agenda to control the meeting. This will enable you to move the meeting along at an appropriate pace. One of the biggest complaints by subcontractors is these meetings "take too long" and "waste a lot of my time."

Client Meetings   The purpose of a client meeting is to review the project. In general, this is to discuss progress and, if needed, to determine what actions are needed to improve progress on the project. This meeting should also be a forum for bringing up issues, identifying problems, receiving input from the design team, and coordinating the interaction of various trades. If the architect is responsible for preparing the minutes from these meetings, be sure to read and review them carefully for any discrepancies. Respond immediately to those discrepancies in writing. Here are some of the typical agenda items to discuss:

- Job progress—overall and short horizon look ahead
- Change orders
- Outstanding RFIs
- Overdue submittals
- Interaction between parties and requisitions to be approved
- Action items and parties responsible

Remember, meetings are a fact of life in construction, but unproductive meetings are by choice, not by chance. Make your meetings productive ones and your efforts will be greatly appreciated by all your project team members.

> Good construction firms use committed cost as part of their job cost calculation. When reviewing job cost, this keeps surprises to a minimum. They can project the cost to complete with more confidence.

Submittals—Approval Means Installation

A free-market society benefits from innovation. Products that perform better or cost less (or both) give projects benefits during construction and many years after. Communicating these types of products is one function of the submittal process. Two other functions of the process are dimension coordination and color selection.

Clearly, a majority of building and road projects require product submittals. Making this a quicker process than your competitors leads to a competitive edge. Allowing others to slow it down leads to schedule impacts that cannot be recovered without a cost.

Most project management software allows the creation of a submittal log with relative ease. In it, submittals and submittal packages can be added as needed. The PM must be familiar with the owner's contract as it relates to submittals. The contract must be reviewed against the plans and specifications, and any corrections should be recorded and reported appropriately. A submittal schedule must be submitted to the architect based on the requirements in the specifications for the submittal of shop drawings, product information, and samples. The submittal log is set up during the start-up phase of construction and it contains every part of what should be included in the project.

A log is set up by division, including the various pieces of work for which shop drawings, catalog cuts, product data, or physical samples will be submitted. The log specifies the date to be submitted and the requested turnaround time. This becomes a historical record of submission, review, approval, and distribution to the subcontractor.

This is an important function where the PM can be aggressive in setting up a schedule that pushes for faster submission and approval of shop drawings. The submittal log also acts as a reminder for the PM to "push" the process along and avoid delays on the project.

Important submittal dates should be included in the project schedule. Report weekly to the designers and client what is pending in their office, what is late, and what they can expect in the coming week.

Submittal Review

The GC is generally responsible for making sure the submittals conform to the contract documents. His responsibility is also to identify areas where deviations exist from the contract documents and to coordinate with any work summarily affected by wrong information. Obviously, the designers have the final approval in the entire process.

If a subcontractor offers an "equal" or a "substitution," the PM must be familiar with the use of these terms and what the owners' contract says in regard to their acceptance. Usually, *substitution* is meant to mean a change in the work called for in the specification.

The designers will send back the submittal either as "approved" or "approved as noted," or as "rejected" or "revise and submit." In either case, this must be logged into your system.

Using a simple process to track the status of submittals can increase your productivity. Simplicity means speed in construction. Elegance is fascinating, but it's hardly profitable. (Some consultants love elegance.)

Figure 3-11 is a copy of a Submittal Index form for your review and use. This basic form should help you start creating your company's unique tracking process.

> Force communication internally and externally by the use of meetings. Periodic formal meetings place pressure on people to accomplish objectives, deliver information, and update action plans.

Submittal index

Specification section	Specification paragraph	Item description	Proposed vendor or sub	As specified	See submittal data page

FIGURE 3-11
Tracking submittals from receipt to approval is a necessary task for all project managers. Approval allows for installation, and thus schedule milestones are met.

Change Order Management

We believe that if all contractors collected their rightful change-order compensation, their net profit would double. I know most of you agree. Discounted and ignored COs by clients are accepted as normal and this is frustrating. Contractors fight this attitude and, while they seem to be holding their own, it is a battle. This means we will have good days and bad ones. However, as a client from Texas said, "Don't let them wear you down."

Changed conditions and/or changing project demands lead to schedule and financial impacts. Both cost the same thing: money. To an owner, GC, SC, supplier, or service provider there is a cost of change. Either increasing or decreasing, both have to be formally managed and documented. Without a process, chaos would consume all project stakeholders.

Changes are an inevitable part of the construction process. But, while the industry has lessened the number of changes, it can never eliminate them.

In managing COs, first, let's say that a contractor's right is this: whenever possible, changes are not performed until they are approved by either the architect or the client. This is a tall order and, sometimes, an unrealistic one. The PM and field supervisor must thoroughly understand the client's contract provisions regarding COs and claims. If a change of conditions occurs in the field and a change to the scope of work is required, the PM or field manager must notify all appropriate parties within the provisions of the client's contract. (See the section "Timely Notice Requirement" in your contract.) In general, contractors should not proceed with the work unless they have received written authorization to do so. Only by establishing and following a policy of refusing to make a change without the proper authorized paperwork, can you reduce your risk of having a claim situation later in the project.

Be careful of "no damage for delay" clauses in your contract. These may limit your ability to charge for general conditions' costs due to an untimely client.

Change orders should be based on the costs submitted by the involved contractors and/or vendors, such as:

1. Direct costs incurred by your company
2. Subcontractor/service provider costs
3. General conditions costs

4. Insurance

5. Taxes

6. Cost of bond premium

7. Office overhead

8. Profit

The PM and field manager must be familiar with the client contract to know the allowable amounts for overhead, profit, and similar items. What is chargeable and what is not? Make sure you review subcontractor pricing for fairness. Do not simply pass along the CO without confirming the costs.

As a small, but important, courtesy, always call your client personally before sending over a change-order request. This can keep your customer from being unpleasantly surprised. If you embarrass your client, the little things this person can do for you will go away.

Your change-order log should show the status of all COs on a project, including the history of their issuance, review, and approval. They should be coded differently and their costs should be kept separate from the baseline-budget figures for the project.

Guidelines Nobody likes to have COs on their project. Clients and design professionals resist approving them. Be prepared and do your homework up front before sending COs.

- Document the impact of the change on the project schedule (duration, impact on substantial completion, and change in critical path) when you submit the CO.

- Use a CO standard release form that reflects your right to claim for further impacts while performing this CO. Also, this document should protect your right to lien the project. (See our sample form in the section "Change Order Release Form.")

- If a client refuses to acknowledge a certain effect of the CO, reserve in writing your right to continue to assert your position.

- Reflect this in the schedule updates. On a separate line, document the CO, the material delivery days (if substantial), the extra work days, and then connect them to subsequent tasks. Leave no orphans. This will allow your CPM schedule to reflect the impacts. This is why we recommend using 100 intervals on a CPM schedule, instead of the default of 10 in most software packages.

- Bill the client for all COs as soon as it is appropriate.

- Do not hesitate to use a national costing or pricing service. When CO costs are in dispute, this can settle some arguments. Three thousand estimators can't be wrong, especially about labor hours per task.

- Monthly schedule narratives are effective in building a case for COs. Every 30 days at a minimum, the PM should be writing a few paragraphs about the progress on the project, submittal handling, and so forth. Much like what the field manager does on a daily basis, this extemporaneously documents project issues. A preponderance of evidence is a key factor in determining fault. Another client said, "You can be right, but if you can't prove it, it doesn't matter."

- The field manager typically has the best relationship with the owner. Usually, they have garnered some goodwill from doing little favors for the client. When a CO situation arises, a field manager might have to exchange this goodwill for cash—the warm feelings generated over the construction project must now be traded for a rightful request for compensation.

Smart construction firms know they are buying an employee's energy, enthusiasm, and ideas, not their time. Companies give their loyalty and caring to individuals until proven differently.

Change Order Release Form

As we all know, COs are a way to recover the cost of a changed condition, a change directed by the owner, a conflict in the set of plans, or a latent condition in the work area. We, as contractors, are due to receive reimbursement of our direct costs and reasonable overhead and profit. Change orders have been around for centuries, such as in Egyptian times, but slaves didn't have the rights we do to file a CO request.

Following is a standard release form for CO acceptance. This form protects you from waiving your right to claim further reimbursement for additional costs associated with the changed condition, including lien rights for nonpayment.

Please consult your attorney for the specific language to keep your rights protected. The standard release form, as shown on page 221, is only a sample.

> Find and keep good craftspeople. Quality construction work done in a timely fashion is a keystone of all successful contractors.

Action Planning

Do you ever feel frustrated with a lack of follow-up by other people (especially after meetings when you had strong agreement on a course of action, only to have people forget their commitments to you)?

Several phone calls later, your time is wasted reminding people to complete their tasks. This is neither productive nor profitable. Well, we have found an effective technique to keep others (and yourself) focused on the tasks that need to be done and that technique is an action plan template.

The use of an action plan template is an effective way to document what has been agreed to, and thus, keep people committed to necessary actions.

Any print shop can print and bind these in a gummed, carbonless pad. They are easy to carry in your briefcase and productive to use as you meet with people daily.

(Your Company Stationery)

Date: _____

To: _____

_____

_____

Project: _____   Project No. _____

Subject: Our Estimate No. _____

Customer Control No. _____

Attention: _____

Sir/Madam:

We propose to increase/decrease our contract total in the amount of $_____ for the following:

PROPOSAL:

To substantiate our proposal, we are enclosing one (1) set of our pricing sheets.

STIPULATIONS: This proposal is based solely on the usual cost elements, such as labor, material, and normal markups. It does not include any amount for additional changes in the sequence of work, delays, disruptions, rescheduling, extended overhead, overtime, acceleration, the cumulative effects of change orders on productivity, and/or other impacts costs. We expressly reserve the right to address any and all of these related items of impact cost, which affect the contractor, prior to the close-out of the contract.

This proposal must be accepted within 30 days, after which time it will be subject to escalation. We are currently requesting a time extension of _____ days in conjunction with this change.

CHECK ONE:

_____ We will be pleased to proceed with this work on receipt of your change order in the above amount.

_____ Inasmuch as we are proceeding with this work, we would appreciate your change order in the above amount.

_____ Inasmuch as this work has been completed; we would appreciate receiving your change order in the above amount.

ACCEPTED BY: _____   BY: _____

Project Manager

Keep one of these pads handy in your daybook or briefcase. When you have meetings or discussions, agreements to perform occur. Simply document them on the attached form, send a copy, but also keep one. This is a simple, but effective approach. We know we must keep our word (this is one of the reasons people buy our construction services) and we know we should be able to expect others to keep their commitments, too. In dealing with others, though, sometimes we have to remind them of their commitments. See Figure 3-12.

What needs to be done	Who	Start	Finish	Resources

FIGURE 3-12
The use of an action plan is an efficient method to accomplish a myriad of tasks. Once written, assignments and their deadlines are clear.

Short Horizon Planning and Scheduling

With 30+ percent wasted time in field and office labor, planning represents the greatest financial opportunity for all contractors. Reducing that average amount of unproductive time is a significant competitive edge, but it takes a belief in the power of planning.

A plan is not a plan if it isn't in writing. In the absence of a document, anyone can "paint the target": in other words, shoot the arrow and wherever it lands, we can paint the bull's eye—wherever that is. The manager can state convincingly, "This is what we intended to do," and he or she will never build a long-term planning skill.

Field managers are the only ones who can put together a plan with any great detail. They are living and sleeping with the job. They know the lay of the land—that is, what material has been delivered, what work is ready, the pace of the job, and so forth.

The average foreman looks ahead about five hours. That is your competition, as well as your field manager and it represents one of the great profit opportunities in construction. Looking ahead farther leads to greater efficiency, less stress on everyone, and better use of labor and equipment.

Industry studies show that an average planning and scheduling effort reduces labor cost by at least 3 percent. Some people say it is more. We have found that it depends on two factors:

1. The consistency of written planning and scheduling
2. The level of detail

The Short Horizon Planning and Scheduling Form is filled out on a weekly basis and looks ahead into the next week. Some contractors use the two-week version. The field manager initially fills out the planner. Because he knows the project details well, it involves less than 20 minutes of time, which is not a difficult investment to justify.

The Short Horizon Planning and Scheduling System (SHPS) is an effective approach to completing construction work efficiently.

SHPS is a method that is specific to field supervisors and/or PMs who are responsible for managing labor, material, equipment, tools, and general conditions with a limited budget and a time deadline.

If we lived in a dream world, we would have unlimited resources with no lead time. Then, the construction business would be easy, but we would have unlimited competition. Everyone, including the long-term unemployed, would be in the construction business. But, because we don't live in that world, we must do some planning.

In contrast, if we worked in a gypsum factory, would we have to do much planning? No. We would stand at a station and cut, stack, reload, and so forth eliminate drywall. This work is a simple, continuous function without variation. We wouldn't need a plan *B* and each day would be the same.

The construction business has no resemblance to working in a factory. It is dynamic, changing with each day. The people are different, each task is different, the supply is uneven, and weather is unpredictable. Planning is a must, but it is difficult to get people to plan consistently and in detail. Fortunately, though, planning has a high payoff.

Yet, in this new century, the average foreman does not plan consistently. This means if your field supervisors do use a look-ahead method, you can be more efficient than your average competitor.

Consistent guidelines and detailed planning by the field manager saves 3 percent wasted time according to one survey. Looking ahead has a significant profit impact:

- A plan is not a plan unless it is written down.
- The foreman has to generate the plan. He knows the most about the project.
- Plan the work in detail, and then schedule it to follow the plan (not vice versa).

- Plan to complete 90 percent of capacity. Don't overload. Overloading leads to mistakes by pushing too hard. Rework is more than four times as costly.
- The farther out in time you plan, the more that plan changes. This is inefficient. Thus, the closer in time you plan and schedule, the more accurate you will be. The minimum look-ahead is one week; the maximum look-ahead is four weeks. See Figure 3-13.

The example below is a starting place to create your own example. All contractors are unique, so all planning and scheduling is different. Most construction companies will modify this form in some way.

The use of a written planner and schedule is done by the best foremen. They know using this process and writing down next week's

Short interval planner

Page_____ of_____   Week starting: _____   Date filled out: _____
Job name:_____   Address: _____   Job number: _____
Foreman: _____   Project manager: _____   Superintendent: _____

Day	Work planned	Man power	Rental equipment	Material	Special tools	Safety/PPE training	Comments (Use back if necessary)
Alternative							

Comments/special needs: _____
_____
_____

FIGURE 3-13
Here is a sample short horizon planning and scheduling form. The foreman fills it out and the contractor reviews it for refinement.

tasks is working smarter. Once the schedule is committed to paper, it can be faxed, copied, or mimeographed to others. From this plan, contractors have the opportunity to coach the field supervisors and make them better managers.

For the field managers, they now have the plan filed in their field book and they can refer to it often. Your company will experience fewer problems and surprises on the project, which translate to better financial and schedule performance. And this is the hallmark of a great contractor.

> Superior contractors emphasize and teach technical and craft understanding to their employees. In other words, they preach field experience, and they glorify craft and technical knowledge in general.

Daily Project Team Meetings

All construction is dynamic and fast moving. Communication is key to keeping work efficient. It is critical for contractors to promote the exchange of information. Some would say it is important to force it and daily project team meetings accomplish just that.

The field manager (foreman, superintendent, or lead man) holds a meeting in the morning to go over the day's work. Just as a quarterback in football huddles with his offense before each play, so does this leader.

The leader asks questions to prompt thinking. A foreperson doesn't have the power to control what people think (no one does), but questions do influence what people think about. The smart foreperson knows this and uses it to his or her advantage.

The field manger covers three essential areas of the day's work:

1. What will be installed today?
    A. What is our goal?
    B. What do we need to get done at the end of the week?
    C. Are we maintaining quality?

2. How do we improve our performance?

    A. Should we stage the material differently?

    B. Do we need different or more tools?

    C. Breaks, attitudes, or work habits?

3. Safety

    A. Things to be aware of, such as overhead hazards, cutting dust, water, and so forth

    B. Safety issues the crew is seeing

    C. Basic safety rules

When starting this new process, the first week of daily huddles is always a struggle. Crews are not used to being asked for their opinions. They will look down and shuffle. After a week, they should start coming up with some good thinking. Once in a while, you'll hear a wise crack or two. There's no need to react. This is construction people being themselves. After a month, everyone will certainly be comfortable with this morning process and, now, you are on your way to working smarter. Your crew members are starting to think like managers. Remember, it's crucial for this to become part of the foreman's daily report or log. These days, you can never document enough.

Construction firms all have different approaches. Some contractors use a dry erase board to write the goals and concerns for the day. At quitting time, a quick meeting occurs and the list is reviewed. Some companies use this late-day meeting to make sure everyone stays on the job and they take attendance.

Other firms make the morning process a stretch and flex meeting and practice a mild form of calisthenics. For older workers, this helps to lessen the chance of injury. With Workers' Compensation insurance still a major cost issue in many parts of the country, this two-for-one approach is hard to criticize.

Some contractors add the following topic areas:

- Behavior—horseplay, inappropriate language
- Paperwork reporting
- People issues—birthdays, anniversaries, workers having personal problems

All these are determined by the owner. The management staff can make these meetings take on any tone they want.

Again, you know you need to promote communication. Half the business is people. You have to keep coaching, teaching, and instructing to keep your crews working on the right things.

> Good contractors don't let their managers look down on field supervisors, craftspeople, or operators. They know field operations is the leverage point for all contractors to make money.

Closeout—Bringing It Home

The closeout phase of the project is one of the most important factors in determining how a project ends. Does it end with a strong finish and with the owner delighted at how quickly they received occupancy? Or, did the last 10 percent of the job drag on forever and it seemed like the job would never finish? Customers most vividly remember the last 10 percent of the project. How you closeout a project will leave a lasting impression in the owner's mind. Unfortunately, he won't remember all the hoops you jumped through to get the job started in the dead of winter, but he will remember it took three weeks longer than expected to patch the drywall or to broom rocks.

An effective PM closes out a project by accomplishing the following tasks in a timely manner:

- Completing the punch-list process
- Delivering all operation and maintenance manuals, as-builts, and warranties to the owner on the date of substantial completion
- Training the owner/client on systems
- Transferring utilities
- Closing out the job files and consolidating all documents for future reference
- Delivering accurate as-built drawings

Punch List

The field manager is primarily responsible for generating an internal punch list to minimize the amount of items on the final punch list. Their internal punch list should be started while construction is in full swing. This type of policing procedure should go on throughout the life of the project by phase, floor, area, or room. Once an area or phase is approximately 80 percent complete, the internal punch list should be created. These are incomplete items that should be addressed and, when finished, inspected by the field manager.

A *punch list* focuses on the quality of the completed work and verifies that it meets contract and specification requirements. After this step, the architect/owner's final punch list is created and fulfilled within 30 days of substantial completion. You should accept only one punch list. Subsequent to the Certificate of Occupancy, the PM is responsible to attend punch-list meetings until such a time as the owner, architect, and your client agree the project is complete. If you and the field manager have done your jobs well, the final punch list should be short.

Only after all work is complete are any subcontractors finished with their work; that is, all requirements are met and all punch-list work has been executed. The PM is responsible for ensuring that all work is done before final payments are made.

Guidelines

Develop a closeout schedule, which outlines the receipt of all closeout documents, 60 days in advance of substantial completion. You will have more financial leverage at this point than you will have when the job is complete.

Include the closeout documentation required by the division in your submittal schedule. Also include any special guarantees, service contracts, warranties, and so forth.

- Tell any subcontractors and distributors exactly what to submit. Don't assume they know what is called for in their contract or purchase order.

- Use the submittal log and meeting minutes to remind sub-contractors and vendors throughout the job of their closeout responsibilities. Reminding them late in the project means delays will occur.
- Ensure that as-built drawings are updated monthly to maintain an accurate set of record drawings.

A contractor's average net profit before tax is less than 10 percent, while common retention amounts are 10 percent. If the close-out process gets delayed, you won't collect your final billing and retainage in a timely manner. Using the your bank's interest rate, you can calculate the profit decrease from this delay. Excellent closeout skills have a financial impact.

> Above average contractors have a yearly session to review contracts and purchase orders. They also educate themselves on client-contract clauses to watch for.

Measurement

Contractors who measure have a high correlation with profitability. Measurement of the contractor's processes allows for consistent assessment of performance without emotion. Why? Because *measurement is not an opinion*.

When you measure, you achieve the following benefits:

1. Keeps you objective about your business
2. Makes your people focus
3. Confirms any improvement is successful or unsuccessful

The best measurements of a PM's or field supervisor's performance are the following:

- Profit forecast accuracy
- Gross profit per man-hour
- Process adherence

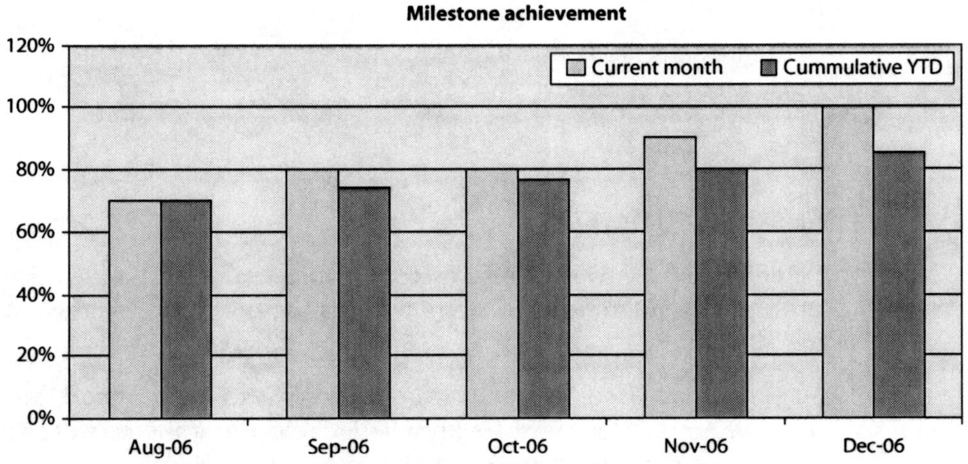

Milestone achievement

FIGURE 3-14
Use the shorthand of graphs or charts to communicate important facts quickly to your employees.

Simple measurements are understood quickly. Not everyone in construction speaks the King's English or has an MBA. Bar charts are effective in communicating an issue with your people. See Figure 3-14.

Guidelines

Measuring is key to keeping companies focused on the right things. Measuring sounds simple, but the list below can keep you out of common traps.

1. Never publicly post an individual's performance. This can embarrass people and eliminate any buy-in you may have earned.

2. Do publicly display company performance measures. This influences what people think about.

3. Keep measurements to a chart or graph. Use something simple (therefore, faster) to understand, such as pie charts or line charts. Remember, we will continue to attract and employ new immigrants to our industry. Not everyone reads English. Pictures translate in all languages.

Create an attitude and a goal to beat each project schedule and budget, rather than just meeting it.

CHAPTER SUMMARY

Planning must always occur before you schedule a work task or project. Careful and practical thinking is the only way to efficiently use resources.

Schedules are used by many owners and GCs to monitor and document progress. You must be knowledgeable about the process, but with today's all-inclusive contracts, a smarter strategy is to try to meet your contract demands, unless you have a compelling reason not to do so. Coordination software helps you place the right people on the right jobs at the right time.

Part of planning is forecasting, which answers the question, "What are my available resources against my expected demands over the next weeks?" Accurate information makes for accurate forecasts. Construction firms can only receive accurate information from the people who are closest to the resources and demands—PMs, field supervisors, and so forth.

Short Horizon Planning and Scheduling is an excellent technique for contractors to keep a project well-coordinated. SHPS starts with the field manager, who knows the project better than anyone. The field manager should start the project's planning and scheduling process, and then communicate his plan to others.

Daily huddles or crew meetings are a best practice to force communication and commitment at the field level. Foremen who consistently conduct them are considered in the top-half of all foremen in the country. These huddles don't take much time, and they keep the crew informed and aware of the requirements of the project.

The construction phase of a project is when a contractor either posts a loss or makes a profit. Direct field costs compose from 70 percent to upward of 95 percent of the contract amount, depending on the type of construction firm. Contractors must be great at building work. Reputations and wealth are made on the job site.

Meetings are a necessary part of construction. While meetings can seem like a waste of time, we cannot do without them, so we must find ways to manage them effectively.

Closing out a project is crucial to keep cash flow and profits strong in your company. Retention is 10 percent and average net profit is 3 percent. Closing out a project quickly and efficiently is crucial.

Measuring and communicating the results has many benefits. As long as the measurements are accurate (and not contrived), we have found that good employees will react and improve their performance.

> Understand financial management. All managers should know the basics and make smart decisions concerning money management.

4

The Keep Track Process

The last phase of the cycle is the Keep Track process. This is also known as financial management. Financial management is critical to the successful operation of any construction firm. It is where we analyze and report all activities of the firm.

From a business perspective, financial management contains two components that can increase the speed of the keep track (also known as financial management) process, while keeping accuracy high.

1. Executing all the duties of the keep track process
2. Transferring the information to the other two components (acquire work and build work)

First, let's look at an overview of financial management for construction contractors.

FINANCIAL MANAGEMENT FOR CONTRACTORS

Financial management is not an exciting subject, except when you are in financial trouble. Then, your blood pressure and heart rate will skyrocket. To the unknowing, this is not the time to study the subject. As sure as the sun will rise tomorrow, lack of financial knowledge can lead to financial distress.

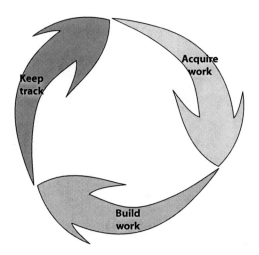

FIGURE 4-1
The Keep Track phase is integrated with the others.

Contractors are different from tradespeople because they view construction as a business. They consistently grow is because they understand all the areas of financial risk and opportunities. Successful contractors know construction is more than tradecraft. Without a keen eye for cost and value, their companies would, at best, stay small and, at worst, no longer exist. Money is the key difference. Without money, no company can stay in business. As I have heard often, "Money is next to oxygen in importance."

Therefore, the subject of financial management is one that journeymen have to study if they want to own and operate a viable construction company. They must deal with the sometimes unpleasant task of managing cash flow and meeting with institutions (banks, sureties, and so forth) about their financial status. Contractors typically dread this. Building a project is why they got into the business. But if you can adapt an attitude of respect for the finances, then certainly your company can continue to operate as a viable firm.

Financial management is not accounting. Accounting deals with the classification of income and outgo (expenses). Financial management is the diagnosis and operation of your finances. Excellent accounting is the first step in the process. Certainly, if your accounting is performed haphazardly, then the financial management will be poor.

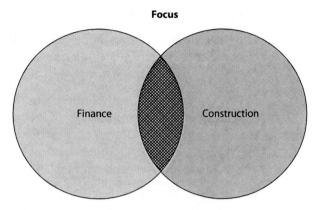

FIGURE 4-2
Relatively few financial concepts apply to the construction industry.

Not all financial concepts apply to construction. In fact, some are dangerous. This chapter focuses on the few appropriate and powerful financial concepts. See Figure 4-2.

> Create job-cost reporting that allows project managers to tie in physical completion percentages to financial results. This is a basic financial principle of construction.

SUCCESSFUL CONTRACTING ORGANIZATIONS KNOW FINANCE

Construction companies have long neglected the idea that their employees should understand financial management. Owners trying to create personal wealth with employees who do not know money management fundamentals is madness. If employees don't know financial concepts, how can they deliberately influence them?

Furthermore, if an employee is causing profit losses for the firm, owners are quick to dismiss him. Simply put, finances are critical to the success of any business. Why don't we do more to further the understanding of finances?

Finances Make or Break a Construction Firm

Superior financial management is a keystone to continued success for each organization. Conversely, the loss of money erodes a company's ability to perform, and then kills it.

Every owner starts with limited funds and a few projects. They quickly learn the importance of good financial management. As the firm grows, others take over the daily responsibility of building projects and managing cash flow. Do they have the same deep understanding of its importance?

Senior managers must have a laser-like focus on financial matters. They know finances affect every aspect of a business. Not knowing enough can lead to a slow, but steady, downward spiral. All activities—adopting technology, hiring, office expansion, and bidder-list qualification, just to name a few—expand or curtail due to money. Well-managed firms keep clients, attract talent, and build value for their owners.

Middle managers make the most money for the construction firm. Profit is made on the project. Field supervisors and project managers make it happen on the job. Shouldn't they be the most knowledgeable of all middle managers?

Look at these statistics that reflect most categories of contracting:

- 3 percent—average profit before tax
- 10 percent—average overhead
- 87 percent—direct job costs

Middle managers influence or control 87 percent of the project. They are critical to profitable construction and, therefore, to profitable companies.

Overall, three people have the greatest impact: (1) the estimating manager (2) the field supervisor, and (3) the project manager. Each of these people has profit-and-loss responsibility, but financial management is more than that.

As an example, cash flow is a key indicator. *Cash flow* involves the sources and uses of funds. Some activities require cash, while others do not. Knowing the difference improves the performance of the firm. In my research, long-term negative cash flow is a precursor to bankruptcy. See Figure 4-3.

> Have a bidding process that includes a "sizer" for overhead application costs. It is an efficiency recognizer. Larger jobs require less overhead as a percentage. Smaller jobs require more overhead as a percentage. Quite simply, costs are added to smaller-than-average jobs, while costs are reduced in larger-than-average jobs. Contractors have a formula to calculate these numbers.

Let's start with some basic questions that lead to improved results.

ABC contracting					
President	Sets budgets, overhead allocation for departments with accounting manager	Determines target markets with company personnel	Sets job sizing formula		
Project manager	Searches for qualified subcontractors/update list				
Foreman					
Estimator	Downloads cost/productivity information from accounting and analyzes labor rates				
Estimating group					
Purchasing manager	Updates suppliers & database	Takes inventory at yard			
Accounting manager	Sets budgets, overhead allocation for departments with president	Reviews billings for client, change orders, retainage, job cost	Matches cash receipts, reconciles billing, & apartment /diem expenses	Creates A/R borrowing balance report	

FIGURE 4-3
Financial processes are probably the best-defined processes in any typical construction firm. The reason: they are normally managed by one person—the Financial Manager—and they are extremely important. The challenge is to make sure they are designed to provide useful and timely information to the build work and the acquire work phases.

What Is the First Rule of Business?

The first rule of business is don't run out of cash. You are taken out of the game for that. The second through tenth rules of business are the same: don't run out of cash. It is that important.

Construction Contracting Financial Fundamentals

We have listed below the four typical issues for construction firms. Solve these and you will have stronger financial health.

1. How do you decrease the cash conversion cycle (days) of your firm?

    The equation has two parts:

    *   Income

    *   Outgo

    Contractors start by making sure they have an above-average paying customer. They give (happily) the poor paying ones to their competitors. Additionally, they make sure they bill and collect from that client per their agreement, not only first billings and follow-on billings, but also change orders and retention.

    The other part of the equation is the outgo. Financially successful contractors make sure they are conservative on their expenses. They do not spend carelessly on investments in their business or future opportunities with customers. (Examples: radon or computer software.) They know that first adopters typically are the beta-testers and they take a financial hit.

    Combine the two and you have a cash flow or a *cash-to-cash cycle*. This determines your financial success.

2. How do you improve the return on investment (ROI) of a project?

    Only if projects are profitable can a company be profitable. Take a look at the cash-to-cash cycle of a construction project and its profit margin. These two are the major parts of a return on investment. Keep these favorable more often and your company's financial performance will be above average.

3. What are the key financial control measures you should review at least monthly?

    • Company profit and loss

    • Job cost with cost-to-complete calculations

    • Cash flow

    • Gross profit per man-hour or man-week

4. Which construction factor is the true profit opportunity for most firms?

Labor is the true profit opportunity. Over the history of the United States' construction market, for some 200+ years, labor management has determined the success or failure in 90 percent of the projects.

Do your senior and middle managers know these answers? Do they actively try to increase the financial performance of your firm? Could education in these areas help them work smarter?

As an aside, understanding risk is part of any financial management improvement. Ignore this at your own risk. The construction industry is one of the top five riskiest industries in the United States based on bankruptcy statistics. Your employees must have this type of financial education to keep you profitable.

Building the value of a firm is the ultimate goal for most owners, but most employees are not given the basic knowledge to help achieve this. Construction companies who address this can win a competitive edge. In fact, best of class contractors are determined by their financial result, not by their technical ability. That is another book for another time.

> **Receive and review credit ratings/financial information for major projects and major clients. This keeps the negative surprises at a minimum.**

The Vocabulary of Financial Management

To comprehend finances, you must first understand the following concepts. They are essential ratios to understand a construction company's financial strength. Banks, sureties, and other institutions use these as a gauge. Therefore, it is doubly important to be knowledgeable if you intend to use banks and bonding in your contracting business.

- **Activity ratios**—These ratios measure how effectively the firm is using its resources.
- **Backlog statistics**—The backlog of revenue is only one feature of this area.
- **Leverage ratios**—These ratios measure the extent to which the firm is financed by debt.
- **Liquidity ratios**—These ratios measure a construction company's capability to meet its short-term obligations.
- **Profit fade analysis**—This area identifies whether a contractor is consistently too optimistic (or pessimistic) about the outcome of construction projects.
- **Profitability ratios**—These ratios measure management's overall effectiveness as shown by the returns generated on revenue.

Definitions

These definitions are used by bank, sureties, and others to measure the relative financial strength of a construction firm. You need to be familiar with these when dealing with these outsiders. More importantly, the ratios listed below objectively show your financial health.

Acid Test Ratio (Also Known as the Quick Ratio)—The *acid test ratio* is similar to the current ratio, except inventory is deducted from current assets. (See Current Ratio.)

Most financial analysts agree that the ratio should be in the range of 1.0 to 1 and 1.5 to 1. This is because of the highly liquid financial character of construction.

Annual Revenue Generated by Each Dollar of Net Property and Equipment—This statistic measures the dollar value of fixed assets committed to the generation of revenues.

Asset Turnover (Net Revenues Divided by Total Assets)—*Asset turnover* is one indicator of management's efficiency in the management of resources.

Average Age of Accounts Payable—This statistic measures the average number of days that invoices remain in accounts payable before they are paid.

Age of Trade Accounts Receivable (Trade Accounts Receivable Divided by Net Revenues Multiplied by 365)—This measure indicates the number of days on average that the company has funds tied up in trade accounts receivable.

If the figure for the average number of days exceeds 45, the company is losing the opportunity to invest funds more productively and management should consider steps to accelerate collections.

Average Age of Accounts Receivable—This measures the average number of days it takes to collect invoices that were billed to customers. This ratio is often called the *average collection period*. (See Activity Ratios.)

Average Age of Overbillings—*Overbillings* are the liability account on the balance sheet labeled as "Billings in excess of costs plus margin on uncompleted contracts." (See Activity Ratios.)

Average Age of Underbillings—*Underbillings* are the asset account on the balance sheet labeled as "Costs plus margin in excess of billings on uncompleted contracts."

Age of Material Inventory (Material Inventory Divided by Material Cost Multiplied by 365)—The *age of material inventory* indicates the number of days the company has cash invested in inventory. As a general rule, for contractors who have significant material inventory, this should be in the range of 30 to 45 days.

Bad Debts as a % of Revenues—Consistently high bad debts experience indicates the company has poor practices when it comes to billing and collecting on work performed for customers. A number of issues may account for this, including:

- Poor follow-up on the collection of billings
- A poorly documented change order process
- Not prequalifying customers to determine if they have the ability to pay on time and if they have a reputation for being adversarial
- Accepting customers who have a poor record of payment just to get work (See Activity Ratios.)

Current Assets—*Current assets* include cash, receivables, under-billings, and prepaid assets.

Current Assets to Total Assets—This expresses how much of total assets are expected to be converted into cash in a short period of time.

Current Ratio—This ratio is the most commonly used statistic to measure short-term solvency. The *current ratio* indicates the extent to which the claims of short-term creditors are covered by assets (i.e., receivables and inventory) that are expected to be converted to cash within a period roughly corresponding to the maturity of the claims.

Debt Service Coverage—This is expressed as the number of times net income (before taxes) is available to cover principal and interest on outstanding debt (that is, net income can cover three times interest expense). (See Leverage Ratios.)

Degree of Fixed Asset Newness—This ratio identifies the age of tools and equipment. The net book value of older equipment is next to zero. The net book value of new equipment is closer to 100 percent of its original purchase price. If this calculation results in an answer that is below 40 percent, the contractor's equipment may be too old.

Depreciation as a Percent of Fixed Assets—This ratio shows how fast assets are written off. As a general rule, purchases of fixed assets (that is, property and equipment) should approximate depreciation. (See Activity Ratios.)

EBIT—*EBIT* is an acronym that stands for Earnings Before Interest and Taxes. EBIT is easily calculated by taking the net income, and adding interest expense and income taxes.

Gross Margin as a Percent of Total Revenues—This measures the profitability of a contractor at the job level for open and closed jobs combined as reported on the income statement. (See Gross Margin from Completed Projects.)

Gross Margin from Completed Projects—This measures the profitability of a contractor at the job level for closed jobs only. Completed jobs that have a higher gross margin than open and closed contracts combined on the income statement may indicate:

- Open jobs are not as profitable.
- This may be a sign of a declining construction economy or a change in management structure that does not benefit the company.
- It may also indicate management is conservative in recognizing profits until the projects are completed.

If the gross margin percent on completed jobs is smaller than open and closed jobs combined on the income statement:

- This may be a sign the construction economy is improving.
- It may also be a sign that management is too optimistic about the profit potential of work-in-process, delaying the bad news until the projects are finished and the bad news cannot be delayed anymore.
- A change in management structure has occurred that benefits the company. (See Profitability Ratios.)

Long-Term Debt to Equity Ratio—A company needs to finance property and equipment with long-term debt. This ratio helps to monitor the relationship between long-term debt and equity. (See Leverage Ratios.)

Marginal Revenue, Marginal Cost, Marginal Overhead, and so forth—Marginal revenue represents the change or difference in revenue from one year to the next. This is the same thought as concerning marginal cost and marginal overhead.

Net Income Before Taxes as a Percent of Revenues—This measures the combined management of jobs and overhead. This standard varies by industry within construction. Some companies are Sub S corporations or partnerships, which have no income taxes. That is why we exclude taxes. This allows the comparison with other companies across the industry. It is important for management to set a goal for the net income they require by establishing an income statement budget at the beginning of the year that reflects their profit goal. Management can monitor their progress toward this goal each month by the review of monthly financial statements. When it appears, the goal will not be met, adjustments to improve gross margin and/or reduce overhead need to be made. (See Profitability Ratios.)

Operating Profit Margin (Operating Profits Divided by Net Revenue)—The operating profit margin is one of the most important measures of management effectiveness. Computed properly, the *operating profit margin* shows how well the company performs its core business, unaffected by tax consequences that may fluctuate with the dollar amount of profit.

Overhead as a Percent of Revenues—The value of this statistic lies in the trend over several years. If revenue remains flat, but overhead increases each year, then the statistic will show an increasing overhead rate.

Total Overhead to Total Direct Costs—The *total overhead to total direct cost ratio* is an important indicator, which shows the total amount that total direct costs must be marked up to recover total company overhead. Most contractors assume that each individual job should be marked up by the overhead-to-cost ratio to recover overhead. Unfortunately, overhead recovery is not so simple, but involves ratios of material to labor, job size, and other factors.

R-Score—This calculation measures the financial risk and strength of a company.

Return on Assets (Net Income Before Taxes Divided by Total Assets)—This measure shows how productively management uses and manages all the assets at its disposal to make money.

Return on Equity (ROE)—In this calculation, the denominator is the stockholders' equity or the partners' capital. Net income after taxes is the numerator.

Return on Working Capital (ROWC) (Net Income Before Taxes Divided by Working Capital)—Return on working capital is a useful indicator when considered with working capital turnover and other measures to determine not only how effectively management uses working capital, but also how productively. We recommend a range of 40 percent to 60 percent return on working capital.

Return on Net Worth (Net Income Before Taxes Divided by Total Net Worth)—Determining which investment out of a number of alternatives to pursue an investor is primarily concerned with the likelihood of a return commensurate with the risk to which the investment is exposed. With more risk, the investor will expect the opportunity for a higher return.

Revenue to Total Assets—This calculation indicates how much revenue is generated by each dollar of total assets. A favorable answer would be a high ratio.

Times Interest Earned—Interest expense plus net operating profit (which is net income before income taxes, gain [loss] on sale of fixed assets and other income) is divided by interest expense. This determines the number of times interest is "covered" by earnings. A low ratio means the management of the business does not have much room for error.

Underbillings/Overbillings Ratio—*Underbillings* is a shortened name for the asset account on the balance sheet labeled "Costs plus estimated margin in excess of billings on uncompleted contracts." *Overbillings* is a shortened name for a liability account on the balance sheet labeled "Billings in excess of costs plus estimated margin on uncompleted contracts." A close relationship exists between these two accounts because their amounts are derived from the same work-in-process data. When this particular ratio exceeds

150 percent, this is a warning sign that a company may be running into financial trouble.

Net Excess Billings or Costs (Costs Plus Estimated Earnings in Excess of Billings Divided by Estimated Earnings)—When negative, this figure shows the company has not actually earned all the costs associated with its billing.

Age Of Costs and Estimated Earnings in Excess Of Billings (Costs and Estimated Earnings in Excess of Billings Divided by Net Revenues Multiplied by 365)—This measure shows the number of days the company has funds invested in job costs, which have not been billed.

Age Of Billings in Excess Of Costs and Estimated Earnings— (Billings in Excess of Costs and Estimated Earnings Divided by Net Revenues Multiplied by 365)—This measure shows the number of days the company has funds from billing customer in excess of costs.

Working Capital—*Working capital* can be simply defined as total current assets minus total current liabilities. To meet current obligations, working capital may be increased, if necessary, in three ways:

1. Generate and retain operating profits
2. Borrow money long-term
3. Sell owned assets and lease them back to the firm

Working capital is subject to certain distortions and misinterpretations because some current liabilities that reduce the working capital number can represent cash (someone else's cash) available for operations. For long-term health and growth, however, the firm's working capital must be sufficient to finance current sales and operations.

Working Capital Turnover—A contractor needs working capital to finance the business.

We recommend a turnover rate of more than 8 and less than 12. If this turnover rate is not available, some reasons may be:

- Too much cash is on hand and not enough cash is in the business. Receivables are high (actively collecting receivables).

- Payables are paid off sooner than necessary. Payables are held longer than 45 days.

- Substantial notes are receivable from the owners. Substantial current notes are payable to the owners. Material inventory may be substantial and other current liabilities may be overstated.

- Claims are recorded as assets.

Z-Score—This calculation measures the potential of a company to fail (it is different from the R-Score calculation). The *Z-Score statistic* is more balance-sheet based.

> Superior contractors rarely miss a first billing opportunity. They know that the first billing is the first chance to collect costs, but also it is a first glimpse at the client's pay practices with a small amount of money at stake.

Financial Statement Format

A snapshot of a typical financial format that many contractors use is included here. This is certainly not the only one to use, but for this purpose, it centers the discussion on the few critical success factors of financial management in contracting.

We present Moonlight Contracting, which you may know as Second-Job Construction. This company is a smaller, and well-managed firm.

The following list of information is for contracting professionals to use when setting up your accounting packages. Construction is a unique business. The right chart of accounts keeps you organized. Also, it allows for efficient financial analysis. See Figures 4-4 and 4-5.

Sample profit and loss statement

	Year XX
Revenues	9,045,445
Direct costs	
Material	3,098,436
Subcontracts	345,987
Labor	2,945,363
Equipment	454,646
Other direct costs	190,343
Total direct costs	7,034,775
Gross profit	2,010,670
Overhead	
Interest expense	224,453
Other variable overhead	34,353
Officers' compensation	190,000
Other fixed overhead	1,232,165
Total overhead	1,680,971
Operating income/(loss)	329,699
Other income	498,061
Other expenses	151,317
Extraordinary items	45,464
Net income/(loss) before taxes	721,907
Income taxes	289,573
Net income/(loss) after taxes	432,334

FIGURE 4-4
A sample profit and loss statement is also known as an income statement.

The numbers here are unimportant, but the concepts are critical. One important concept is the trend. This year compared to previous years gives clues as to current performance.

> Profitable contractors are expert at change orders. They know what is appropriate, how to document it, and how to collect them. For any contractor, change orders can make the difference between a poor year and a good year.

Sample balance sheet

Assets	Year XX
Cash and cash equivalents	8,287,029
Accounts receivable-progress billings	7,425,195
Accounts receivable-current retention	8,134,024
Other current receivables	16,331
Materials inventory	40,000
Cost and estimated earnings in excess of billings	599,445
All other current assets	191,252
Total current assets	**24,693,276**
Buildings, equipment and vehicles	2,388,568
Accumulated depreciation	1,746,178
Net depreciable fixed assets	642,390
Land	4,213
Total fixed assets (net)	**646,603**
Joint ventures and investments	503,262
Intangibles (net)	8,000
All other non-current assets	1,449,423
Total assets	**27,300,564**

Liabilities and net worth	
Short term notes payable	4,000
Accounts payable-material & subs	5,512,329
Accounts payable-current retention	6,894,121
Billings in excess of costs and estimated earnings	9,261,808
Accrued expenses and liabilities	45,178
Current maturities-long term debt	13,331
All other current liabilities	40,000
Total current liabilities	**21,770,767**
Long-term debt	4,213
Deferred taxes	4,000
All other non-current liabilities	3,000
Total liabilities	**21,781,980**
Net worth	5,518,584
Total liabilities and net worth	**27,300,564**

FIGURE 4-5

A sample balance sheet. This represents the overall financial health of a construction contracting firm at a point in time.

Our Industry Is a Variable-Cost Business

Construction is a variable-cost business. Many other businesses have a fixed-cost structure. The determining factor in classifying a business is a look at the percent of fixed cost and *variable cost* (cost caused by a sale) of the business. Add these two percentages together, subtract the total from 100 percent, and what remains is profit.

To make this more clear, let's define two terms:

- Over 50 percent fixed costs—We consider this a fixed-cost business, such as airlines, computer software manufacturers, and restaurants to name a few. They have to drive volume to make the economics work. To pay their fixed cost every month, they must have a certain volume.

- Under 50 percent fixed costs—We consider this a variable-cost business. As a side note, many service businesses are considered in this category. A *fixed-cost business* means that most of the cost of the product or service is caused by the sale. See Figure 4-6.

Construction is under 20 percent in fixed-cost to variable-cost ratio. In reality, a majority of contractors are under 10 percent. That places a huge premium on taking the right work, not cheap work. Furthermore, you must insist on a margin that is reasonable for the job.

In this business of contracting, we cannot use volume as a way to earn profits. We are not an airline. Our resources (good people, your expertise) are too scarce. We have to demand a value for these factors. Thus, we should have a profitable job.

> If projects are profitable, then the firm will also be profitable.

One of the lessons of our business is not to turn it into a fixed-cost business. As an example, if you are a young utility contractor and you buy (instead of lease or rent) a backhoe in your first year, you now have fixed costs or a nut to cover. This places more pressure on you to sell another job to cover this cost.

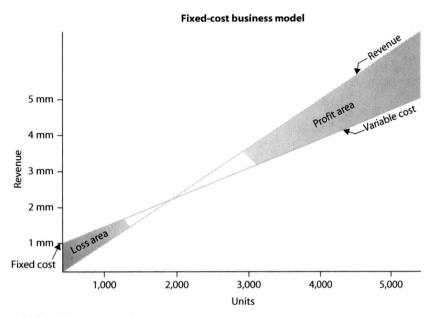

FIGURE 4-6
Once a company covers its fixed costs or *nut*, then the company enjoys greater profits. They grow both as a percentage and total dollars.

Crews can be a de facto-fixed cost if you promise them a future. Just like buying a backhoe, this commitment puts pressure on the contractor to sell another job and keep it busy. With commitment to your people, there must be a consistent stream of revenue. Otherwise, you have to lay them off from time to time. We know well that, at some point, they will choose not to return.

One of the keys to the variable-cost model is that you can break even (earn profit to cover your fixed cost) with a minimal amount of volume. This gives contractors some flexibility in finding the right kind of work. You don't need to sell every customer, just a few who pay well. This is evidenced in that hit rates of financially successful contractors is less than 20 percent. Well capitalized construction firms are not low bidders and low bidders are not consistently profitable. See Figure 4-7.

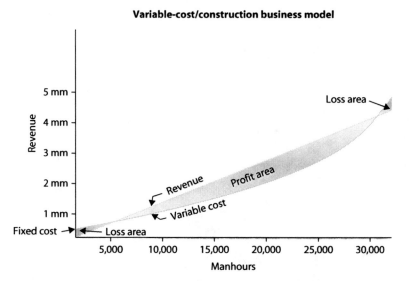

FIGURE 4-7
Construction is a variable cost business that has a lower fixed-cost percentage to cover. However, if volume is too great for labor man-hours to efficiently execute them, cost will exceed revenue (see the right end of the graph), spelling financial trouble.

> Be financially disciplined and keep debt out of your company. Be conservative in your buying habits.

We should also mention that, with all the risk involved, this extra margin gives a contractor a cushion to pay for unforeseen and uncompensated costs. If a client won't pay, the contractor still has some funds to buy the extra labor, material, and so forth.

Think of it this way: if you keep your break-even costs low, you have the ability to walk away from an unfair or an overly demanding negotiation.

On the other end of the scale, if contractors take on too much volume, they will certainly have costs rise and profit margins shrink. In other words, costs and profit will cross over at the high revenue end of the curve.

This is due to two factors:

1. The last 50 percent of volume has to be sold cheaper than the first 50 percent of volume. Extra revenue has to be sold at discount.

2. Adding extra, unproven people makes our business inefficient because mistakes, rework, and a general slowing of the process occur. This drives the cost up.

Again, the cost and revenue curves will cross. Financial losses will add up.

As people in the industry have said for many years:

Volume is for show, profit is the dough.

This brings up the point of our section. The construction business rewards those who are detail-oriented and time-sensitive. This applies to craftsmanship and management. If you are one of the contractors who believe as I do, then you will always be in demand. Construction buyers value good and timely work.

For this kind of contracting firm, it is just a small matter of price. If the economy is strong, prices stay high. If the economy is struggling, a good contractor can always lower his price and win any job he wants. Craftsmanship sells.

Here are three principles all contractors should consider:

1. **A high return on investments means you are efficient in your financial choices.** That is, contractors who earn 40 percent or more in return on equity are making great business decisions. Many times, they practice conservative financial habits. This high ROI has little to do with volume.

2. **It is not how much you make; it is how much you save.** Substantial money in the bank with no debt gives you greater options in your personal and professional life.

3. **We make money in the field and at the bid table.** Good financial management doesn't make money, it *saves* contractors money. So, if you don't make any money in the first place, you have nothing to save or manage. Keep the focus on the field (doing work) and the bid table (getting work).

> Savvy contractors know the average financial ratios of peer companies in their market sector. This keeps them competitive in overhead costs and balance sheet assets/liabilities.

You Cannot Ignore Financial Management

Recently, I was presenting to several contractors and their executives. In starting this seminar, I asked some questions to understand the group and its composition. Then I asked "What part of contracting do you enjoy most?" In this session, the following results were (these are common):

- Building projects—more than 50 percent
- Acquiring work—less than 40 percent
- Accounting/finances—less than 10 percent

This is not a surprising result for most people, but any for-profit business must pay 100 percent attention to its finances. This is not an option. The ability to pay its bills determines solvency. As stated earlier, money is like oxygen to a business.

One business legend said it this way: "There are ten rules of business. The first is don't run out of cash, the second is don't run out of cash, and rules 3 through 10 are not that important." You may not agree, but our most important focus as contractors is financial management. It makes our arteries constrict or dilate, depending on the state of our bank accounts.

> Demand that all daily job consumables be called into the supplier by the field supervisor at noon the day before—at a minimum. This reduces wasted time.

Budgeting

In any financial management process, a budget is the first requirement. Before the start of a business, the business plan with a budget must be created. Let's look at why budgeting is critical.

- Requires planning
- Forces communication and coordination (essential for contractors)
- Provides the framework for measurement of performance
- Clearly educates about business costs

For contractors who keep their volume the same year-in and year-out, the budgeting process is less of a mystery and less work. But, for companies growing or decreasing their volume, budgeting is a must. With a changing business, planning takes on a new importance.

Let's look at a typical construction budget in Table 4-1. We can use this as an example for upcoming discussions. What we observe is that costs behave in a fairly narrow fashion for most contractors and we want to use that to help our budgeting process.

TABLE 4-1
A Simple Construction Budget. This is a fairly typical breakout for a labor-intensive contractor. There are no surprises here. In the following, we introduce a powerful concept called "bottom-up budgeting." A high correlation exists between profitability and budgeting. There is only one way to budget in construction from the bottom up.

Contract Revenue	$1,000,000	100%
Labor	$350,000	35%
Material	$350,000	35%
Equipment	$50,000	5%
Subcontract	$100,000	10%
Other Direct Cost	$20,000	2%
Gross Profit	$130,000	13%
Overhead	$90,000	9%
Income Before Taxes	**$40,000**	**4%**

> Smart contractors plan the use of any asset they want or need. They never purchase on impulse. This is especially true when it comes to software. The amount of unused or underutilized software in the construction industry is legend.

Bottom-Up Budgeting   *Bottom-up budgeting* reflects the goal(s) for an organization. Through its cost and revenue calculation, it derives cost and revenue requirements for the target. What is the goal for the organization? Let's look at a simple example. The owner wants to make $100,000 net income before tax (other times, it might be to launch a new division but, right now, let's keep the discussion on a clear example). You can see how we form a budget for growth in net income in Table 4-2.

We start with the *knowns* of our business, which are the historical percentage costs of the company and a desired profit for our business.

We place the number of $100,000 at the Income Before Tax (IBT) line. Then, we multiply this number by an acceptable net income percent. This might be 8 percent or 4.2 percent, but not 10 percent. Ten percent IBT would reflect a 25 percent gain in efficiency and/reduction in cost at the current revenue. Unless there is a compelling reason, we would argue against it.

TABLE 4-2
An Example of a Beginning Template for Bottom-Up Budgeting

Revenue	?	
Labor		30%
Material		25%
Equipment		5%
Subcontracts		10%
Other		2%
Overhead		20%
Targeted Net Profit	**$100,000**	

TABLE 4-3
Resulting Preliminary Budget

Revenue	$1,250,000	100%
Labor	$375,000	30%
Material	$312,000	25%
Equipment	$62,500	5%
Subcontracts	$125,000	10%
Other	$25,000	2%
Overhead	$250,000	20%
Targeted Net Profit	**$100,000**	**8%**

So, let's say we use 8 percent because this is a number we have consistently accomplished. By multiplication, the new top-line or revenue number is $1,250,000. See Table 4-3.

Now we use the normal or reasonable percentages of direct costs to perform the rest of our calculations. Again, this percentage should not be a wish or a stretch goal. History of the firm's performance must justify these numbers. If you are a new firm, look at the industry financial statistics.

We have calculated the numbers based on our history. Now, we should "what if" as part of our yearly planning and budgeting discipline. See Table 4-4.

Review these direct costs, and then see the following planning questions.

TABLE 4-4
This reflects the first iteration of budgeting. These numbers will change as management decisions are made in the planning process.

Labor	$375,000	30%
Material	$312,000	25%
Equipment	$62,500	5%
Subcontracts	$125,000	10%
Other Direct Costs	$25,000	2%

Now we need to have a discussion. Here are some questions to ask:

1. With our existing field forces, can we take on the additional work and deliver the same cost percentages?
2. If we have to hire addition crews with supervision, can we expect the same performance as with our proven crews?
3. If we are proceeding with a new building process and/or equipment, what will the effect be?
4. If not, what is the new overhead percentage? Possibly, 21 percent or 22 percent (ominously, overhead should grow as a percentage due to more work and creeping inefficiency).

As a word of advice, always be conservative in your assumptions. In other words, keep growth small and expense-impact higher. This will make your budgeting surprises positive ones.

We have not discussed the overhead issue, so let's do that now.

> Safety conscious contractors have additional safety standards to OSHA's Publication 1926. This book is the minimum. Requiring more allows the contractors to be safer, thus enjoying the benefits—business, personal, and moral.

Overhead Budgeting

Overhead budgeting is a line-by-line exercise. In some firms, there may be more than 100 different overhead categories, which would be considered a detailed approach to budgeting for most contractors. Table 4-5 shows the typical overhead-budgeting categories. You may have more or less.

You can e-mail clientservices@stevensci.com or fax 419-828-5026 to request a detailed explanation of these categories. The number of these categories can be limited by you. Some small contractors have less than 15 line items. This is no great sin. They keep their business simple and they still know everything about the business.

TABLE 4-5
Typical Overhead Budgeting Categories

Advertising	Oil & Gas
Bonuses	Postage & Freight
Cell Phone	Propane
Commissions	R&M—Building
Computer Expense	R&M—Trucks & Equip.
Depreciation—G&A	Rent
Discounts Given	Safety & Recall Incentives
Donations	Salaries & Wages
Dues & Subscriptions	Shop Supplies & Tools
Employee Recruiting	Taxes—Other
Insur—W/C, Office	Taxes—Payroll, Office
Insur—Auto	Taxes—Property
Insur—Other	Taxes—Franchise
Interest Expense	Telephone & Pagers
Legal and Professional	Training
Licenses, Permits, & Plans	Travel
Meals & Entertainment	Uniforms
Mileage	Unapplied Labor & Overhead
Miscellaneous	Unapplied Materials
Office Expenses & Supplies	Utilities

Overhead budgeting starts from:

1. Previous experience if you're just starting out in your contracting business.

2. Last year's budget results if your business is ongoing.

In any event, these are numbers that must be determined by you. No one knows your plans for the new year except you. And, certainly, no one prioritizes business expenses except you. A great example is bottled water. Who would have thought bottled water would have a value 10 years ago? What about computer services or e-mail expenses? Some contractors still don't have e-mail and, yet, they are quite happy and productive.

So, our conclusion is this: you must be the one to determine what business expenses you are willing to pay. In reality, this is your job. The business decision has to be centered on the question "Does this have a compelling benefit to my business?"

Let me spend a moment on the following concept: it's a business expense, so it is a write-off on my taxes. I have heard many young contractors who believe they are doing themselves a financial service by having lots of business expenses. This is an idea I'd like to stamp out and here's why. All expenses are a 35 percent write-off against taxable profit. That is, you are paying for 65 percent of the cost of the purchase. This is no great opportunity. However, truck salespeople and computer consultants, among others, continue to imply it is a 1 to 1 trade-off between income and taxes. It is not. You can't save enough money. The economy will be fine without you buying products and services that are not appropriate for your business.

> Use graphics to communicate simple, but powerful, ideas to employees. Examples: using a loss-revenue chart (shown later in this chapter) or productivity improvement expressed in minutes (see Chapter 3).

Overhead Rightsizing

Overhead will always be a hot topic among contractors. Being too fat in your office support of projects is a constant concern. It takes away from your profitability. Additionally, it is natural. We grew up in a hard-bid world where being low was important and keeping overhead lean was religion.

Overhead in *unnecessary* expenses is a sin. Keeping the nonproduction-related costs reasonable is a worthy goal. Items such as cell-phone expenses, copy costs, software investment, travel, and the like typically don't add to the on-time and on-budget production of projects. This seems to be a necessary evil and a drag to our business. Conversely, having enough people to manage the details of a job can make money for a contractor.

Different types of contractors have different office/support needs; therefore, they have different overhead cost percentages. Getting right-sized is necessary for profitable operations.

Where can you find solid overhead costs to compare them? Here are three resources:

1. Peer groups
2. Industry associations
3. Banking information

Peer groups are an excellent place to find out what other companies do and how they do it. A *peer group* is a voluntary gathering of noncompeting contractors who get together for the express purpose of gathering and disseminating information. Typically, they meet every quarter with a predetermined agenda in the home city of one of the members. This is usually an all-day affair. Contractors enjoy fresh ideas from each other and, sometimes, the value of "done that, it doesn't work" can save a company thousands of dollars and hundreds of hours of effort.

All *industry-association* data are voluntarily reported information. These data are confidential from each company, but not audited by anyone. So, such data are not as defendable as banking information. Still, trade-association financial statistics are good data from excellent contractors in the country, even though it is not the best information.

Banking information is available to contractors at a cost. This kind of financial data allows them to review high-quality industry results against their own information. This banking information is from thousands of contractors. The source documents are loan applications, and the like, which a bank receives, and they are carefully submitted by contractors. Reporting publications sell these summaries, so these data are not hard to find.

From this research, it is now easier to determine an appropriate overhead cost for our companies. Thus, we can keep our operating cost and our bidding at a competitive level.

Once we know the cost of a project, then we know our *break-even point*, that is, we know the direct cost of the job, plus the overhead cost to support it. From that point, the poker game begins. The smart contractor thinks to himself, "What is the highest price I can offer, while satisfying the owner's perception about my construction service value?" In a hard-bid environment, success is the low number, but in other bid environments, there is some opportunity to play poker.

Take a look at your overhead numbers, compare them to your peers, or review them against banking information. You will benefit by keeping your overhead costs competitive. This should be a yearly exercise.

> Excellent contractors reestimate bad bids to correctly set a reasonable budget to work against. From this, the field supervisor and project manager know what it is possible. This keeps the company from revisiting the problem estimate time and again. It cuts off all excuses in the future.

Allocating Overhead to Two or More Types of Work

In Figure 4-8, we show you not only budgeting, but also how to determine overhead-cost allocation to two or more types of work. This is a powerful concept when it comes to determining the profit and loss of individual departments. All owners are faced with the decision of discontinuing a type of work due to its profitability. Conversely, this can give to you some insight into whether you should enter a niche. With this process, you can project revenue versus costs quite nicely.

For our purposes, let's take a few overhead categories and discuss the effects on them with this growth. There are certainly more than these four items, but we'll use these as an example.

1. Technology

The technology cost category contains every changing expense for keeping current with labor-saving devices, such as PDAs, laptops, software, and so forth. Yearly maintenance agreements, upgrades, and new software purchases add to this cost every year.

2. Training

Training increases with headcount. Having untrained employees can lead to more problems than you are experiencing now. The cost must be budgeted, otherwise, you won't add to your wealth.

ABC Construction Company operating budget - sample

		Work A		Work B		Total
	Revenue	1,100,000	100.00%	700,000	100.00%	$1,800,000
	Cost of revenue					
	Materials	302,228	27.48%	234,361	33.48%	$536,589
	Labor	563,530	51.23%	126,432	18.06%	$689,962
	Equipment	10,891	0.99%	12,335	1.76%	$23,226
	Subcontract	24,505	2.23%	135,683	19.38%	$160,188
	Other	1,000	0.00%	1,000	0.00%	$2,000
	Total cost of sales	902,154	81.92%	509,811	72.69%	$1,411,964
	Gross profit	197,846	18.08%	190,189	27.31%	$388,036
	Overhead costs					
A	Advertising	611		389		1,000.00
C	Bonuses	8,168		1,832		10,000.00
C	Cell phone	3,267		733		4,000.00
D	Commissions	5,099		4,901		10,000.00
A	Computer expense	3,056		1,944		5,000.00
A	Depreciation - G & A	7,944		5,056		13,000.00
A	Discounts given	306		194		500.00
D	Donations	510		490		1,000.00
D	Dues & subscriptions	1,020		980		2,000.00
D	Employee recruiting	510		490		1,000.00
D	Insur - W/C, office	2,549		2,451		5,000.00
D	Insur - auto	4,079		3,921		8,000.00
D	Insur - other	7,648		7,352		15,000.00
D	Interest expense	510		490		1,000.00
D	Legal and professional	2,549		2,451		5,000.00
A	Licenses, permits & plans	1,222		778		2,000.00
D	Meals & entertainment	2,549		2,451		5,000.00
D	Mileage	510		490		1,000.00
D	Miscellaneous	0		0		0.00
D	Office exp. & supplies	5,099		4,901		10,000.00
A	Oil & gas	9,167		5,833		15,000.00
A	Postage & freight	917		583		1,500.00
C	Propane	4,084		916		5,000.00
D	R&M - building	5,099		4,901		10,000.0
C	R&M - trucks & equip.	14,276		5,131		28,000.00
D	Rent	6,118		5,882		12,000.00
C	Safety & recall incentives	1,785		641		3,500.00
D	Salaries & wages	43,339		41,661		85,000.00
C	Shop supplies & tools	12,251		2,749		15,000.00
D	Taxes - other	127		123		250.00
D	Taxes - payroll, office	4,589		4,411		9,000.00
D	Taxes - property	510		490		1,000.00
D	Taxes - franchise	1,020		980		2,000.00
C	Telephone & pagers	3,569		1,283		7,000.00
C	Training	4,084		916		5,000.00

FIGURE 4-8

The key to allocating two or more types of work (or departments) is to use a rational factor of expense allocation. As you see, using more than one is necessary (see the left-hand side).

3. Estimating Costs

The estimating cost category is different for each company, but it captures those overhead items that are the cost of plans, overnight delivery bills, software, and so forth.

With a 25 percent increase in revenue, will the cost for estimating increase? Certainly, it should be the same cost percent or 9 percent. You can only look at the cost on a dollar-for-dollar basis. From my experience, this is neither a huge expense nor does it grow faster than the revenue.

4. Salaries

The salary cost category is all project management, estimating, administrative, field salaries, and so forth. Typical positions are project manager, estimator, general superintendent, human resources (HR), and the like. This category is also known as office positions.

The increase in volume will certainly affect the salary in more than one way. First, the extra revenue with the same staff will cause extra work. This is dangerous in construction where your deep understanding of the contract documents and construction requirements gives you the best chance of success. Intensity of focus captures opportunities and/or threats to profits. If there is no intensity, then luck must be on your side.

Estimators lose accuracy working longer hours and this is a recipe for financial loss. In a business that historically provides less than 5 percent net profit, mistakes are unforgiving.

Whether they're project managers or estimators, hiring extra people also has its potential problems. New, unproven staff does not consistently perform. Just ask anyone who has hired 10 or more people over the years. A majority of those hired have not lasted in the contractor's employment.

Our conclusion is that overhead budgeting for salaries should be reviewed closely. The review may change the owner's mind about increased profit and, thus, revenue and that is not a bad thing.

Summary

Budgeting in the construction industry is different than most other business segments. The bottom-up budgeting technique has been in use for many years and it has stood the test of time from the contracting community.

The process forces people to consider real world issues. Line by line, the historical and rational facts guide people toward realistic expectations.

While bottom-up budgeting doesn't give you all the answers, it is a superior method to start the conversation between executives whose job is to carry out the plan.

> Superior construction firms have organized financial information, so it is easy to create mini profit and loss statements for any equipment or project manager. This indicates whether they are earning an acceptable ROI.

What Does a Good Project Look Like (Financially)?

As we strongly believe, contractors always have to search and solve for financial reward. Money is the life blood of any contractor. Without it, a construction firm is in technical bankruptcy. Additionally, construction projects are where a contractor makes money. There is no other place. If all projects are profitable, then a construction company is also.

The following is a template that solves for ROI of a job before you bid it. Of course, your costs and other information have to be accurate to receive truthful results. In this example, we compare three projects and solve for ROI. This template measures only financial result.

As we have said, though, if a project doesn't make financial sense, we need to be aware of that to make a wise decision.

We suggest you use this example and the template (see Figures 4-9 and 4-10) before you consider bidding any project to make sure it meets your ROI goal. If it doesn't, then you certainly have to look

Job selection analysis

This tool can be used to evaluate the true return on investment of a job or jobs. It takes into consideration the length of the job, the time it is estimated to get paid on the job, the accounts payable commitment (in days), etc.

Use of this tool is at user's risk.

Instructions

1. Input the following (only shaded cells):

			Job 1	Job 2	Job 3
Contract or bid amount of job			$ 500,000	$ 460,000	$ 520,000
Costs:					
Material			$ 228,000	$ 282,000	$ 270,000
Labor			$ 189,000	$ 109,000	$ 165,000
Overhead on materials	rate =	8%	$ 18,240	$ 22,560	$ 21,600
Overhead on labor	rate =	15%	$ 28,350	$ 16,350	$ 24,750
Total costs			$ 463,590	$ 429,910	$ 481,350
Profit expected in dollars			$ 36,410	$ 30,090	$ 38,650
Profit expected as a percent of contract			7%	7%	7%
Length of job (in months)			3	4	2
Expected lag in receipt of funds after billing customer (in months)			3	1	2
Supplier (for material) credit terms (in months)			1	1	2
Current working capital (in dollars)	$ 287,000				

FIGURE 4-9
This example shows that the cash demand coupled with the profit margin leads to a smaller-than-expected ROI in projects. Calculation of this template helps a contractor look at a job from a financial perspective.

at other factors, such as being located next to your office or for a high-profile client, to justify pursuing it.

> Create a compensation system that has a variable component. This is also known as a *bonus*. In some firms, a bonus can comprise a 25 percent or more addition to the base salary. It makes employees act more like owners.

Determining Your "Walk-Away" Number

All contractors are helped by the ability to play "poker" once in a while. Negotiating is the highest and best use of any business person's time. The owner of a construction firm is no different.

Job selection analysis

	Job 1	Job 2	Job 3
Length of job (in days)	90	120	60
Length of receivables commitment (in days)	90	30	60
Length of payables (in days)	30	30	60
Net material cost days	60	0	0
Net labor cost days	90	30	60
Net investment rate per day	$ 5,151.00	$ 3,582.58	$ 8,022.50
Material costs per day	$ 2,736.00	$ 2,538.00	$ 4,860.00
Labor costs per day	$ 2,415.00	$ 1,044.58	$ 3,162.50

Investment in each job

	Job 1	Job 2	Job 3
Total investment in material	$ 164,160.00	$ –	$ –
Total investment in labor	$ 217,350.00	$ 31,337.50	$ 189,750.00
Total working capital investment	$ 381,510.00	$ 31,337.50	$ 189,750.00
Profit generated	$ 36,410.00	$ 30,090.00	$ 38,650.00
Job payback period (in days)	180	150	120
Return on investment (annual)	19.09%	230.45%	61.11%
Working capital situation assessment	EXCEEDED	OKAY	OKAY

FIGURE 4-10
These results show that financial results of a project are driven by (a) profit margin and (b) terms and conditions of that project.

Part of the ability to successfully play poker is to know your *walk-away number*, which is knowing the minimum you will accept. Just as we all have a high price that we would accept for doing something unpleasant, we have a dollar value that is the least we will take.

The following is a calculation example for your review.

As we indicated, the major contributors to the ROI of a project are:

1. The profit margin
2. The timing of cash flows

Other factors also affect this, such as the cost of money, but these two are the critical success factors. You need to make these your shorthand calculation for determining a financially rewarding job.

The shorthand we are alluding to can be stated in the following formula:

$$\frac{\textbf{Profit}}{\textbf{Amount of Working Capital + Its Cost}}$$

Profit is the gross dollar amount you derive from the project before you subtract overhead (office) costs. *Working capital dollars* is the amount of money you have to "rent" to the job and "+ Its Cost" means interest cost.

All contractors have different financial perceptions. They require a lot of money or a little bit of money to live on. They perceive their own value differently. Some feel they should be paid above the market, others feel the market price is fair. Some want to get ahead of the customer on payments, while others bill as they build the job.

Whatever your financial perception is, it is certainly your choice and your business decision. From the template and its calculation, though, we can show you the effect of your decisions.

As a practical matter, we recommend that you don't let the customer make you finance the construction project. Payment has to be made in a prompt fashion. Again, if you finance the project, this will have a substantial effect on the financial outcome.

Financially successful contractors attain ROIs north of 40 percent. This makes all the sense in the world. We are in a risky business and we should be compensated for it. See Figures 4-11 and 4-12.

> Use bonus/incentive plans to encourage good business practice, as well as profits.

Marginal Contribution

What is the first question to ask about any potential strategic move? It is not about marketing, sales, or any other potential benefit. The first question to ask is "Does it make financial sense?"

	A	B	C	D	E	F	G	H	I
1						**Reward analysis**			
2									
3		This tool can be used to evaluate the true return on investment of a company or division. It takes into consideration the length of the job, the time it is estimated to get paid on the job, the accounts payable commitment (in days), etc.							
4									
5		**Use of this tool is at user's risk. SCI assumes no responsibility for its accuracy, completeness, correctness, or usefulness.**							
6						Instructions			
7	1.	Input the following (only shaded cells):							
8									**Company**
9		Revenue							$ 2,500,000
10		Costs:							
11			Direct material						$ 1,000,000
12			Direct labor						$ 500,000
13			Direct equipment - rent						$ 30,000
14			Direct equipment - own						$ 30,000
15			Subcontractor						$ 600,000
16			General conditions						$ 100,000
17			Overhead						$ 100,000
18				Total costs					$ 2,360,000
19		Profit expected in dollars							$ 140,000
20		Profit expected as a percent							6%
21									
22									
23		Average client payment time in days after billing (in days)							30
24		Supplier (for material) credit terms (in days)							30
25		Supplier (for equipment) credit terms (in days)							30
26		Total working days per year (in days)							30
27		Billing cycle by your company (in days)							30
28		Company/division working capital (in dollars)						$ 100,000	
29									
30			Assuming paid when paid to any subcontractors						
31			Owned equipment is cash out from day one.						
32			If neccesary, input division by division numbers.						
33			Please normalize overhead costs, e.g. owner's bonus, salary, expenses.						

FIGURE 4-11
These inputs determine the reward for the risk. As varied as construction companies are, so, too, are the ROI calculations. This is a good place to start.

Reward analysis

	Company
Average length of receivables commitment (in days)	45
Average length of material payables (in days)	30
Average length of equipment rent payables(in days)	30
Net material cost days	15
Net labor cost days	45
Net rental equipment cost days	15
Net owned equipment cost days	45
Net general conditions cost days	45
Net overhead cost days	45
Material costs per day	$ 33,333.33
Labor costs per day	$ 16,666.67
Rental equipment cost per day	$ 1,000.00
Owned equipment cost per day	$ 1,000.00
General conditions cost per day	$ 3,333.33
Overhead cost per day	$ 3,333.33

	Investment
Total material investment	$ 500,000.00
Total labor investment	$ 750,000.00
Total rental equipment investment	$ 15,000.00
Total owned equipment investment	$ 45,000.00
Total general conditions investment	$ 150,000.00
Total overhead investment	$ 150,000.00
Total working capital investment	$ 1,610,000.00
Profit generated	$ 140,000.00
Cash to cash cycle (in days)	45
Return on investment (annual)	69.57%

Working capital situation assessment	EXCEEDED

FIGURE 4-12
The calculation of financial return is a complex one, but with a spreadsheet, variables and formulas can be changed to reflect your specific business. This shows the power of cash flow and net margin on ROI.

As long as there are contracting businesses, there will be the harsh reality of profit and loss. Profit and loss is the primary score-card for any business, and construction is no different. Whether you have continuous losses or one big one, you will be working for someone else, which is not a great prospect for a contractor. We all cherish working for ourselves.

More positively, consistent profits reward you with numerous personal and professional options. Consistent profits give a contractor access to several roads he might take.

How do you go about making a strategic decision and vetting the potential financial problems or gains? Part of this discussion must encompass marginal contribution.

Marginal contribution is a straightforward concept. A portion of revenue pays for the fixed costs (and for any contemplated expenses). *Marginal contribution* states that for every dollar of revenue, a part of it pays for direct project costs, such as labor, material, equipment, subcontractors, and so forth. Costs for marginal contribution are caused by building the project. They are directly related to the project and, without the job, we would not spend the money.

Indirect costs also occur. While *indirect costs* are related to the project, they can be spread over several projects. So they are not directly related to one project. If we didn't have any projects, we couldn't justify having the cost, such as a general superintendent or a payroll clerk.

Fixed costs also occur. *Fixed costs* are those things that are commitments of a yearly nature, such as a salary or office rent. The commitment might be longer, but it is usually for at least one year.

> **The direct cost plus the variable costs less revenue divided by the revenue is the marginal contribution.**

Let's say that the resulting percentage for your company is 17 percent. To add a $50,000 estimating position means you have to generate $295,000 to break even. To be more exact, because the construction industry is risky, we should target a return on this investment of, say, 30 percent. That makes our target revenue rise to $421,000.

There is more to this discussion than we can state at this time. Please be aware that contracting is more of a business than ever before. The revenue, direct costs, overhead, net profit, and other like indicators tell us if we are beating the competition. There is no more basic report card than these. Pay close attention. They will tell you if you're winning.

Above average contractors have an accurate picture of the cost to complete on all projects. They consistently use cost reports and cost-to-complete projections.

Cash Flow—Keep Water Out of the Bottom of the Ship

A cash-flow problem is a drag on the performance of a construction firm. Just as a foot of water in the bottom of a ship would cause it to ride lower, move slower, and be a foot closer to sinking, a cash-flow problem is problematic for a construction company. Cash flow is a primary economic factor of whether a contractor does or does not do well. Understanding this issue can keep your company profitable and, thus, make your management easier.

How important is understanding cash flow? It is a top-five issue. Why? Negative cash flow is the *leading* predictor of construction contractor bankruptcy. See Figure 4-13.

As a company grows, it becomes even more important for each project manager to manage the cash flow on all projects. Think of each project as its own separate business, with its own profit and loss statement. Typically, that is equivalent to the job-cost summary

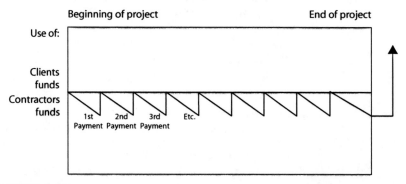

Typical cash flow

FIGURE 4-13
Typically, contractors finance projects with their own working capital. They only catch up at the end of the job. The challenge is to change this for the good of the contractor.

you get regularly to update the status of the job. It's important to understand the difference between the concept of profit and cash flow. Profit is the contract revenue less the cost of the contracted work, and cash flow is the timing of those revenues and the payments of those costs.

Let's start by stating that some bills exist that are nonnegotiable. What are these? Payroll is one. If you cannot pay your employees, then you have crippled or killed your construction firm. Your firm is about people. Not having the money to pay wages and salaries is the reason cash flow is such an important concept.

There are cash and noncash items. On an accrual basis of accounting, there are items we don't write a check for, but they do tell us whether we make a profit. As an example, depreciation is not a negative on cash flow. However, most contractors do book it yearly, but they are not poorer in cash for doing so.

On the revenue side, the promise of future work is also a noncash item. It is nice to hear, however, that you cannot pay expenses with it unless you can bill it and collect it. Construction firms have been stung by this type of promise. They have paid for certain design or estimating costs only to have the contract go to someone else.

The difference between cash and noncash is a clear concept to anyone who has managed through any of the recessions in the last 30 years. The danger is some items cause you to have less cash to pay your nonnegotiable demand payments.

The basic cash-flow problem is that clients tend to pay us in 45 days from billing (cash in), while vendors want to be paid in 30 days and employees want to be paid quicker than that (cash out).

To further complicate matters, no contractor has unlimited working capital. That is, no construction firm can be continuously cash negative and stay in business. The only business to have unlimited working capital is the federal government.

This difference in timing of cash in and cash out is not a problem as long as we are small and static. Once you take on more and/or bigger contracts, the gross dollars needed to fill that difference in timing can be huge. Unless you have substantial cash reserves or a credit line, someone will go unpaid. Therefore, you stand the chance they will enforce their right to payment through the court system. At a minimum, vendors and subcontractors will charge your firm higher prices while limiting your purchases.

Recently, a young man approached me for counsel on starting a construction firm. After going through a checklist of necessary business and legal requirements, we turned to his cash needs. He is an underground contractor and he felt he would need to buy a backhoe. We discussed this for a while and we concluded that, because he didn't have contracts in hand, he couldn't predict the utilization and, therefore, the billing for this piece of equipment. To start, he is going to do some work for his former employer. Again, he has some work, but he has no locks on any other business. In his first year, he has chosen to rent. From a cash flow perspective, it is a smart thing to do. When he has a predicable revenue stream, he can cut his cost by buying instead of renting. However, he realizes that if the demand for cash exceeds the inflow of cash, plus his cash reserve, he will fail.

By renting in his first year, he additionally benefits by not having pressure to get a job. There is no onus to cut the price to get that job. This allows him to ask for and receive a fair price. He can be patient.

Project cash flow in the construction industry is defined as total billings less our obligations to pay for the work performed. Sometimes, projects have negative cash-flow situations. Here are some scenarios that could cause this to happen:

- **Underbilling the Client**—This can be prevented by creating a schedule of values that is front-end loaded to pay for the cost of work early in the project.

- **Inaccurate Project Budget**—If the budget isn't current, comparing the field projections with financial figures will show some disparity and provide numbers for reconciliation.

- **Special Payment Terms**—Agreements made with subcontractors and distributors are sometimes necessary, but they can cause the project to be in a negative cash position.

- **Project Started in a Negative Cash Position**—We hope this is a temporary situation and is eventually worked out as the project progresses. Otherwise, there has been a budget bust of a large proportion.
- **Overpaying Subcontractors**—This occurs when you pay the subcontractors before you are paid by the client. If you approve payments to vendors that have not yet been funded by the client, you are in a negative cash status on that item. Remember, only pay before being paid in special situations.

Financial profits are derived by calculating the percentage of completion on a job times the estimated project gross profit.

> The percent complete figure is equal to total job costs incurred ÷ (total job costs incurred + projected costs to finish the project).

Profits are like oxygen to a company. If those profits are never collected, our economic success is nonexistent. The ability to keep financial demands satisfied (positive cash flow) allows our company to deliver profits. This funds our salary, bonuses, and dividends, which makes our personal financial independence grow. See Figure 4-14.

> Don't let managers or supervisors hide costs in unrelated cost codes. This doesn't give the estimator an accurate picture of the costs of the project for the next bid.

Company Cash Flow

As we said previously, if the projects don't do well, then the company can't do well. As far as cash flow, the company must do a good job to project the cash flow. The following is a typical format of a corporate cash-flow projection.

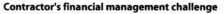

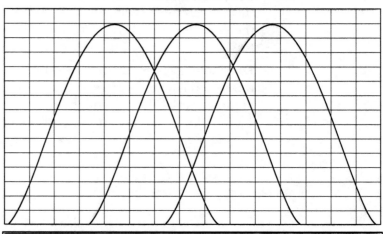

- Contractor's cash outflow
- Billing to client
- Payment from client

FIGURE 4-14
The lag between costs expended and revenue received makes contractors an investor in construction projects. The challenge is to shorten the lag.

You can see several cash-flow classifications that help identify and forecast the need for cash. Two critical ones are:

1. Cash receipts
2. Cash disbursements

Both of these provide the net cash flow. If positive, then the cash has to be placed somewhere. It can be invested in the business activities, taken as a dividend, put into a checking account, or hidden in a mattress. See Figure 4-15.

The next set of places to put the money is in:

1. Investing activities
2. Financing activities

	For the years ended December 31,			
	2006	**2007**	**2008**	**2009**
Cash flows from (used for) operating activities:				
Cash receipts from sales	$ 11,066,890	$ 13,917,822	$ 17,225,613	$ 15,720,148
Cash disbursements for cost of sales and overhead expenses	(9,713,481)	(12,011,255)	(14,139,773)	(13,902,580)
Net cash provided (used for) operating activities	1,353,409	1,906,567	3,085,840	1,817,568
Cash flows from (used for) investing activities:				
Proceeds from the sale of property and equipment	60,132	56,299	51,917	62,575
Purchases of property and equipment	(551,434)	(479,830)	(1,807,472)	(773,814)
Repayment of mortgage receivable	6,061	6,416	7,205	92,929
Net cash provided (used for) investing activities	(485,241)	(417,115)	(1,748,350)	(618,310)
Cash flows from (used for) financing activities:				
Additions to debt	189,155	–	606,701	549,427
Debt service payments (principal paid)	(212,246)	(400,387)	(118,341)	(626,118)
Dividends paid	(773,000)	(281,992)	(805,398)	(872,737)
Net cash provided (used for) financing activities	(796,091)	(682,379)	(317,038)	(949,428)
Net increase (decrease) in cash	72,077	807,073	1,020,452	249,830
Cash, beginning of period	61,153	133,230	940,303	1,960,755
Cash, end of period	$ 133,230	$ 940,303	$ 1,960,755	$ 2,210,585

FIGURE 4-15
This company has continued to be profitable and, thus, has built its cash. From there, it has paid down debt and taken some dividends for its shareholders.

Savvy contractors don't use litigation as a way to resolve client issues. That is always a last resort. Unless the claim is extremely large and the circumstances unusual, attorneys and claims consultants make this a waste of time and money. Furthermore, these contractors don't want a judge deciding their fate unless there is no other alternative.

Retention

Because retention is typically paid some time after a construction project is completed, the subcontractors place among the phases of a project can affect his credit facilities, such as long-term debt.

If you are unclear about how this affects you and your competitor's debt, then the following chart should help. This indicates different debt needs for different trades. As you may know, banks or other lenders' attitudes do change, depending on the type of contractor they are working with.

It should come as no surprise that specialty contractors who work in the (typically) early stages of a project carry (and are allowed) more long-term debt. Especially civil and structural contractors who pay large material and equipment costs at full invoice, and then wait for the owner to release their retention after other, later phases are completed. They wait in line with everyone else, only the total duration of their wait is longer. See Figure 4-16.

Many contractors wish retention would be abolished by constitutional amendment. Because this will not happen in our lifetimes, we will have to manage it as best as we can.

There are several variations in retention practices. Some owners offer partial releases of retention, such as in the case of strip shopping centers or projects that can be completed in distinct, freestanding phases.

Government officials and others have experimented with 5 percent retention and even with no retention. Nevertheless, a 10 percent

L/T Debt as a % of total assets	1980	1985	1990	1995	2000
Concrete work	12.9	16.3	14.6	16.6	17.7
Excavation and foundation	19.8	19.9	19.1	22.0	26.6
Drywall and acoustical	11.5	10.9	10.2	9.4	10.4
Painting and wallpaper	11.8	11.2	13.8	14.0	19.7

FIGURE 4-16
Contractors in the earlier phases of the construction process have larger amounts of debt. Notice that long-term debt amounts (retention) have grown.

retention policy remains the norm. Couple this with a 4 percent average net profit for a construction firm and you can see why it will not change.

Sometimes, the next best strategy besides trying to reduce retention is trying to gain acceptance of parts of the project, such as floors on a high rise, where access can be controlled or given outright to an owner.

We have observed many contractors using a punch-as-you-go method to ensure fewer punch-list items remaining at the end of the job.

Some contractors discourage the client from using multiple punch lists. The contractor's goal is to receive only one and to focus on that to completion. Thus, the job is quicker to releasing retention.

We cannot predict any change to retention practices. It is powerful leverage, in assuring a fast, quality, and completed project for the end user. If we build for our own account, we would be foolish not to use it. After all, what better lever is there for ensuring satisfactory completion than holding back double the net profit?

> Good contractors know that great clients are a minority in the population and, once found, they keep these clients satisfied and returning for more business. Also, they believe they have to "fire" problematic clients.

The Fallacy of Operating Leverage

This is a fact: Gross profit dollars will increase or decrease with the amount of construction volume. That fact is an example of operating leverage. It can be a wonderful insight for a company owner or investor. The more we do, the larger the reward to the shareholders.

Some people see all businesses benefiting. In some cases, as volume increases, the percentage of gross profit increases. It doesn't occur in all business types, though, only in some. For a few sectors of the economy, areas such as airlines, e-commerce, software, restaurants, and other fixed-cost businesses, this is a real business opportunity. The business principle simply stated says: "Once you cover the start-up costs, there is little expense for each additional dollar sold." This is the beauty of the fixed-cost financial model.

For a variable-cost business, the model is different. There is little fixed cost and, for each additional dollar sold, there is a large expense. In construction contracting, this is exactly the case. The gross profit percentage does not grow with volume, instead, it shrinks. In other words, the percentage decreases as the volume increases and vice versa. Unless there is an under-capacity issue, this is factually correct. Why? Because we are in a variable-cost business, not a fixed cost one.

Additional production outside our proven "norm" causes us to:

- Sell to unfamiliar clients
- Use unknown labor
- Use unknown suppliers

We reach for revenue as we have never done before. We will certainly have some surprises and general miscommunication due to these new players.

This will make your variable cost increase, thus, decreasing your gross profit and, subsequently, decreasing your net profit.

Operating leverage is a mathematical technique to measure the effect of sales on profits. In other words, what percentage of each revenue dollar is profit, and then how much does it change with a decrease or increase in sales?

As you know, part of a contractor's cost structure includes fixed costs. By definition, these costs stay the same, despite changing volume. Variable costs change greatly with a change in volume. Most of our costs—over 80 percent—are tied to a construction project and, hence, are variable.

The operating leverage indicator is the amount of net profit before tax divided by the gross profit dollars. Typically, this results in a number below 10.

Let's take the example of a contractor who has the following financial statement, as shown in Table 4-6.

TABLE 4-6
This table reflects a typical operating leverage for a construction firm.

Revenue	4,000,000
Direct Costs	3,200,000
Gross Profit	800,000
Overhead	700,000
Net Profit Before Tax	100,000
Operating Leverage	8.0
(Gross Profit / Net Profit)	

Operating leverage is dangerous in construction. It implies that a correlation of revenue (or the amount of gross profit) to net profit exists. There is no question that higher volume does not bring an equal or higher gross profit. The implication is this: if revenue is raised or lowered, the net profit should closely follow the operating leverage ratio. Certainly, it holds on the side of decreasing volume. Smaller contractors make a greater percentage of profit than larger contractors.

The dangerous implication is that higher profits should follow higher revenue. This is simply a brutal assumption to make. Expanding volume has been the death of most ex-contractors. The majority of the time it has been the search for volume or a larger job that has created a difficult end for a construction business.

Gross profit increases as costs decrease. Gross profit analysis provides clues about management's ability to control costs and increase profits. This leads to a refined operating leverage ratio.

Declining gross profits with constant revenue are indicators of:

1. Unplanned overtime
2. Uncompensated changes to the work
3. Excessive materials waste
4. Rework/shoddy workmanship
5. Defective materials
6. Inefficient labor

Because construction is variable cost, our means of production (craftsmen, supervision, and equipment) must be increased immediately if we take on higher revenue. Unless an undercapacity issue exists, we cannot take on another job cavalierly. When "book smart" managers start to look at operating leverage closely, it is time for "street smart" managers to intervene.

> Encourage communication with project staffs by holding formal meetings concerning the status of jobs. Don't let managers and supervisors keep problems under the radar until it is too late.

Compensation

Let's review executive compensation first. Owners of construction companies do worry about how much they can pay themselves in benefits, expenses, and salary without unduly overcompensating themselves. This is a constant issue with governmental authorities, banks, and bonding companies. Owners have averaged 4 percent of revenue for their salary compensation in the last 20 years.

The highest paid principals as a percentage of revenue are:

1. Glass and glazing (highest)
2. Flooring

The lowest paid principals as a percentage of revenue are:

1. General contracting—industrial buildings (lowest)
2. Bridge tunnel and elevated highway

The Internal Revenue Service (IRS) is sensitive to the compensation issue. It especially focuses on expense reimbursement. Banks are vigilant about the executive salary and compensation issue in the loan area. They see a red flag if overall compensation is high and job profits are lower. This would include bonuses and reimbursed expenses. Bonding companies look at this area as well. Because losses are difficult and costly to collect, extra time is spent trying to stay ahead of any losses. And, in the area of leases, some owners may overcharge for leasing equipment to themselves as a way to take operation profit out of their company. All external parties review such arrangements.

Personnel Administrative Services (PAS) gives well-respected information about executive compensation, including perks. This information is seen as a good guide for salary, benefits, and other items in an executive package.

> Understand that morale equals communication. In my work as a management consultant, I find a high correlation between morale and communication. In company surveys, they move together incrementally. Improve your morale and you will improve communication.

Employee Compensation

"How much should we pay our employees?" This is an emotional question whether you are an employer or the employee. As an example, any tenured contractor has gone at least once without a paycheck. And, this was done while risking his financial future managing his construction firm.

No man is an island and no man is all-powerful. We need employees to build work. People are a necessary ingredient to construction. However, seldom do contractors see the kind of effort that they, themselves, have given. It is easy to become frustrated with anyone on a guaranteed salary (just ask the owner of a sports team).

Employees, on the other hand, are never satisfied with their pay package. In their opinion, they are seldom justly compensated and, thus, they feel as if the owner doesn't realize their full value.

Compensation is an age-old question that has been answered by local customs, current markets, and in the last 20 years, accurate salary surveys. Thus, the question of the amount of pay has been answered. There is little mystery as to what the range is.

Finding out the appropriate wage amount is easier today than it was years ago. Wage and salary surveys are available in this country and are furnished by some conscientious researchers.

These surveys contain hundreds of data points that statistically provide "95 percent confidence." These guides are just that—guidelines to assist us in making decisions based in reality. The construction industry has its own salary surveys, some for-profit organizations and some nonprofit ones.

As a caveat, these compensation surveys are valuable in the open-shop environment for management salaries, but they are not highly useful for hourly employees. In the open-shop environment, too much variability exists among hourly wages.

The information is sorted and analyzed by several factors, including:

- Region—the country is segmented in up to 10 regions.
- Contractor type—general, electrical, design build, construction management, and specialty contractors.
- Bid type—cost plus and firm price.
- Size of firm—from less than $5 million, in increments to contractors over $250 million in contract revenue.
- Construction performed—building, highway, heavy, industrial, municipal, and residential.

As we manage from year to year, salaries will increase on an individual employee basis. Why shouldn't they? If a manager continues to work for a company, they are more valuable in experience in each successive year. We, as contractors, expect to reward them for their tenure.

The amount of salary raises have decreased, in part because of the economy, and in part because of the use of variable compensation pay packages in construction. We were averaging approximately 5 percent at the millennium and this has declined with each passing year.

Contractors have long understood that the low-price employee is much like the low-price supplier—high maintenance affects your critical path on a job negatively (can't tell time, can't count, and can't understand directions).

A better question is "How should we pay our employees so they act more like owners?" That is the new reality. Contractors are seeing the power of this question all around them. People with a stake in the outcome do focus more deeply on doing a great job.

> Have at least quarterly project postmortems. These are positive meetings done in a summary format. They go over the good, as well as the bad, jobs with all company personnel in attendance, such as administrative, accounting, HR, project, field, and so forth. As a result, the company works collectively smarter.

Use of Variable Compensation

New thinking in compensation has evolved in the last 20 years. Contractors and the managers who work for them don't want a day's wage for a day's work.

Contractors need not the time, but the energy, ideas, and commitment of their salaried staff. They are a leverage point for all other parts of the company. The owner is trying to build wealth for himself and his family. He wants his team to deliver good project results consistently.

The management staff wants to innovate, grow as people, and win at their jobs. Certainly, compensation is a concern and greater salary is a desire.

If you use *variable compensation,* which is another term for incentive pay or pay for performance, it instills an ownership mentality. As salaries continue to increase, are we seeing a comparable rise in productivity? Do we see a commensurate rise in entrepreneurship? I think the answer is no. Therefore, to use an "at risk" bonus plan, we sow the seeds of focus and hard work. This is just what every contractor wants.

> Superior contractors only collaborate with other firms or individuals who can help them. They don't partner for the sake of partnering.

Pay for Current Performance, Not for Past Performance

How much we pay our people and the process of how we pay our people are equally important in getting superior performance. The formula for fixed and variable compensation in a company can make your staff act more like business people and less like employees.

The construction industry has traditionally paid management personnel a majority of compensation in salary and a minority in bonus. This should be a concern to most contractors.

Historically, salaries have risen with inflation or because of it. The reason isn't important. There are not many years when compensation hasn't increased. This is expected. If most of your payment to people is in the form of a monthly salary, then it must rise, regardless of job or company performance. It is not a given that fixed compensation has to increase every year, though. If your compensation plan is more variable, then there is less pressure for salaries to rise.

Bonus or incentive compensation makes employees think and act like owners. This is a welcome change for some contractors who have an uninspired staff.

Bonus Programs

Smart contractors know it is better to pay for current performance (bonus) than to pay for past performance (salary). Sports teams would do well to follow this advice.

All bonus programs have two parts:

1. **Funding mechanism,** that is, job profits, project savings, and company profits. This is where dollars are gained by the company owner. In the absence of a rational funding source, the contractor will pay it out of the company's net worth.

2. **Disbursement mechanism,** that is, the formula that decides what amount is paid to individual employees. This is a formula that can include such factors as individual performance, tenure, or a person's rank.

Variable compensation plans vary somewhat in the construction industry. Here are some generic types:

1. Company-based bonus system
2. Job-based bonus system

Company-Based Bonus System   As in most incentive programs, this compensation system can make people perform well. A company-based bonus system causes employees to act more like owners. Its foundation is in a shared pool of funds, which are earned by profitable operations.

One critical detail is this: The owner must be paid for his risk first. That is, any compensation program is not only a retention tool for employees, it is also a financial method that requires the shareholder(s) be compensated for their capital being at risk.

A key is that the company must have an "open book" policy, otherwise seen as discretionary. In other words, employees need to see how the bonus fund is doing throughout the year, including how the bonus calculation is made. From this, greater confidence in the process can result. Again, if this is not part of the system, your staff will conclude that the program is an arbitrary one determined by you and not by factors in their control.

> Leading contractors know that project-specific Web sites are useful and powerful to construction projects. However, they know they are only a value if the project owner insists on their use by all parties.

Job-Based Bonus System   A job-based bonus system also gives your people an incentive to perform well, but in a different way. Why? Because as the specific job they control profits, the employee gains. The funding mechanism is job profits and/or job savings.

As a caveat, job-based bonus systems can be a detriment for your best field supervisors and project managers. How? If you make an estimating error on a job and it is extremely low, who will you designate as project manager and field supervisor on this job? Your best or your average people? Your best people, of course.

As you know, if the formula is based on profits or savings, there might not be either, unless you reestimate the project.

In the same vein, a project-based bonus program can be a windfall for your average field supervisor and project manager. How? From change orders, additive or deductive, it does not matter. You will need to treat change orders in a different way.

After some bonus cycles, you might hear grumblings about people being lucky. The thoughtful contractor knows this and makes an adjustment.

In any variable compensation system, a contractor must have some discretionary component. Whether someone is lucky or snake bit, the company owner should have subjective power to designate an additional bonus for these hardworking, but unlucky employees. The owner should also retain funds from those who are lucky or who take advantage of a quirk in the formula.

Some percent of a bonus should be based on behaviors. This may be part of the discretionary bonus system or it may not be. The logic is this: Say one of your staff does all the right things, for example, they are timely, hardworking, and conscientious, but your fiscal-year results are mediocre at best. Shouldn't you still give this person some financial encouragement? A one-time bonus instead of a pay raise is a better long-term practice.

Any bonus must be tested against "what-ifs" before rolling it out. The contractor must test the formula against different scenarios before announcing it. Not to perform this step might lead to a retraction of the program. In other cases, several changes might have to be made in the first year. This leads to a lack of confidence in the incentive plan and an erosion of your creditability.

Defer bonuses for your high-level employees. As you know, people are constantly recruited. Spread the payment out over three years. Why? Because, then, they have less incentive to leave. And, if they do leave, they leave behind some bonus money.

Spread the bonus out over three years because if you experience a bad year and no bonus, there is less of hook to keep valuable staff (as in a two-year plan). Logically, they would only be giving up one year of a bonus on a two-year plan.

Variable and deferred compensation can deliver most of the behaviors that contractors want from their employees. Take your time in formulating yours. You only get one chance to get it right and, if you don't, your field and office staff will see it as just another "flavor of the month." Getting it right can energize an organization and put some spring into the step of each employee. Yes, it can even make contracting fun again!

> Have an employee-review process be defined and consistent. This gives employees a good sense that they are valued. This does not stop companies from demanding that employees perform consistently at high levels.

Effective Cost Reporting

As construction has become more complex and demanding, the importance of timely and accurate information has increased. Twenty years ago, contractors had to be convinced of the benefit of job-cost reports. The investment was substantial and the value was unclear. Many contractors trusted their "gut feel." It was a simpler time and the approach worked. Now, any sizable contractor would be foolish not to use a cost-report methodology.

Still, in this century, the standard job-cost reports in several software packages lack the practical approach to construction, which is surprising. We have to customize our reports further to make them effective predictors of job cost of a construction project.

Quite a few software programs were created to serve more than the construction industry. We, by our nature, haven't deserved a dedicated approach by a software developer. We are too fragmented and each fragment doesn't have enough buying power to justify a sole approach. The two most common markets these companies target are real estate and engineering. These businesses bear scant resemblance to a contractor's enterprise.

Cost Overruns

Early prediction of cost overruns is a critical measure. Most job-cost software is weak in this area.

What two areas are the biggest risks for cost overrun?

1. Labor
2. Time (which translates into general conditions cost)

If you are a general contractor or a specialty contractor, either (or both) of these have been a culprit in 90 percent of your projects that have broken the budget. For equipment-intensive contractors, labor overruns mean equipment cost overruns. It all starts with managing labor.

To let you know how difficult a task it is to predict construction cost, you could hire a dozen auditors from one of the big four accounting firms and, in two weeks, they still couldn't tell you where the project was in terms of costs versus physical completion and time. The only people who know are the field supervisor and the project manager combined. Without interviewing these two people every week, we have to rely on job-cost and labor-productivity reports.

How do we predict problems earlier in the cycle? In our opinion, that is why some software packages' reports have to be rewritten.

Here are data fields that we recommend you place in your cost reports. We will share man-hours reporting (labor) and job cost (time) reports. Some of these items are not news to some.

> Use software that allows estimating files to be read by accounting and project-management software and vice versa. This ability to translate and transfer information is key. The most common software in the country is a spreadsheet. Some savvy contractors use it for it flexibility. Interestingly, over half of estimating software is self-built by the contractor per a recent study.

Man-Hour/Labor Productivity Report

Here are the basic cost categories your cost reports need to reflect. Some variation to these is needed for some contractors due to their unique business, but this should be a good starting point. See Figure 4-17.

- **Cost Code**—The numerical identifier for the type of work. This can be numeric or alphanumeric.

- **Sub Code**—This typically designates the five direct costs: labor, material, equipment, subcontract, or other.

- **Description**—As it implies, this describes in words the type of work. Careful consideration should be given to using assemblies instead of task-by-task line items.

- **Current Total Man-hour Budget**—Man-hours is what the field understands. We use this measure as a way to plan and forecast with our field crews.

- **% of Total Job**—What percent these line items are as a percent of the total man-hour budget.

- **Percent Complete This Period**—An inputted number by the project manager. It is their judgment how much work the particular line item has been done for this period. This in an inputted (not calculated) number.

- **Percent Complete Job to Date**—An inputted number by the project manager. It is their judgment how much work has been completed. This in an inputted (not calculated) number. Again, the PM determines this amount.

- **Man-Hours Earned This Period**—The percent completed this period times the man-hour budget.

- **Man-Hours Earned Job to Date**—The percent completed job to date times the man-hour budget.

- **Man-Hours Expended This Period**—Actual man-hours incurred. This information is captured from time cards for this period.

- **Man-Hours Expended Job to Date**—Actual man-hours incurred. This information would be captured from time cards for the project.

Man-hour performance report

Job number
Project name

Report period start date
Report period end date
Original completion date
Current completion date

Cost code	Sub code	Description	Current total man-hour budget	Percent complete	Man-hours earned	Man-hours expended	Man-hour variance	Performance factor	Remaining hours
			% of Total job	This period	This period	This period	This period	This period	@ Budget performance
				Job to date	Job to date	Job to date	Job to date	Job to date	@ Current performance
								@ Current performance	To budget

FIGURE 4-17
Here is a sample man-hour report. This is a key report to effectively manage field labor.

- **Performance Factor This Period**—The ratio of hours expended to hours earned—a measure of productivity—1.0 in on budget, 1.1 is overbudget (inefficient), and 0.9 is under-budget (efficient) for this period.

- **Performance Factor Job to Date**—The ratio of hours expended to hours earned—a measure of productivity—1.0 in on budget, 1.1 is overbudget (inefficient), and 0.9 is under-budget (efficient) for the job to date.

- **Remaining Hours Job to Date**—The project manager assesses progress and estimates man-hours needed to build the rest of the job. This in an inputted (not calculated) number.

- **@ Current Performance**—Rate of work × amount of work.

- **@ Budget Performance**—The cost spent to date, plus the hours left at the estimated production rate.

- **To Budget**—The budget hours restated. This is for comparison to the @current performance and budget performance.

Man-hours are the largest consistent opportunity to make money in the construction contracting business. A specific report that monitors and measures this area is invaluable. This is doubly important to labor-intensive contractors.

This is a sample format of an excellent cost report. The boiler plate information is at the top. The critical pieces of information are:

1. Current Total Man-Hour Budget is the number of hours the estimator calculated for the job.

2. Percent of Total Job is how significant this line item is in the total project.

3. Percent Complete tells the total progress you are making by installing the total job.

4. Man-Hours Earned is the result of the percent complete multiplied by the man-hours budget.

5. Man-Hours Expended is captured from weekly payroll.

6. Man-Hour Variance is the difference between expended and earned hours.

7. Performance Factor is the result of the man-hour variance: it is either a positive (good) or negative (bad) number. This alerts management to a problem or an opportunity.

This is important information if we are to project the final cost. These two columns are key alarms for action. A large overrun projected is where executive attention is best focused. Caught early, similar to cancer, serious consequences may be avoided.

- Current Performance and Budget Performance—These two give the range of projected performance: excellent or poor.

- To Budget—This is a restatement of the budget and a quick comparison to the previous two measures.

> Savvy contractors track their construction equipment with GPS to know where it is. This includes company trucks. This is good risk-management practice, which is especially important today.

Job-Cost Performance Report

Overall cost reports are equally valuable to the man-hour reports. The following are the basic categories for you to consider. See Figure 4-18.

- **Cost Code**—The numerical identifier for the type of work. This can be numeric or alphanumeric.

- **Sub Code**—This typically designates the five direct costs: labor, material, equipment, subcontract, or other.

- **Description**—As it implies, this describes the type of work in words. Careful consideration should be given to using assemblies instead of task-by-task line items.

- **Cost Estimated**—This is the cost budgeted for the work task.

- **Quantity Estimated**—The item count or measure of work to install.

Job performance report

Job number

Report period start date
Report period end date
Original completion date
Current completion date

Cost code	Sub code	Description	Cost estimated	Quanity estimated	Quantity actual	% Complete	Earned value	Cost to complete	Total cost at completion	Over and under	Job to date	Remaining cost @ Current performance	To budget

FIGURE 4-18
This sample job performance report focuses on all costs and predicts cost at completion.

- **Quantity Actual**—This is recorded by the field or project manager. If the quantity is different consistently, it is an indicator of an estimating weakness.

- **% Complete Quantity Estimated/Quantity Actual**—Yes, this can be over 100 percent. This is for practical reasons. The man-hour rate or lineal foot cost should be close to the estimate. Otherwise, it indicates a productivity issue in the field or a unit cost error in the estimate.

- **Earned Value**—The percent complete multiplied by the cost estimated.

- **Cost to Complete**—This should be estimated by the project manager. It is an inputted (not calculated) number. This can also be where the committed cost is included or it can be in a separate column.

- **Total Cost at Completion**—The cost-to-date plus the estimated cost to complete.

- **Over and Under**—The difference of the budget and the total cost to complete.

This is a sample format of an excellent cost report. The boiler plate information is at the top. The critical pieces of information are:

- Quantity Estimated—What did the estimator count or measure for the job?
- Quantity Actual—What is installed on the job?

A consistent and substantial difference at the end of the job is a red flag to either the field or the estimating department. Also, this clearly calculates the percent complete on the job. This is important information if we are to project the final cost.

- Total cost at completion
- Over and under

These two columns are key alarms for action. A large overrun projected is where executive attention is best focused.

Caught early, as with cancer, serious consequences may be avoided.

- Job to date
- Remaining cost @ current performance
- To budget

These calculations give the contractor a range of projections. As we all know, tasks start out slowly, inefficiently, and costly. This information gives the contractors a sense if the work is in danger of overrunning cost.

One consistent difference is the use of measurable and completed assemblies. This makes the system work efficiently. The project manager calculates all his inputted numbers by assembly. There is no heavy detail work.

The report organizes the cost the same way we build, that is, apples to apples and oranges to oranges. For a specialty contractor, this might be lineal feet of footing, square feet of wall, or duct. Several of these assemblies are on the cost reports. We don't pay attention to screws, rebar, or pipe yet, but if there are overruns, we delve into the detail.

This type of cost reporting is an effective macro look at the job progress and cost. It is intended for project managers, field supervisors, and executives.

What these two reports do is give the contractor information to predict losses or overruns. Most financially successful contractors manage by exception. They have great people, but they can see a problem job quickly, act on it, and correct it. Certainly, most of their projects deliver the estimated profits and better. However, the current rule of thumb is that it takes four good projects to pay for one bad one. And that is *just to break even*. This makes catching the problem jobs even more important.

Every contractor is different and this section doesn't pretend to represent all types. For decades, though, time and labor have been the two largest risk factors in construction (material increases over the last years are noted). These reports alert us to any red flags in these two areas, so we will have only positive surprises.

Use GPS as a way to improve utilization. The rule of thumb for service contractors is a 10 percent productivity improvement due to better coordination and logistics. For other types of contractors, the percentage is not confirmed, but the opinion is that savings does occur.

Break-even Revenue

How do we proactively plan our business if we are changing our cost structure dramatically? And how do we judge whether an additional cost or investment has been a financial success? There are various methods in the general business environment, but in construction contracting, we must use break-even analysis.

Our goal is to know how much volume we must earn over the year to keep from losing money. Knowing how much revenue we must earn is a critical success factor. It is legend that too much volume will kill a contractor faster than too little. Knowing when to stop (or at least slow down) can mitigate this danger.

Profitable equipment intensive contractors make sure they charge themselves market pricing for their equipment even though it may be paid off. This keeps them receiving a dividend for maintaining old equipment or for paying off equipment early.

How to Determine the Minimum Volume to Breakeven on Your Costs

The basic formula to determine the minimum volume to breakeven on your costs is to determine the gross profit percentage expected from the work. Take that number and divide it into the fixed costs.

You need to determine your overhead cost (assume $1 million) and a planned gross profit percentage (say 20 percent).

Therefore, $1,000,000/0.20 equals $5,000,000.

This is harder than it seems. This equation may sound simple and it is, but several traps might trip you up on the way to executing the plan and realizing the financial results.

Will you need extra overhead to pay for the additional volume? Is there a savings opportunity due to this investment? This is where business judgment and plain old "gut feel" are valuable.

This is analogous to determining the total cost of building a project. We have costs that are both direct and indirect, plus overhead. Once we arrive at that number confidently, then dollars added to it are profit.

A further step is to separate fixed overhead from variable overhead. That is to determine what will increase (or decrease) greatly due to volume and what is relatively fixed. As an example, telephone costs will directly rise with volume. More work, more minutes on the phone, more faxes, and more cell phone usage increases. Rent and the president's salary would be fixed. So, the gross profit percent plus the percent of variable overhead less 100 percent gives you the variable contribution.

Here is the calculation:

Total Revenue	100%
Less	
Direct Costs	80%
Variable Overhead	5%
Results in	15% variable contribution
Fixed Overhead Costs	$1,000,000
Breakeven is	$1,000,000 divided by .15 or $6,666,666

The planned gross-profit percentage has to be what is collected. Again, this can be a tricky formula. In contracting, discounting of change orders by clients is common. In addition, nonpayment occasionally occurs. Hence, being conservative (meaning worst case) is the best strategy. Change orders are often held to the closeout phase where the client's leverage is the greatest.

Nonpayment will happen to a contractor in his career. We hope this happens only once, at the most, but the odds are it could happen more often than that.

There is no easy way to perform this budgeting and planning process. It is iterative. A contractor must look at it periodically and after some sleep. The good news is a contractor's profitability is highly correlated to financial planning. This is the reward. However complicated, this is the good news of going through all this financial hard work.

> Above average contractors know they will use less than 10 percent of the utilities of software. They don't buy the bells and whistles. They buy software that is stable, reports information plainly, and is exportable to other software, such as that of the client and supplier.

Using Purchase Orders

Purchase orders are a necessary progression from a small contractor to larger one. As a contractor grows larger, they will experience losses of material (hence, money) and unnecessary conflict with suppliers about past invoices. All this takes away from what a contractor needs to do, which is to work in the present. Minimizing these interruptions is a benefit of a simple, but thoughtful purchase-order system.

Purchase orders set the conditions of sale. Price is primary in most negotiations, but terms and conditions of that sale are equally important. The terms and conditions (Ts & Cs) answer the question posed by the six wise men of Rudyard Kipling. Who? What? Where? When? How? Why? Conditions of sale determine payment. Merchants know these guiding questions make for good business. The cash-to-cash cycle is one of the important metrics in calculating ROI. The big picture tells us that a poor project ROI also makes the contractor's ROI poor.

Review your terms and conditions of sale. Standardizing these can keep all your projects on better footing. Homebuilders have seen the power of pay by purchase order and its effect on profitability.

For commercial, industrial, and other contractors there are other effective terms. Again, good business practices dictate us being careful with money. Thoughtful purchase-order language protects us against wasting that precious resource.

Some standard language might include:

1. Delivery on our request.
2. Billing terms 2/10 net 30 (net 40, if you can get it).
3. Warranty by distributor against defect (not only by manufacturer).
4. Order-filling errors are the distributor's responsibility. We will charge 5 percent of the cost of unfilled quantity pricing.
5. Material to be protected when delivered by distributor.
6. Credits to be issued within 72 hours of receipt of returned material.

These types of terms and conditions make sure that contractors get the material that they want when they want with the billing conditions they desire.

We cannot build without material and we cannot operate without working capital. These are not exclusive of each other. We can manage each. To be clear, no one has unlimited working capital, so careful contractors adopt conditions of sale that keep material and equipment purchases from draining profitability. Contractors have seen the power of placing the responsibility, such as requiring more timely material deliveries and invoice dating, of sale back to the distributors.

> Timely financial reports, including job cost reports, are a critical success factor. Delays in this area give bad projects time to fester and become unrecoverable.

What Is the True Cost of Loss, Theft, or Mistakes?

The true cost of loss, theft, or mistakes is up to four times the cost of the original construction depending on the situation (see Figure 4-19). Certainly, it is expensive and it must be avoided at

Loss/mistake	Your net profit		Revenue needed	
	% before taxes		to pay for mistake	
$100.00	1%			$10,000
$1,000.00	1%			$100,000
$10,000.00	1%			$1,000,000
$100,000.00	1%			$10,000,000
$100.00	3%			$3,330
$1,000.00	3%			$33,300
$10,000.00	3%			$333,000
$100,000.00	3%			$3,330,000
$100.00	5%			$2,000
$1,000.00	5%			$20,000
$10,000.00	5%			$200,000
$100,000.00	5%			$2,000,000

FIGURE 4-19
If we use revenue to reflect the cost of loss or theft, our field staffs
should realize the high cost of loss, theft, or mistakes. In my experience,
this chart has helped make that point.

all costs. A journeyman must have the true cost explained in terms
of revenue to break even. This is certainly more realistic to people
in the field. The following gives you a complete explanation.

CHAPTER SUMMARY

Superior financial management in construction is embodied in
three things:

1. Conservative financial approaches
2. Realizing that we make money in the field and the bid table
3. It is not how much we make, but how much we save

There is no black magic in the construction business. We leave that
to the magicians of Wall Street. Solid financial habits will consistently give positive results.

Experienced construction firms know that good financial management is mostly about keeping an accurate score card. It doesn't make a profit, but it can identify where profit and losses are. Certainly, understanding construction's unique financial dynamics can keep us out of common traps. Contractors make a profit in the field and, sometimes, at the bid table. Solid financial management skills allow us to consistently keep job losses and business problems to a minimum.

Cash flow and profit margin determine our financial health. Without both, our business will eventually die. If we make a profit, but are never able to collect it, this spells doom for our employees, creditors, and, eventually, for us. Without profit, our cash flow forces us to use our own personal wealth to stay in business.

Most contractors don't love financial management. They are thrilled by getting work or building work. The mental disposition it takes to be in construction doesn't translate well into financial management, but we all must find a way to cover the basics. The basics can make or break a firm.

Contractors can use some solid informational sources to see what financial ratios and other metrics similar companies are achieving. These sources should be "must" reading for startup business planning or yearly strategic planning.

All contracts are based on price, speed, and quality. Successful contractors know they can only deliver two of the three. Superior contractors don't negotiate quality, it is not part of any discussion with a client. They either deliver speed or cost. To try to deliver all three is a recipe for disaster.

Cost reports must report and calculate certain critical information. The typical construction cost report does not contain the data to make sound decisions. Having a complete picture earlier helps contractors act quicker and more decisively.

> Smart contractors use software and systems to predict preventive maintenance schedules and overhaul dates. The software does the calculation, and the contractor does the analysis and coordination.

5

People

F inding and keeping good people can make the business of contracting more efficient and more profitable. Construction consists of two parts: people and processes. This chapter describes half the battle.

GOOD PROCESSES LET PEOPLE SUCCEED

Does anyone you know really want to do a bad job? Do they want to be demoted or, worse, fired? Would they like to take a cut in pay or lose the respect of their peers? Of course not! Over 90 percent of people want to do a great job and receive the benefits for doing so.

This begs the question: "Why are we frustrated with the performance of our construction staffs?" (And, don't forget our construction staffs are sometimes frustrated with us.)

The answer is simple. It is the process. Look around your office and you will see people doing the same things differently. Most of the time, people either do things the way they learned from their first boss or they are self-taught. In any case, they do not do the same task in the same way as others in your office might do it. So, problems occur—miscommunication, missed timing, or just plain thoughtless approaches (also known as bad habits).

What if a new person is hired? Think how confusing new procedures are for them. New hires learn to do a task a certain way under a previous boss, but then, when they begin a new job, they hear they "ought to do the task" another way.

How to address this? Contractors report superior results by approaching the business as a process. That is, creating one thoughtful and consistent process for doing most things (see Figure 5-1). Because the procedure is a process, it can be both monitored and measured. And, even more important, we can use it to coach our people and bring them to a level of superior performance.

On a piece of paper, write how many different parties are involved in each project you build. The list would include several subcontractors you work with as a peer or in a contractual relationship: the owner, the owner's representative, designers, governmental authority, suppliers, insurance entities, and on and on. Typically, you'll have a dozen or more names on your list. If you don't have this number of parties to deal with, count your blessings.

Now, because you transact with all these people, this means you are passing information, money, material, and other essential business items to them. Without these items, you and they would be in trouble.

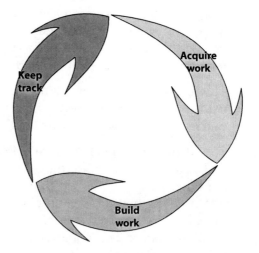

FIGURE 5-1
Good processes allow people to work faster and more efficiently.

Let's take the example of the field manager and the payroll clerk. Early in the week, the site supervisor gives a list of information to the payroll clerk, so he can issue checks later in the week. If the information is correct, that is, if it adds up, cost codes make sense, and the like, the transaction goes smoothly. If not, it will take longer to correct the information.

Later that week, checks are cut and sent out to the job site. If the paychecks are there on time and in the right amounts, if the names are correct, and if the checks are honored by the bank, no one notices. If even one of these things is wrong, time, money, and energy are spent fixing the problem. And personal reputations can be damaged.

All contractors have this process mapped out, communicated, and monitored. Why? You know why. If we pay our employees as promised, they will stay with us. If not, there will be a mass exodus.

Other processes, such as submittals, pay requests, scheduling, planning, and so forth, are not as well-mapped out. Not done consistently well, they are a drag on operations, so we are slower both in building work and in getting paid for it.

> Rarely remove the field manager from a project before closeout. This keeps quality high and gives a project a timely completion. Otherwise, the next field manager is "drinking from a firehose" and will be slow to pick up speed on the project.

Reactive versus Proactive Behaviors

Our business is demanding. It is remarkable that we get anything done in only 24 hours a day. Contractors who realize the difference between proactive and reactive behaviors have a decided advantage. Why? They know that firefighting (reactivity) is an honorable profession, but not a well-rewarded one.

Because of our limited time, we cannot check and recheck our work and communications. Most of the time, doing well once is all we can manage. This leads to problems and, subsequently, less total time in managing.

If your son or daughter is not working to their potential, what is the process to help them improve their academic performance? Studying and doing their homework, good nutrition, good behavior in the classroom, and the parents following up consistently to assure things are being done. If the child's behaviors are the right ones and are consistently performed, then better grades will follow.

Being reactive is not the best approach to your professional or personal life. My sister reacts to her weight. She is a horse trainer and a good one. (One of her students recently won a national championship.) At 6'3" and 140 pounds, the horses pay attention. Well, when she looks at the scale in the morning and sees she is five pounds overweight, she reacts with more salads, more exercise, and generally better things for her body. This lady has taken off 900 pounds in the past 10 years this way!

Proactive and forward-thinking processes—planning, scheduling, early print review, and the like—all force decisions and, thus, uncover problems early.

> Discourage the use of multiple punch lists on projects from the client, designer, end user, and so forth. This makes the close-out/punch-out process much easier and less time-consuming to manage. Thus, a construction company is closer to receiving their retention.

Guidelines for Process Improvement   Every contracting firm has four cornerstones to process improvement:

1. Planning—The time spent reviewing and deciding how to build the job and beat the budget.
2. Communicating—Passing that planning information on to others who will build it.
3. Measurement—Measuring the progress against the contract, the schedule, and the budget requirement.
4. Feedback—Communicating to the people who are building the project about how they are doing.

The cycle repeats itself as the feedback allows people to plan with current information.

Controllable versus Uncontrollable   In our adult lives, we became aware of what areas we can influence or control and what areas we cannot.

The greatest uncontrollable item is the weather, another is freak accidents, and the third is the secret agendas of others.

Some controllable items are our attitude, effort, consistency, and the ability to look ahead with two or more options. Knowing these is the difference between a good manager and a great one.

The process is the key; people are not the key. Contractors have fewer problems with their people because they have weeded out the incompetents and the malcontents, sending them over to their competition. The real challenge is to create, map, and monitor efficient ways of doing things to keep their company ahead of the rest.

> Have merit-based employee promotions. All managers have earned their rank, regardless of relationship to company executives. Hold all managers accountable for their actions and results.

Successful People in Construction

We have studied success in construction over many years. Nightingale, Carnegie, Tracy, Ziegler, and others have all written about it extensively, but we feel there is more to add to their work for the construction industry.

We know and have worked with hundreds of construction people. Our clients and their employees make for a small sample size considering that employment is somewhere above 7 million professionals. However, this data set is from over 30 states and dozens of market sectors.

As a guide to this discussion, let's start by reviewing how one group of people—new immigrants—defines success. As a side-note, all Americans would be wise to review the following two points:

1. Provide for your family. Family is primary and, as adults, workers view their responsibility to provide food, clothing, and shelter for their loved ones, whether their families reside here or outside the United States.

2. Keep your family together. Keeping close to your family and communicating with them on a regular basis is important. The natural desire is to have your family with you but, sometimes, this is not possible. In the southwestern United States, construction projects are all but halted in December as many workers head south. They do so to keep close to their families and to participate with their loved ones during the holidays. This has nothing to do with cars, clothes, or memberships. It has everything to do with your ancestors and successors.

As we studied professional success, we found outstanding construction people are excellent at their jobs. No surprise. Statistically, they perform their function better than 75 percent of others in the same position. In other words, they would rank in the top quartile of like professionals in job performance.

How Do You Accomplish This?

You accomplish this by focusing on continuous improvement. The most common approaches are by studying and by plain hard work. Savvy individuals compete with themselves. They don't worry about how others might be doing. They know that what matters is what they, themselves, do.

As you well know, commonalities exist among the best professionals in every industry.

Successful People Worry About Controllable Events

Successful people know they can only do something about controllable events, so they spend minimal time on uncontrollable events.

As our world becomes more and more complicated, this is especially important. We can worry about how things are changing, but we can continue to search for things to help us improve in the construction business.

Successful Construction People Are Independent Thinkers

Successful construction people take time to quietly think through a problem or an issue. They resist making snap decisions. Certainly, they seek counsel from smart and trusted friends, but they think in detail about the reasons for which they should or should not do something. And this thought process includes considering unintended consequences that may bite them later.

Successful People Know No 100 Percent Solution Exists

Successful people manage the negative of any direction they take. They know there is no perfect answer or 100 percent solution. Without exception, highly performing people do the best they can, and then they "turn the page" and focus on tomorrow's challenges.

Successful People Have Minimum Standards

Successful people have performance standards for themselves and others. They require standards in all areas of their lives, such as timeliness, manners, appearance, promises, and productivity. Minimum standards are adhered to. This is no secret. If they don't adhere to their minimum standards, it can lead to a dysfunctional life. Successful people know strong and good people are out in the world. They are not afraid to cut off people who violate their standards and find another person.

"Best of Class" Contractors

You have probably heard the term **"Best of Class"** contractors, which is a consulting term that has been thrown around like the word "Superstar." What Best of Class means in the mainstream press and what it should mean are two different things.

Best of Class contractors are judged by the financial ratios achieved in their business. That is, they are financially successful. There is no consideration for technical knowledge. The Best of Class construction firm is one that does well fiscally, but not necessarily personally. Additionally, there is some correlation to technical construction ability. Specialty contractors have a higher correlation between technical ability and financial success.

Does Anyone Beside Me Believe They Are Personally Successful?

Most of us believe we are personally successful. Hundreds of thousands of contractors have dinner with their loved ones every night, go to little league games and dance recitals, and generally participate in the lives of the people they love. So, would you agree we should start using the term "financially successful" instead of Best of Class? Financial success is about money management and not about building work. In these days of political correctness, the former title accurately describes the fiscally savvy construction firm. It does not guarantee the firm can build work any better or faster than a personally successful one.

Success is not a fuzzy concept. We conclude that it means you are better at what you do than three-fourths of others who do the same thing. Whether you are a project manager, a foreperson, or a contractor, being excellent has many rewards, including personal satisfaction.

What is professional success in construction? To answer this, I think we can't look at financial success, even though it is very American. Wealth building is important to have independence in our later years, but after the first couple million dollars, it doesn't help. We need to have a definition that can apply to all situations in life, so this is my definition: *professional success is the respect of intelligent people.*

These intelligent people are the people whom others respect and they know the construction business deeply. They know how complicated and how demanding the business is, and how unfair it can be. If you show them that you conduct yourself with solid reasons and values, they certainly will respect you, regardless of your station in life.

> **Back up managers in their decisions. Managers are not second-guessed publicly by company executives.**

Understanding Personalities

To understand the personalities of different people, we are best served by using a proven system of analysis. Several are on the market and available to contractors, but none is more simple, tenured, or defendable than the DiSC system. The *DiSC Profile Methodology* is a helpful device to understand an individual's behavioral pattern and what emotions they might feel. This system provides labels, definitions, and a structure to explain different visible behaviors and internal emotions. This aids contractors, so an employee's personality strengths can be directed, while weaknesses can be augmented for everyone's benefit, including the employee. The DiSC is equally as valuable when you're analyzing a prospective employee. Many contractors have experienced "We hired him based on his resume, but we fired him on his behavior!" DiSC helps project the future employee's behavior on the job.

DiSC Helps Explain the Mysteries of People

Several caveats should be kept in mind when you analyze DiSC information. First, no one should attempt to change their personality profile as a result of DiSC information. To do so would probably be a waste of effort. It might work for a short time, but the strain would eventually force you to go back to your natural self. People do undergo rapid personality changes, though, in what psychologists call psychological trauma, such as what would result from an event of extreme good luck or, conversely, misfortune (for example, the death of a loved one, or a divorce).

Second, there are neither "superior" nor "poor" profiles. We have found successful, incompetent, happy, miserable, personable, and unfriendly people with every one of the DiSC behavior profiles. An ingredient that appears frequently in people who are successful in their jobs is not any one personality type, but the person's awareness and accommodation of the strengths and weaknesses of their personality, whatever the type, that is, self-awareness. The DiSC process aids in self-awareness and can recommend tactics to accommodate a person's personality, so they can win at their job more often. Certain behavioral patterns adapt more easily to certain types of jobs and the DiSC is particularly useful as one source of information for making staffing decisions. However, be careful: All behavioral patterns have proven successful at work.

Third, the information contained here is general, so it should not be used as the sole criterion for making personnel decisions. The DiSC does not measure IQ, experience, or talent. That determination is made by checking references, administering intelligence tests, and trusting your gut feel.

The DiSC Profile Methodology is based on the work of behavioral scientists William Marston and John Grier. Marston wrote a breakthrough book named *The Emotions of Normal People* in the 1930s, in which he asserted that a personality has four dimensions:

1. D = Dominant or Driven Personality
2. I = Influencing or Inspirational to Others
3. S = Steady or Systematic about Work
4. C = Compliant or Conscientious of the Rules

Each individual uses each of these dimensions to relative degrees, which may or may not vary, depending on the state under which the individual is functioning. The behavioral states that the DiSC evaluates are perceived expectations of others (and job), pressure, and perception of self. Most individuals will use one of the four dimensions more than the others under a state of pressure. This dimension is called the "high" or major characteristic for the purposes of this explanation.

Dominant or Driven Individuals *D dimension,* or *dominant or driven individuals,* attempt to shape the environment by overcoming opposition to achieve results. These persons may be quick decision makers, good problem solvers, unafraid of uncertainty and new challenges, and adept at getting results. They may also be impatient, pushy, easily bored, quick to anger, and uninterested in detail.

Highly driven persons usually prefer to work in situations where they have authority, challenge, prestige, lack of supervision, a variety of tasks, and opportunities for advancement. They often are effective when working with others who are more inclined to calculate risks, more cautious, and more patient with others.

To be more effective, highly dominant individuals should seek difficult assignments, which require techniques based on practical experience, make an effort to understand that they need cooperation from others to succeed, identify reasons for their conclusions, and pace themselves. Occasionally, they need a shock if it becomes necessary to make them aware of the need for different behavior.

Highly Influencing or Inspirational Individuals *I dimension, or highly influencing or inspirational individuals,* attempt to shape the environment by obtaining the alliance of others to accomplish results. These persons put effort into making a favorable impression, helping and motivating others, entertaining people, generating enthusiasm, and making personal contacts.

These inspirational individuals usually prefer to work in situations where they have social recognition, group activities, freedom from controls and details, freedom of expression, and favorable working conditions. They are often most effective when working with others who speak out candidly, research facts and details, and concentrate on follow-through. They prefer to deal with things or systems, rather than people.

To be more effective, highly influencing individuals should make an effort to manage their time if their dominance or steadiness dimensions are low, meet deadlines, apprise others on more than people skills, be more objective, and be more firm with others if the influencer's dominance dimension is low.

Highly Steady or Systematic Individuals *S dimension,* or *highly steady or systematic individuals,* cooperate with others to carry out tasks. These persons are usually patient, loyal, good listeners, and slow to anger. They may dislike noisy arguments and will calm excited people. They are capable of performing routine or specialized work.

Highly systematic individuals usually prefer to work in situations where they have security, little infringement on personal style, infrequent changes, identification with a group, and sincere appreciation for their contribution. They are often most effective when working with others who delegate, react quickly to unexpected events, work on more than one thing, apply pressure, and are flexible in work procedures.

To be more effective, these steady individuals should condition themselves for change before it occurs, seek information on how their efforts contribute to the overall organization, seek coworkers in whose competence they have confidence, ask for guidelines to accomplish tasks, and seek out those who encourage creativity.

Highly Compliant or Conscientious Individuals *C dimension,* or *highly compliant or conscientious individuals,* attempt to promote quality in products or services under whatever circumstances may exist. These persons usually follow directives and standards, concentrate on details, comply with authority, criticize and check for accuracy, and behave diplomatically or formally with others.

Highly conscientious individuals usually prefer to work in situations where they have others who call attention to the high-compliance individual's accomplishments, security and standard procedures, identification with a group, and the absence of frequent or abrupt changes that might compromise quality. They are often most effective when working with others who delegate, seek more authority, make quick decisions, compromise, and use policies as guidelines instead of hard rules.

To be more effective, highly compliant individuals should seek out precision work, tolerate some conflict, appraise people on more than their accomplishments, ask for guidelines and objectives, and set deadlines for planning and deliberating.

As a rule of thumb, most people possess two personality traits above the *midline* or average emotion. And, obviously, they have two traits below the midline. If three traits are above or below, this may be an indication of change of circumstance—good or bad. If all four personality traits are close to the midline, then the same is also true.

DiSC does not discriminate against people due to their creed, color, race, or national origin. In the parlance of human resource (HR) management, it meets the four-fifths' rule, which is valuable in today's employment climate.

We completed a recent study using the DiSC instrument process. The focus was what makes the best laborer or craftsperson? Some analysis was done of hundreds of individuals who work with their hands in hourly positions. The industry studied was construction, and the results do point to insights that cannot be ignored.

Our study asserts that the best employees have the following attributes:

- Safety conscious and have an above-average safety record
- Loyal and have been with their employer for a number of years
- Neither wasteful nor make many mistakes in their work

This sounds like a perfect construction craftsperson or laborer. Personnel records and other employment information were collected. A review of the best employees was completed.

The results state that two DiSC emotions correlate to the three previous attributes.

1. A low *D*—This person seeks a lot of information. They do not fly off in a rage, but take careful assessment of the situation. Hence, they do not quit abruptly. They take time to make decisions.

2. A high *S*—This person is a nice and process-oriented person. They do work in a methodical fashion, therefore, they create less waste and fewer mistakes. Again, being nice lends itself to being forgiving of people, including when you might say or do something offensive.

If you do have a choice of people to hire in a laborer or craft position, DiSC can help you make an informed choice for the long-term benefit of your company. To be clear, this profiling method should be used in concert with other information such as interviews, background checks, drug testing, references, and skill testing.

In summary, the DiSC methodology can join other tools and techniques to make managers work better with people. The classifying system can be an important aid for:

1. Increasing awareness of others and yourself
2. Selecting people to work together
3. Conflict management

A DiSC assessment takes about 10 minutes to complete and half a day to understand the system and process. Its value is that it saves the contractor years of trial and error in working with people.

> Calculate gross profit per man-hour or man-week as a financial indicator. This measure allows companies to compare financial results to manager effort. They can also see the profitability of a customer. This is a key measure.

Generations We Deal With

Have you ever heard yourself say, "Young people! What a shame youth is wasted on the young!" We all know each generation differs in attitude. Influences are many and they vary for each generation. Such influences include economic times, heroes, world events, family composition, and the like.

We see distinctly different demographic groups that most contractors deal with. These people can be a client, employee, subcontractor, supplier, or peer. All these people approach their responsibilities with a different attitude. The secret to working with people better is to understand what that approach is, and then couch your communication in respect to that attitude. If you don't, you can ruin a relationship before it even starts.

The War Generation

The *War Generation* includes war veterans and their spouses. This group was influenced by several remarkable events, including World War II, global economic depression, and the spread of communism.

Jobs were scarce for most of this generation. They believe in working to fend off going hungry and becoming homeless. Savings are important to them and to help with their saving, frugality is a habit.

I can remember my uncle using the same sandwich bags again and again. His view of money was that you couldn't have enough of it. He taught me "It is not how much you make, but how much you save."

Many in this generation experienced the armed forces chain of command, so a hierarchy in the workplace is familiar to them. Working in a structured format is expected and doing what their superior says is normal. The people in command—Eisenhower, MacArthur, and Roosevelt—were trustworthy.

Keeping the same job for all of their careers is a mark of honor, but other generations think differently. They don't talk as much about personal issues. The term "rugged individualism" was coined by this generation. In essence, that kind of self-disclosure is considered a sign of weakness. To discuss personal problems makes this generation uncomfortable.

My godfather won the bronze star at the Battle of the Bulge, but I didn't know it until his funeral. His generation didn't talk about such things because they believe it cheapens the honor to discuss it. Also, they had many friends who died in that war. To discuss the war is simply not their style.

Baby Boomers

Sociologists place the birth year of this group, known as "Baby Boomers," at a time between 1946 and 1963. In other words, the end of World War II, plus nine months and the first year of reliable birth control—the invention of "the pill."

This group sees work as a means to an end. They are not overly enthusiastic about working the necessary hours to get ahead financially, but they do see financial security as a top priority for themselves and their families. They tend to work hard, but they don't invest themselves totally in being a craftsperson or a project manager. Pride in their work is not an attitude they possess.

When the Boomer generation came home from school, mother was usually home and there to share the day. They experienced a more nurturing environment than later generations. After school, the son or daughter went out to play (they would build forts and tunnels that OSHA would shut down). Why didn't they have to go to work after school? Because of good economic times, children didn't have to help meet the family budget.

This generation grew up on rock music, scandalous leaders, and the Vietnam War. Institutions were not to be trusted on everything and leaders are suspect until they're proven worthy.

College was not an economic stretch for the Boomers. Grants, loans, student aid, and their parents help made a college degree attainable. But, as soon as graduation finished, it was off to work to pay back those student loans.

Generation X

This group was born between 1964 and the mid 1980s. *Generation X* is marked by the ability of mothers to have a choice of family size, if they wanted a family at all. The pill was in use around this time and it allowed women to have a career. Mothers could work outside the home without interruption, giving them more financial independence than previous generations. Divorce rates soared.

Xers are affected by a different family structure: a one-parent home and that one parent was working. This young person grew up coming home to an empty house and they had to seek their own fun. These "latchkey" kids learned quickly that finding something to do was up to them. In other words, they are independent.

As you can imagine, divorced parents sometimes did not stay in the area and the nonresidential parent moved away. This left the Xer with a sense of disloyalty. In the workplace, though, this group has an attitude of loyalty, but it is loyalty to themselves.

They saw their parents laid off during corporate "rightsizing" during the 1980s. Dad or mom worked for the same firm for most of their career, only to be laid off in this decade. Their parent(s) then sought employment at a vastly reduced salary and compensation package: tensions and conversations typically flowed. These sons and daughters quickly learned the high price of loyalty to a corporation.

Xers grew up with many hours of television while their parent worked, so they are not a physically active bunch. Television exposed them to world events as no other generation before them.

Computers were coming of age in the 1980s and later. Technology intrigues Generation *X*. They did witness the fallibility of technology, however, in the Space Shuttle Challenger accident.

This generation experienced tremendous economic times. If they graduated college in 1992 or later, they have never worked through a recession. Their attitude sometimes reflects this phenomenon.

To retain this generation, you need to recognize several things:

- Let them be one of the first employees to look over any new technology. They grew up in the era of computers and typically know a lot about them. Certainly, they can help make the new technology more productive faster.

- Create a sense of family. The majority of this generation experienced a loss of one parent in the home. They do seek a sense of family. Research by the U.S. Army led to the slogan, "An Army of One." This portrays the Army in family terms.

- Give them their time off. This group does have an attitude of "working to live." They will not act as the War Generation does and value that they have work to do.

- Be aware they might go over the heads of their immediate supervisor and talk directly with the owner. They consider this normal. They have less respect for seniority and position than do other generations.

- Recognize them for a job well done and for a job not well done. Xers believe if they achieve good results, they should be rewarded. You might need to temper this with subtle recognition of mediocre work.

Like any important personal relationship, knowing the family along with the person is always better. As in marriage, if someone comes from a combative and destructive home environment, the person will be affected. The behaviors they exhibit should come as no surprise. With a consistent and tight-knit family, any person will benefit.

Recognizing the generational differences helps us understand more about how each group will approach their job. This information is an overview and is not meant to be conclusive, but it is factually correct for a majority of each group. Knowing how they might act and, thus, changing your management style with that person can be effective.

> Make the compensation plan follow the strategic plan. Companies know if it is in the best interest of the company to do certain things, they also need to make it in the best interest of the employee.

Management Styles

What is your management style? If you are a small contractor and you have just a few employees, it can be any one of a number of styles and still be effective. You don't have to be a management expert to lead a low-volume construction firm. Why? Two reasons: (1) the margins are higher on small work and it gives the contractor room to be nonscientific about his management style. (2) Over the years, contractors will hire and keep people who can work under their management style. They don't need many employees to start with or to operate a company this size.

I have seen contractors who are highly vocal (and sometimes abusive), and their people don't seem to mind. Everything has worked itself out over the years and the projects get built.

Some small contractors have a sales attitude toward everything. They don't worry about cost as much as volume. Somewhere in their organization, though, is a frugal, worrisome person who keeps a rein on expenses. This person might be a spouse or an office manager. Again, small contractors enjoy a lot of latitude.

An extremely large contractor must have greater flexibility in his approach to people. If he has 500 employees, he will have to know dozens of methods to manage this group effectively. Add to that dozens of clients and suppliers, and he must carefully use all his skills to keep the business profitable.

Management style	Positive aspects	Negative aspects
One-at-a-time boss	• Clear instruction • Focus	• Time wasted walking from worksite to supervisor and back • Most people don't like to be instructed this way
200-Pound tiger	• More work done • This type of manager consistently achieves cost and schedule	• Workers quitting • Will drive off talented people
School marm	• Careful communication	• Slightly condescending
Coach	• Makes people think • Talented people will grow under this manager	• Extra time it takes • Potential problem: thinking out loud

FIGURE 5-2
Each management style has its strengths and weaknesses.

Most contractors use four basic approaches (see Figure 5-2):

1. **One-at-a-Time-Boss**—This manager is careful with assigning people a lot of work. He may assign one or two tasks at a time. He sees focus on a task as more important than having a lot of concurrent demands, which is the opposite of a multitasker personality. A person who doesn't like the pressure of a list of duties will like this management style.

2. **200-Pound Tiger**—He is strongly involved in giving several assignments and/or more work than a person can do in one day. On the job site, the term is a "pusher." He tells people what to do, how to do it, and how much to get done. He gets a lot done through others, and workers either tolerate him or quit. Employees who stay may experience burnout. The good news about the 200-pound tiger is he consistently achieves budget and schedule goals.

This supervisor type is valuable, although he can be costly in terms of losing employees.

3. **School Marm**—This manager is careful about communicating correctly and completely. He tells you what to do, how to do it, and then asks you to repeat the plan. Communication is a concern of this person. If a lack of clarity is in an instruction, it isn't because the effort wasn't there.

4. **Coach**—This manager feels that most people want to do a good job and he attempts to guide workers to that goal. One of his techniques is to ask questions that make people think. The same question repeated over several months makes people think about the subject in question.

Parents use this same method with their teenagers. While mom and dad don't instruct openly, they do ask questions that help their youngsters think, plan, and execute better.

The coach has no hesitation about using this approach. As a manager, however, he must demand that the work needs to be done and by when. So, he tells the team what to do and involves them in a discussion of how to do it and how much to do. The coach might ask the following questions:

- Do we have everything we need?
- How long should each task take?
- How much should we be able to get completed by the end of the week?
- Does anyone have any questions or ideas?
- What would make this easier?
- Does anyone see any quality/safety issues?

Smart contractors make sure to keep separate the pay of shareholder employees. They don't overpay the salary of an employee just because they are also a shareholder.

The Evaluation of Each Style

The one-at-a-time boss can't be a long-term strategy because too much time is wasted (some research suggests up to 6 percent). This is an expensive style. The manager must start giving a list to the employee. This will free up more time for both people to accomplish more.

More management training happens from the second row—the 200-pound tiger down to the coach. The bottom three styles have a lot of value. In our opinion, getting your people to think more like managers is powerful. They will become more sensitive to schedule, cost, quality, and safety. Your company will attain a better performance.

> Keep job-cost reports straightforward and easy-to-read. Then, field people can quickly know where they stand, and then they can do something about it.

Recruiting Good People

Finding and hiring good people can make the contracting business much easier. Having the wrong kind of people can certainly bankrupt even the best contractor. The following is a list of ways to find and/or recruit people you might not have thought of:

- Did you know 45 percent of people who start college don't finish? Think of that civil engineering or construction management student who doesn't care for the classroom. They may be your next field superintendent. Certainly, their education level is higher-than-average. Get to know the dean of your local college(s). That person may be able to direct or refer you to a soon-to-be former student.

- Some of the best construction firms use the "black book" method. The process is as follows—the president or other senior executive maintains a recruiting list or black book of people who have the qualities the company desires. In conversations with employees and other people, the president constantly asks "What quality people do you know?" "Why are they good?" "Where do they work?" and so forth. They routinely maintain and add to this list of names. At some point, the executive will contact one or several of these people, starting the relationship. Eventually, this evolves into a conversation about employment. Good people are so critical to a contractor's success that senior executives need to lead the effort.

- A major materials' supplier is recruiting from the local "boot camp" for younger people who have made mistakes early in life. The supplier recruits selectively and offers about 25 hours of training to the young people. Retention is about 75 percent. This supplier is also a founding member of the Construction Workers Coalition, a group of local construction-related businesses that seek to improve the construction industry's image as a viable career. They also recruit individuals to become employed in the local industry.

- A contractor has recruited about 40 Eastern Europeans. They can legally immigrate to the United States because they are viewed as politically persecuted. These individuals have proven to be reliable and hard-working employees. You might consider looking into Bosnia and other Eastern European countries, where this method of immigration is possible and sponsor some individuals. Several of the Bosnians are being groomed for leadership positions; they are buying houses and beginning to live out the American dream. Consequently, they are loyal employees.

- Consider recruiting Canadians. Most Canadians already love the United States, they can move here freely, and most of them already speak English.

- Some contractors have arrangements to share employees with others, as necessary.

- A contractor in Denver is working with people who haven't gotten off to the greatest start in life: he particularly targets high-school dropouts. His company attempts to communicate the potential long-term income potential from learning a trade. Most kids today don't realize how much you can make working with your hands. They provide training and mentoring, and they require classes. The retention has been high and morale is great. This story was in one of the local papers a few weeks ago.

- A company has staffed an operation in the south by running ads in depressed parts of the country. It has also run ads in the sports section, as opposed to the classified section of the newspaper.

- Contact the National Center for Construction Education and Research in Gainesville, Florida. They have programs that currently target exactly the type of person who, when trained, can raise the caliber of contractor employees.

- Another possibility is to conduct a series of industry-oriented training programs for the vocational schools in the local area. By taking the lead, the company positions itself as a firm to consider. Another possibility is to develop and present a qualified training program for the local vocational school. The training is run at the contractor's office or training facility, and the students get credit for a school-to-work program. Both of these take some effort, but they do work.

- Consider signing and referral bonuses. One company offers a $1,000 bonus to any employee who recommends a hire who stays for at least one year.

- One company has taken advantage of the excellent military resources available. They have had great success at creating alliances with various military bases. They began by contacting the outprocessing center, and then went from there. The military releases thousands of trained people every month who are looking for work. This is an unbelievable source of top-quality people.

- A building company has had good results marketing through churches in the area. Their culture is very much Christian-based, and they have sent flyers and called churches asking for members who may want to become a part of their company. They have recruited at all levels with this approach.

- A company in one part of the country is considering renting a billboard and using the slogan "Why end your vacation?" on an interstate around the attractions. They have talked about advertising in the theme park stands at hotels and other tourist hot spots that have racks with brochures for local sights and activities.

- Participate in local high school- and college-career days. Sponsor a science fair award at local high schools. Sponsor work-site visits to expose young people in high schools, community or technical colleges, and universities to the mysteries of the complex and rewarding construction industry. Include an office visit as well.

- Issue carefully targeted radio advertising. A local ad is touting the benefits of working in the construction industry. It is a powerful, well-positioned message.

- Use the Internet. *Blogs* (web logs) are popular. The constant outreach of blogs and other Internet tools is good for marketing to clients, as well as to prospective employees. The software is free from several sources and content can be found almost anywhere. You don't need to earn a journalism degree. Offering a free form(s) in an Adobe format or some sort of other service can start a conversation for almost nothing and one of your staff can keep it updated. Something you may not realize is that blogs have a lot more key words for search engines to find. By the nature of blogs, they have more words, including words that reflect the construction industry, so you'll have more hits from your target audience.

- County jails can be a place to find a few field employees. County jails encourage it and inmates (nonviolent and nondrug-related) want the privilege of working. Contractors report consistent work habits and also, little difficulty in managing them.

- Develop a group of contractors (of diverse trades) and speak to groups that have access to the high school or recent immigrants. Usually, school groups meet on a regular basis. Getting in front of these kinds of organizations and presenting your organizations and opportunities is a positive approach. And, asking for feedback on how to reach these groups can help inform you, as well as give you an introduction into other areas.

- Get in front of influential groups, such as the PTA and other parent groups. Proclaim the virtues of starting a career by learning a hands-on trade. See Chapter 1.

- How about internships? We often think of coops only with college students, but with new class scheduling, these opportunities are open to high school seniors. Many seniors have large blocks of time available for coops or internships. They need to have a focus and be mentored, so take advantage of this. Remember, though, these kids may also be interested in extracurricular activities.

- Be active in trade associations. This can lead to contact with potential employees that no other forum will afford. The yearly convention has a history of people deciding to change jobs.

- Timing can be everything. Bonuses are typically paid at the end of the year. If someone is disappointed in their bonus and your message arrives, that may be the start of a conversation with a potential new hire.

- Here is a preventive idea. Some contractor's don't take their employees to association conventions. Even though this is a nice gesture, some construction companies have found that other contractors have and will recruit your people at these meetings.

Once you find a prospective employee, it will be time to interview them. Remember, you will never be satisfied with all your hires. People are earnest in job interviews. They would like to have a better situation. But, somehow between the time you offer them a job and the first day on the job, a change takes place. Contractors state that it takes five hires to find one good craftsperson. When hiring a manager, it is less risky. As in all endeavors with people, the more information you have about them, the less mistakes you will make in working with them.

Here are seven tried-and-true techniques that can improve your success rate in finding long-term employees.

1. Constantly recruit. It takes a lot of candidates to find one great person. The number of prospects has a strong correlation to finding one good hire.

2. Ask your current, most-respected employees who they know and who they would recommend. Press them if they don't give you an answer. Keep track of these recommendations in a book. As you find out more information, such as their phone number, place of employment, and so forth, you can write everything down in the same place.

3. Use an assessment tool(s) of the person's personality. (See "Understanding Personalities" discussed earlier in this chapter.) Given the time and money wasted on a bad hire, this is worth the expense.

4. Ask the potential new hire the following questions:
   - Ethical questions, such as "What would you do if. ..."
   - Who is someone you dislike and why?
   - Who is someone you are friends with and why?
   - What would your former employers say about you?
   - What are your strengths and weaknesses? (Everyone has both strengths and weaknesses.)

5. Run the background checks on the candidate that are legal in your state.

6. Ask other people you trust to interview the candidate and see what they think.

7. Take the candidate out to lunch or other social setting. In a relaxed atmosphere, they will tend to be themselves. One contractor takes a prospective employee to a buffet. He swears that the candidate's decision-making ability shows if he looks over all the lunch choices.

> Have a process that requires the person who generates the percentages/gross dollar billing to be the first person to call on the client to collect.

Managing People Better

Managing people well is half the battle in contracting (some people say it is more). The business, as we have said, consists of people and processes. In managing people, older contractors make fewer mistakes in working with others. They have the experience (or scar tissue) to know how to do this better than their younger brethren.

This section applies to everyone in your firm. If you are an executive, you already know some of these guidelines. The stakes are high here because they are all your projects and that is worth many times more than a single job.

If you are a project manager, you typically control more than one project. Your leverage is not as great as that of an executive, but it's more than the project field supervisor or foreperson.

If you are a foreperson, people are important to your success. Good, disciplined craftsmen who like your management style can make your professional life enjoyable. Some say the quality of the foreperson is directly linked to the level of gross profit a contractor enjoys. The field supervisor is a resource manager, taking the demands of the job and matching them with limited resources. At the end of a project, the foreperson who thinks more as a manager will win.

For any construction professional to win more often, they must psychologically take off their tool belt and assume the role of business owner. The business is the construction project. The average construction project in the United States is about the same as the revenue of a small business. Any project supervisor is responsible for it, just as small business owner is.

For everyone who is part of the contracting business, these guidelines apply:

1. People are fragile. Deep down inside, your people want to be taken seriously. This is no mystery to HR executives. Respect is the number one human need. Take your people seriously and they will respond positively. As a starting point:

    A. Take time to teach and understand each subordinate.

    B. Never use their nickname. People will never be offended by using their given name or a shortened version of it.

    C. Paychecks and/or bonus checks should be handed out with a "thank you for your efforts."

    D. Always assume people are trying to do a good job until proven otherwise. Don't spoil anyone's attitude until they spoil yours.

    E. Make sure your people have what they need or, at least, fight to get it.

2. Just because things are true, doesn't mean they need to be said. If something is true and positive, certainly say it,

but keep the negative comments out of your conversations. This keeps the workplace atmosphere professional and forward-thinking. Because of influences in our society today, you might be tempted to comment on someone's obvious shortcoming. Don't do it, unless you are on your way to fire them. Even then, it is still a hazard.

3. Well-organized beats smart every time. Success in construction is based on a good, thoughtful process executed on every job every time. Daily organizational skill can make anyone look smart. Planning weekly, training people in small increments, knowing the contract documents, and keeping material constantly in the work area are typical processes that reward supervisors and managers. Smart, disorganized people in construction are common and neither well compensated nor respected.

4. The process is the problem, not the people. The number of people, the amount of products, and the conflicting goals cause problems on most projects. People come to work wanting to succeed. They would like a raise, to be considered for a promotion, and to go to the next big job. Success comes from having a thoughtful, proactive process.

5. You are buying people's energy, ideas, and enthusiasm, not their time. Do the things that keep people in a positive state of mind. Being appreciative about your journeymen will encourage them to follow you. Having a sense of humor never hurts anyone's outlook. Giving a well-deserved compliment won't hurt your leadership. Being a fake will come out in the wash.

6. People want to be included in the plan. Thirty years ago, people just wanted to receive their instruction and go to work. Today's typical worker wants to know what to do and why he should do it. Include them in the information that is appropriate to share.

7. Talk about bad situations only once. Yes, strongly voice your disappointment behind closed doors. Make a point of showing your displeasure. Use the opportunity to raise the performance bar, but once the door reopens and you walk out, that should be the end of the verbal spanking.

No one wants to, or should be made to, stay in the penalty box for days, weeks, or years.

8. Money doesn't buy happiness. We know this, but your people will constantly talk about their paychecks. Why? Because it is easily measured and hard to argue. What do they really want? To be appreciated. To go to a good job. To have a bright future. In surveys, compensation ranks at the middle of all variables concerning job satisfaction. You guessed it, being included in the plans of the company, along with appreciation and a bright future, ranks ahead of pay.

9. Don't think out loud. In other words, don't tell people what you are considering or what you plan to do. The armed forces teach that this confuses the troops and starts rumors. Be clear in your mind and well-reasoned in your thinking. When you speak, state a direction you have chosen and don't change your mind, unless it's absolutely necessary. Don't voice your thinking and you will keep your crew's distractions and gossip to a minimum.

10. Don't forget to tie any raise to improved performance or skill. For open-shop situations, raises should be mentioned as a concept. State this in the months preceding the raise date. The smart foreperson talks about ways to maximize the raise by acquiring skills or showing improvement, such as competent person training, being independent, or the ability to install so much work in a day. When raise time comes, then nothing else needs to be said. You either give them a minimal or maximal raise.

11. People notice the little things. Remembering their concerns and interests tells them they work for a good person. Football coach Bill Parcells is the greatest example. Parcells knows several things about each player and mentions them. Even when he cuts someone, they don't take issue with it because they know it is not personal. Parcells cares about his players as people. Take another look at all these guidelines. Sincerity and caring wins with people, even if you cut someone.

12. People work for people, not for companies. Most great contractors are great people. If you are someone people can believe in, they will stay and work hard for you.

The loyalty will be there. As an aside, it is clear to me that most great contractors are "mud on the boots" types. The crews in the field have a great respect for someone who has done their jobs. A friend said it better: "You can't run a construction company by e-mail."

13. Compete with yourself, not with others. Great professionals do not worry about other projects or their peers. They compete against themselves and focus on that. If it takes them an hour to do something, they try to finish the job in 55 minutes. Frankly, they don't concern themselves with the Joneses. Teach this concept to your people.

14. Get ugly early. When a true professional sees a problem, they identify it and communicate it. Great people don't hide from the truth. No one ever lost respect for someone who had the courage to communicate a rock in the road ahead. Once everyone calms down, their minds will start thinking of a plan *B*. Early detection always gives people more time to research and consider options. Having to make difficult decisions in an hour is a recipe for subsequent problems down the road.

15. Values equal actions equal culture. When a leader believes in a value, it is expressed in actions and subordinates can't help but see it. People can say anything, but what they do speaks their heart. If you value hard work, you don't care if the hard worker is your least popular worker; you mention it. People who value courtesies from people are not taken for granted. If someone fetches a tool or a cup of coffee, thank them for it. If you value someone's organizational habits, notice them and point them out to others. A true value(s) builds a culture in your team. Certainly, when raise or promotion time comes, you speak your values though actions. Conversely, if you have limited values, your people will do all manner of things. If a manager is weak or too laid-back, his team will not focus on a few things. They will be all over the board with their priorities. The crew and, thus, the manager will not produce. Pity the mild supervisor in our industry. The construction business only rewards safety, production, quality, and cost.

If the manager doesn't change, they will have a difficult time growing in their responsibilities.

16. Break up cliques. Allowing cliques on the job site does little to enhance teamwork and learning. As we move people around to work with others, we do a service for ourselves and to our people. A new partner adds perspective to performing tasks in different ways. In addition, the practice gives a person an understanding of different personalities. In summary, people will develop a better sense of other people. This is inexpensive management training for your next foreperson, superintendent, or project manager. The best ones tend to come from inside companies, rather than those who are recruited from outside.

These principals are the major attitudes I have identified over the years working as a management consultant. The great people have either stated or done (or both) the previous actions. I certainly consider these actions to be the best practices of people.

> Superior contractors don't start unnecessary conflict. The construction business has plenty of conflict, so there is no need to add to it. They try to find ways to keep their personality (and that of the other person) out of the business.

The F Words to Use in Managing a Construction Contracting Firm

This is a good model to keep things simple and moving forward. Managing people is still the greatest contracting challenge.

1. Friendliness. Relationships and people grow in a friendly atmosphere. Human nature seeks friendly atmospheres and turns away from unfriendly ones. Let your place of business have a positive air without any negative tension.

   Your managers and supervisors will certainly look forward to coming to work. They are half-way to wanting to do a good job for you. See the following four *F*s.

2. Frankness. It pays to be frank. Although it is uncomfortable for everyone in the first half hour or so, the healthy discussion of what happened and why makes your people better performers. Of course, you'll want to be friendly in the process.

3. Fairness. Don't play favorites. Always seek the answer to "what is the right thing to do?" versus "who is right." This keeps all your employees and other people you work with treated equally. They will return the favor to you and treat you fairly.

4. Faithfulness. Always assume that your people and business partners have the intent and capability to do a good job. Do this until proven otherwise, and then be frank. After that discussion, forget the past and start on a blank page. If they don't have the intent and capability to do a good job, however, read the following.

5. Firmness. Have minimum standards of performance, including behavior and quality, that apply to all people. Use the other four Fs to communicate this to others. In the short-term, you may have some late nights but, in the long-term, you will polish your reputation and performance.

> Project and measure cash flow. This is one of two determinants of return on investment (ROI) on a project and for a contractor. Clearly, this is a critical factor.

Job Descriptions and Yearly Reviews

Job descriptions can be an arduous task for most contractors. Good people do want to know how to do a great job. The paperwork involved in such a task encourages some construction firms to be slow about giving job descriptions and slower yet to give yearly reviews. Again, true professionals want to know how they are doing and how to do better. These kinds of employees are the difference between average and excellent companies.

A sample job description follows. You can use this for almost any position. The tasks outlined are less important than the form. This layout can help a contractor quickly create an effective position narrative for their employees. Just fill in the appropriate information.

Take this structure and apply it to all the positions in your company. What most contractors are looking for is an effective, but time-efficient, way to manage employees. This process does it. You can determine an employee's rating by using your subjective opinion. A contractor who signs the paychecks has the power to do this. A company can use this objective process to evaluate employees, but know in advance this is a time-consuming process.

Both kinds of employee evaluation systems can start an argument. There is no guarantee. All people are emotional when it comes to their performance. Taking the more efficient system (the one shown here) may make sense for your organization.

Guidelines

Use this as a yearly exercise for your employees. Have your employee fill out the same form and submit it to you before the review meeting. This gives you a good idea about their perception of their work. Then, a beneficial (not superficial) discussion can follow concerning their current performance and future improvement.

Some work tasks will change. This seems to be the case with many contractors and their business. To anticipate this, the language "other duties as designated by the president from time-to-time" is appropriate.

As in all employee evaluations, keep a copy. You may never have to prove what was said or documented in a yearly review, but you never know.

Field Manager (Sample)

(1 of 2)

Report to: President

Supervises: Subcontractors, Suppliers, Service Providers, Employees as designated

Works Directly with: Company's Building Client and Our Project Executive

Basic Function:

Plan, organize, direct, and control the building aspects of the company and jobs in such a way as to meet company objectives of costs, quality, time, and safety, as well as other duties as designated by the president from time-to-time.

Duties and Responsibilities:

1. Hiring/Training

- Hires needed personnel
- Oversees the coordination of personnel
- Establishes and implements a new-hire orientation process
- Participates in establishing company objectives
- Participates in establishing goals and objectives for the construction area
- Gains buy-in on company objectives from subordinates

2. Planning

- Participates in the pre-job planning process
- Participates in establishing goals and objectives for the company
- Oversees planning and use of company resources
- Assures the planning process is followed
- Prepares job descriptions for subordinates
- Coordinates and plans with clients

3. Organizing

- Oversees the organization of the field operation areas
- Sees that administration of the jobs is effective and efficient
- Sees that the field is well-organized
- Makes recommendations for organizational changes
- Helps with client demands, such as access or storage space

4. Directing

- Troubleshoots difficult construction problems
- Establishes ways to motivate and keep personnel/subcontractors/suppliers/service providers' morale at a high level
- Reviews subordinates periodically and makes recommendations for improvements and wage adjustments
- Gives directions to subordinate managers

5. Controlling

- Sees that construction cost targets are met
- Helps establishes strategies and action plans to meet the budget
- Establishes action plans and oversees such plans as to achieve goals
- Makes sure job-cost feedback is furnished to subordinates
- Oversees the terms and conditions of construction agreements
- Oversees job schedules and makes sure they are updated and reported
- Keeps clients satisfied, but not at the substantial detriment to the company

Key Results:

1. Punch list coordination
2. Customer satisfaction
3. Professional appearance
4. Job cleanliness
5. Schedule adherence
6. Paperwork
7. Teamwork
8. Improvements to operations
9. Safety
10. Quality
11. Cost savings

The president will grade a field manager's performance on each of the previous factors, using a 0 to 100 percent scale. The resulting cumulative average will be multiplied by the total maximum incentive pay per completed home. The result will be the bonus earned by the superintendent. The bonus will be paid 30 days after completion of the punch list and the closing of the home, whichever is later. If the superintendent leaves the employment of the company before this date on any home, then the incentive pay is not due to the superintendent from that home.

Primary Working Relationships:

1. Company's clients
2. President
3. Financial manager
4. Subcontractors
5. Suppliers
6. Service providers

Field Manager (Sample)

Name: _____ **Date:** _____

QUALITATIVE

		Unacceptable	Poor	Satisfactory	Excellent	Outstanding
1.	Punch List Completion	1	2	3	4	5
2.	Customer Satisfaction	1	2	3	4	5
3.	Subcontractor Coordination	1	2	3	4	5
4.	Professional Appearance	1	2	3	4	5
5.	Job Cleanliness	1	2	3	4	5
6.	Schedule Adherence	1	2	3	4	5
7.	Independence	1	2	3	4	5
8.	Paperwork	1	2	3	4	5
9.	Teamwork	1	2	3	4	5
10.	Improvement	1	2	3	4	5

GOALS:

- _____
- _____
- _____
- _____
- _____
- _____

RECOMMENDATIONS FOR IMPROVEMENT:

- _____
- _____
- _____
- _____
- _____
- _____
- _____

When contractors have concerns about a person's status as an independent contractor, use the IRS form SS-9. The person in question can fill out the form, while they do the same, and then the form can be sent to the government for a decision. This gives the construction company almost bullet-proof evidence (if the independent contractor is deemed so) against any later claims.

Training

We know from the past 20 years that the path to bettering a company's personnel is through training. Contractors have used recruiting firms (commonly known as *headhunters*) to find and help recruit potential management personnel.

In our experience, this option has been a mediocre one for most contractors. For high-level personnel, however, recruiting firms do an excellent job in finding a quality person with deep construction experience. This kind of person is rare. If you have that specific kind of need, you can't ignore using a recruiting firm.

For middle management, though, the successful use of headhunters is mixed at best. So, we believe that for project managers, estimators, and field supervisors you have a higher payoff and less risk to growing and promoting internally.

Certainly, instances occur when a dismissal or a resignation means you have to act quickly. In this case, there is no other alternative. If you don't have someone ready to go into battle, you would be better served to seek talent outside of your firm.

One company discussed the need to replace their superintendents who would retire in 5 to 10 years. As you probably guessed, these employees were from the War Generation—they were the steady, dependable hands whose excellent work ethic the company had benefited from.

The company discussed all the possibilities and determined that an internal program to train potential middle managers would be the best course of action. On a side note, the company made sure if a well-qualified outsider became available, it wouldn't hesitate recruiting them.

The program involved one-time incentives and training to bring people up to the caliber needed. For existing supervisors, they would be paid one time for training an existing employee for a superintendent's position. The bonus was large enough to make it worthwhile. For the trainee, the same one-time incentive rule existed, although the dollar amount was smaller.

The result? Superintendents, assistant superintendents, field engineers, forepersons, and the like were spending time after work teaching and learning. The company reports that steady progress is being made toward the goal of replacing proven field leadership.

Growing people takes time. Some feel the horizon is five years, which makes sense. Teaching and learning are both long-term processes. Companies have to make sure the employee has the knowledge and is capable of using it under pressure. The consensus is that you have to be patient. The good news is the challenge is the same for your competition.

> Savvy contractors know that the construction industry average of wasted time is in the 30 percent range. They also know people are not trying to do a bad job. It is simply that the process is not being defined. They define the major business processes at a minimum.

Your People's Safety

The Occupational Safety and Health Administration (OSHA) is a help to construction contractors. They are an ally to contractors, but most contractors would disagree on that point. However, let me share some insights and conclusions that strengthen this argument.

What are some of the largest cost categories to contractors today? Workers' compensation and general liability insurance. Certainly, there are others, but these are the major expenses, whether you are a specialty contractor or a general contractor.

How does OSHA help in reducing this cost? Let's step back for a moment and look at a job site. Would you agree there are unsafe behaviors? I'm sure you would. Every road or building project has journeymen, laborers, and others who don't follow the OSHA

Safety Requirements explained in Publication 1926. Consciously or unconsciously, people on job sites are not as careful as they should be.

If you agree unsafe behaviors occur on job sites, then you would have to agree there are incidents, near hits, and accidents caused by this unsafe behavior. Risky actions produce adverse effects. The law of probability catches up to the perpetrator, and then someone is hurt.

The immediate business effect is a rise in the cost of workers' compensation to your company. If a nonemployee is injured, you have a potential claim against your general liability insurance. Revenue stays the same, but expenses increase, so marginal contribution (gross profit) decreases.

OSHA spends most of its time focusing on improving behaviors. Of all the duties the agency executes, enforcing the rules of Publication 1926 is the majority of effort. As a result, unsafe behaviors are reduced. If unsafe behaviors are less, then near misses and accidents are also less. If the recordable injuries, claims, and lost days are reduced, the contractor benefits from stable and, in some cases, lower premiums. OSHA is your friend. It wants the same thing you do: a safer worksite.

Federal OSHA is made up of 2,200 people. Not a large staff considering the Environmental Protection Agency employs 18,000. From all sources, qualified opinions believe the nitpickers are gone and OSHA is focused on the major safety issues (and not on stickers on hard hats) of the construction industry. See Figure 5-3.

The agency certainly wants changed behavior on job sites. As an example, once a fine is levied on a contractor, OSHA allows an "informal" settlement conference, which occurs within 15 days of notice, and allows the construction firm to discuss the fine and its actions in compliance with OSHA's regulations. Once the agency is convinced that the contractor has improved the safety behaviors, it is not uncommon for the fine to be reduced by 50 percent or more for first-time offenders. OSHA cares more about safe projects than collecting large fines. We are all in this together.

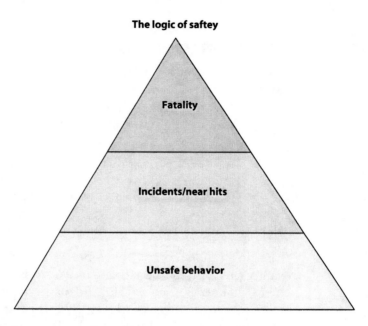

The logic of saftey

Fatality

Incidents/near hits

Unsafe behavior

FIGURE 5-3
Unsafe behavior leads to accidents and deaths. Reduce the unsafe behaviors and those problems will lessen or be eliminated.

Some of the entities we work with in the construction industry are not helpful and they can be our adversaries. OSHA is clearly not one of them.

1926 Is Not a Safety Plan

Contractors are fighting the increasing cost of safety. From workers' compensation to general liability to OSHA fines, construction firms are constantly feeling this headache. Some contractors cannot find private workers' compensation insurance and are forced to resort to governmental pools. This is the harsh reality of contracting. But, there are some ways to improve the cost and availability of insurance. You must realize that OSHA Publication 1926 is not a safety program. It is the law or the absolute minimum of what is expected of a contractor. In other words, if you are using Publication 1926 as your safety program, you are not distinguishing yourself as an above-average contractor.

As far the insurance industry is concerned, you are losing on two fronts:

1. Your insurance company may be viewing you as "just another contractor."

2. Your staff is probably behaving as unsafely as average construction employees, so you will have the same number of accidents as expected by the actuaries.

Neither of these issues bode well for any contractor.

The insurance company is being rational when it sees your safety program is undistinguishable from most other construction firms. It knows that day in and day out, you will have average incidents, near hits, accidents, lost days, and even fatalities. The underwriter will not see the logic in taking a gamble, which means your premiums will increase on the same trend as most of your competitors.

What to do? Formulate a safety program that goes beyond the requirements of law. Add to the safety requirements of your people on your jobs. Put it in writing, and train on these rules and police accordingly. The insurance industry is always looking for safe contractors to insure. They make money when people are not hurt, while contractors continue to pay their premiums.

In addition to the moral responsibility a contractor should feel about safety, preventing accidents is simply good business.

> Understand that the "big don't eat the small," but the "quick eat the slow." Big construction firms have less of a competitive edge in the market. For any contractor, big departments and crews are not desired. Smaller groups of people tend to be more proactive and efficient.

Are Your People Independent Contractors or Employees?

Do you have independent contractors working for you who are actually employees? As most construction firms know, this is a huge danger. If this is determined, you are liable for state and federal employment labor burden or taxes. In addition, you will be required to pay the workers' compensation of that employee(s) for the period of time in the determination. Your firm might be liable for months or even years of payroll. This is not something to ignore. Ignoring this is perilous to your contracting business.

An independent contractor is what most construction subcontractors are; however, there is some confusion about what attributes determine one.

To decide if one or more of your subcontractors is an employee, you need to use a multipart test. No one answer conclusively determines the status of a relationship as a contractor or employee. Understand that this is not a substitute for legal advice. The purpose here is to alert you of a potential, major problem.

The test has two general rules:

1. The employee is not subject to the will or the control of the employer.
2. The employer does not control the method of construction installation.

Furthermore, an independent contractor is one who:

1. The client does not furnish materials or labor.
2. Has a written contract.
3. Is not trained by the client. The existence of training points toward an employee/employer relationship.
4. Has temporary or nonexistent integration with the construction contractor's service.

5. Is free to assign anyone to do the work. In other words, they do not have to do the work themselves as a requirement.

6. Hires, supervises, and pays their workers; this is not done by anyone else.

7. Determines the hours of the day the business is open.

8. Is free to choose for whom and when they work. An independent contractor is not tied to a single client.

9. Can work where they please.

10. Does not set the sequence of work to be performed.

11. Does not have to provide oral or written reports to their client(s).

12. Are paid by the job, no matter how long it takes.

13. Estimates expenses ahead of time.

14. Is at risk of profit and at risk of loss.

15. Can work for any client, including one of your competitors, anywhere and at any time.

16. Must complete the project that is contracted and is liable for damages if the job is not completed.

No one question can determine the classification of "independent contractor" or "employee." Some case law and some bureaucracy is involved. And, more to the point, contractors don't make money fighting bureaucrats or employing lawyers.

As previously stated, one powerful practice is to use IRS Form SS-9. This is the form that clears up any confusion and it is your strongest defense against a reclassification. The danger of reclassification is a one way street—from independent contractor to employee. Think of it: if one of your employees were determined to be independent, you would have a refund coming from several places, including the IRS. That is not a bad day. Be careful, though. Our industry likes the idea of using these types of contractors. They are a less-risky proposition than hiring an unknown employee. However, the power of this type of relationship is not without peril, even if it's unintentionally misused.

The projected profit of a job is a good measure of project manager's skills. Over a project's life, a PM may project an increase or decrease of profit. Analyzing this trend on several jobs is called profit fade analysis. Smart contractors use profit fade analysis as a key measure for project managers and others. If there is a negative trend, it shows the tendency not to address problems early and/or not having a clear grasp of the project and its demands.

Negotiating with People

We offer these points of view to help contractors negotiate more effectively with clients, peers, and others. If you read this entire section, it can give you a better understanding of how other contractors negotiate more effectively.

1. Ask for more than you want. You deserve to be compensated richly. You can never ask for more later.

2. Never fall in love with a product or an idea. If you do, the other side has an enormous advantage.

3. Try not to accept the first proposal. There is more where that came from.

4. Don't make the first major concession.

5. Listen to words first, look at body language second, and then talk.

6. Do your homework and anticipate questions you can ask.

7. Don't volunteer information (such as funding sources or timing) unless you have a compelling reason to do this.

8. Practice the magic words of negotiation, "I don't understand."

9. Excel at the art of compromise. Don't let your ego get in the way of getting "half a loaf" of what you want.

10. Don't trample on the other side's ego. Allow them to save face and go home in one piece emotionally.

11. Don't make a lopsided deal. People will either renegotiate or interpret the agreement differently than what was intended.

Good negotiators are not afraid to do the following:

- Take a break during negotiation. A time-out enables you to focus on what has transpired.
- Reach out for information. Adults can ask any questions without fear. Sometimes, the other side will answer.
- Talk through a third party. This might be appropriate if you feel a face-to-face conversation will be a losing proposition.
- Demand an agenda. This structures the discussion with starting, finishing, and break times. Also, it structures who attends, what the subtopics are, and in what order those subtopics are discussed.
- Force the first concession. This sets the floor or ceiling for subsequent proposals and this limit will not be exceeded.
- Negotiate tough. Strong effort in all professions is rewarded. Negotiation is no different.
- Know the difference between positions and principles. Positions are negotiable, principles are not.
- Craft long-term agreements. This is a principle that will give others a reason to trust you the next time.
- Satisfy the legitimate interests of both parties as much as possible.
- Efficiently use time and resources, whether yours or theirs. This builds trust and leads to respect.
- Improve or, at least, mend the relationship. People do want to help their friends.
- Separate the people from the problem. No one is trying to do a poor job. Reasonable people want to agree and make the bargain work.
- Focus on underlying concerns. The reasons people want things gives you a more complete picture. In other words, ask why.
- Generate a variety of solutions. Consider them carefully before you decide what to do.
- Keep the process of fair and equitable dealing in the forefront. If someone does not follow your lead, there is little to do but end the negotiations.

- Have a Plan *B* in advance of current negotiations. If the deal is unfair to you or if the other side threatens constantly, you should have another opportunity in your pocket.
- Have and keep leverage. Time is a good one, having some alternatives is another. Pledging to do nothing (not to buy or sell) is also effective (if it's true). This is sometimes called the "walk-away" or the "take-away."

Come up with solutions that:

- Are better than your best walk-away alternative.
- Use external standards to judge the fairness of any agreement. These would be the blue book, standard AIA language, or your company's written policy.
- Bind everyone to realistic commitments. Do not overdemand and keep people working for 72 hours straight.

In negotiations, you have to work with people, so:

1.   Put yourself in their shoes.
2.   Don't deduce their intentions from your fears.
3.   Don't blame them for your problems.
4.   Do discuss each other's perceptions.
5.   Give them a stake in the outcome. Have them participate in the process. Get their buy-in.
6.   Make your proposal consistent with their values. Values are motivators.
7.   Look for opportunities to show them who you are. Give them a reason to think you're flexible and a decent person.

People have emotions:

Understanding people is critical to consistent success in negotiation. People can agree to anything. Making your proposal make sense emotionally to the other side is key to gaining agreement.

1. Recognize and understand emotions—both your emotions and their emotions.

2. Acknowledge emotions and make them a focus of discussion, if necessary.

3. Allow the other side to let off steam—don't react. Know that frustration can be high, and releasing it allows the other side to think more objectively about your ideas.

4. Don't react in kind to emotional outbursts from the other side.

5. Use thoughtful gestures. Invite the other side to join you in side events, such as dinner or coffee. Show that you care for them as people. Demonstrate you are interested in a good relationship, no matter what happens.

Because we use words and because words are sometimes inaccurate:

- Listen actively and acknowledge what is being said.
- Understand them, and then speak to be understood.
- Keep confidences and communications private. Everyone should be on a need-to-know priority as an initial understanding.
- Speak about yourself and not about them. Use the first person.
- Don't react. Be a cool customer and be purposeful in your words.

Eleven Lessons I Have Learned

Scar tissue is a great teacher. Here are some wounds or lessons I have learned from my mistakes.

1. Be hard, but be fair. Have some sensitivity to fairness. Great negotiators have often said, "The bargain will not occur again if it is not a value to both parties." Sometimes, we burn bridges only to find that, in the long term, we need as many bridges as we can get.

2. What goes around comes around. Your reputation precedes you. Others will prepare accordingly. If you lack scruples, others will have no hesitation to make you a victim.

3. Use sugar. What you say and how you say it go together in bargaining.

4. What you don't say (gossiping, dismissive talk, and so forth) speaks volumes about you.

5. Have high aspirations. Set the mood of your negotiations to a high level. The other side will be more excited about bargaining with you.

6. A good offense is a good defense. Keep the other side thinking about your proposal and less about their counter-proposal.

7. Do the hard work. The way to get the most complete agreement is to do the hard work during the session.

8. Be prepared. Doing your homework is essential. Unprepared negotiators frustrate the other side and they will look for other options immediately because of this rookie mistake. And, the chance is good that those options don't include you.

9. Timing is everything. Great negotiators know the bargaining can last for hours, weeks, or months, but there are moments when the other side will be receptive to a counterproposal. Watch body language and voice inflection for signals.

10. Use support. After you propose your idea, augment it with common-sense logic, fact supported by proof (in writing).

11. Use strategy. Not to use strategy makes you less than an effective negotiator. The three components of every construction contract are price, scope, and speed. The subsets to these are where strategy comes into play.

For some contractors, knowing the Pay by Purchase Order method decreases paper work and, thus, increases the speed of the business cycle, while it maintains accuracy.

Negotiating Is the Best Use of Any Construction Professional's Time

We make or save the most amount of money in the shortest period of time by negotiating. In my experience, everyone has said yes or no at the right time and made $1,000 in 20 minutes. If we all could do this on an hourly basis, we could retire early, and the construction business would be our hobby.

These are basic rules that must be observed if you are to have an above-average negotiation. Do all these things and you will reap the benefits. Guard against the gambits that others will use against you. Remember, what you deserve is what you negotiate. The following list of rules gives you some of the tactics to be wary of in your negotiations:

1. Make small talk first. It doesn't cost a dime to talk. Start an interesting conversation about a nonconstruction issue. Observe body language, emotions, attitudes, and so forth. This is your final homework before the actual business negotiations start. Do this homework and you will be better prepared.

2. Always have the other side give the initial price. This is an easy win for any negotiator. Have the potential client set the price benchmark. As an example, if you are the seller, they (buyer) name the price. You have now set the "floor," and the price goes up from there. As you know, sometimes the buyer will name a high price and you'll be glad you followed this rule. If you are the buyer, the opposite is true.

3. Have a walk-away number. Professional negotiators do their homework and know the limits of their proposals. They calculate cost, price, cash flow, and value, among other things.

A professional's overall goal is to receive value in the negotiation. *Value* is the benefit divided by the cost. Benefits can be noneconomic and they are judgment calls. Because we are amateurs, we must remember to take our emotions out during the process and focus on what we will not accept. This objective approach helps keep our eye on the ball and keeps our goals clearly in mind.

4. Have multiple options. The person with the most options usually succeeds in reaching their goals. As in sales, negotiations are no different. Conversely, if you have only one project to sell or no Plan *B* in your discussions, the pressure is on you. But, if you have several jobs, you have less pressure and you can say no more easily. Even if you have no other options, acting as if you do gives you more power.

5. The successful contractor has many qualified prospects when they're selling work. They have several choices and possible outcomes for the future when they are selling work. In other words, the successful contractor has multiple options. We define a qualified prospect in the following way:

    *   Has a Deadline—That is, they are kicking tires. This person has to make a decision in a limited amount of time.

    *   Has a Budget—They have money set aside to spend. The old saw is "you can't get rich by dealing with poor people." The time spent on unbudgeted bids and proposals can ruin a contractor.

    *   Can Build a Relationship—People from the same part of the work tend to have more to talk about. A U.S. Marine has more in common with their brethren. The lack of commonality leads to less personal interest by either party and this person may see you as just another contractor.

    *   Has the Authority to Make the Decision—Many books are available about how to identify, and then to negotiate with the decision maker. When a married couple is buying the house, the decision maker most of the time is the wife. The husband writes the check.

- Has a Need—The other side has a compelling reason to buy your construction services, such as employees' cars are parked in adjacent fields (this means a manufacturer is busting at the seams), sales at a distributor are at record levels, or the lease on a home is up in a year. Clients who have this problem are motivated and are not casual about it.

- Is Ethical—If the other side has all of the above, the final test is one of personal character. You cannot ignore this and to do so is at your own peril. There are two serious reasons for this. First, is the high probability at the closing table that you will feel cheated. Second, is that the agreement will span some length of time and has to be implemented. An unethical person will agree in principal and spirit, but fall short on the letter of the agreement. In summary, an unethical person by definition will say and do anything for their own benefit.

6. Always say "pass" and don't say "no." Keep your negotiation alive. People may come back with a better offer. Don't cut off negotiations prematurely.

7. You should not negotiate with some people. It would be unbalanced. Not many people have negotiated successfully with Donald Trump. To try to do so would be foolish.

8. Never say "never" and never say "always." Either statement commits you to a course of action that limits your options. Whether in war, peace, or contracting, if your opponent is uncertain about what you will do, you have more power. There are times when you have to decide. Be sparing and certain in doing so.

Use a bottom-up budgeting process, which is driven simultaneously by the goals of the contractor and reality. (See Chapter 4.)

Tactics

The following list of tactics will be used against you in your career at one time or another. Take the time during your negotiation to identify them, and then to counteract these ploys. This will keep the horse trading going on an even basis for you.

1. Country boy. The rule here is "dumb is smart." The one party who acts as if the world is going too fast sometimes frustrates the other side. At other times, we feel sorry for them and make a more generous offer.

2. Good cop/bad cop. The use of both a friend and an adversary produces pain and relief for the other side. This is a motivator to give more than you planned to give. We see this on TV, but. it is a little more subtle in a developer's office.

3. False deadline. The other side has suddenly stated that the deadline to conclude negotiations is now sooner. You are surprised. This is related to "time is money." Your opponent is using pressure to force you to concede more.

4. Funny money. Sales professionals and other people sometimes explain price in a multitude of ways, but rarely as one that is high. Some sales training teaches to divide the price by the number of months or to use percentages. This makes our bank accounts and investment portfolios seem less important. *Always* use dollars. Think in terms of this: "if I negotiate for just one more hour with this person, then I can shave $1,000 off the price." Now, that is just compensation for a contractor!

5. Strawman. This is a tactic that emphasizes a small possibility or detail as having high importance. Major league baseball used the threat of franchise closing, which became a valuable chip in the game and helped close the labor agreement quickly. In retrospect, the court would have ruled in the favor of the fans. For a contractor, your new client may ask about the superintendent managing the project. His reaction could be to complain bitterly about your choice. The client may only be angling for a further concession and may not have a care about the superintendent.

6. Lack of authority. The other side says they must have the approval of another person before they can agree to anything. You are told to give your proposal in writing and you cannot meet with the decision maker. You will always receive an answer to your proposal through the intermediary with some changes to it. There is neither explanation nor logic to this, but the messenger doesn't know this. Again, this is a tactic meant to put you in an awkward place.

7. Reluctant buyer or seller. They are thinking about buying or selling, but they have no deadline. This tactic tries to force you to give a great deal to spur interest on their part. That proposal, as you know from the previous section is now the floor or ceiling to any further negotiation.

8. Use of anger. Some negotiators will feign emotion in trying to place the other side on the defensive. As you have learned and, sometimes, now believe *what you see, you believe*. Keep your cool. In 100 percent of all instances, if someone is undeservedly upset, there is no reason to react.

9. Flinch. This gambit is related to the previous one, but it is different. It is used immediately after a proposal is given. Because most contractors are visually attuned, we are susceptible to such a gambit. The idea is to make your proposal or counterproposal seem insulting. Logic must take over here, such as the market reality of what is normal.

10. Vise. This is a ploy that, the majority of times, is used on the first proposal. The phrase uttered after the price/terms are delivered is "you will have to do better than that." This means you are out in the parking lot and not even in left field. Be careful not to react.

11. Use decimal places in your price. As you look at the price over the years, the numbers rounded off to the nearest $1,000 have more cushion or room to change. Prices that are calculated to a decimal point seem to be more carefully reached and have less fat in them. They are more believable. You have to do your math homework and know what the number should be.

12. Third-party testimony is more believable than yours. A credible source who has no affiliation to the negotiator carries more weight in determining fact or truth than you do. Certainly, you need to be careful about who the third party is. "Industry studies" or "common knowledge" does not qualify. Written testimony is many times more credible, so make the other side prove it on paper.

13. Time is money. Some negotiators will extend negotiations, so you have increasing amounts of time (which is money) dedicated to the negotiation. This becomes an investment that some people will not walk away from. Smart negotiators will see no progress being made and feel this tactic is being played. Their next move is to stop this negotiation and go to their next option or client.

14. Nibbling. This gambit is used after an agreement has been reached. The other side will ask for a small concession or convenience item with a straight face. If you are flush with success, this tactic might just work. Given the fact that we are in a business of less than 5 percent net profit, this is brutal to the careless contractor. Don't let this gambit fool you.

> Efficient contractors insist on a process where (1) your invoice, (2) the supplier's purchase order, and (3) the delivery ticket all match in terms of quantities, price, and other information. If in agreement, approval and payment should be made. Requiring further approval by field supervisors or project managers only slows down your business process. Furthermore, it frustrates these key management positions.

CHAPTER SUMMARY

The construction business is made up of processes and people. Effectively recruiting and leading people cannot be ignored if you plan on running a premier contracting business.

Managing people well is a process. Some people have an innate sense of how to do it, while others have to learn it. Either way, being successful in leading people involves following proven steps.

Recruiting good people continues to be a challenge for all contractors. The rain falls on everyone. Consistently finding and hiring above-average people is an involved process. We have to use many different tools to quickly understand the potential employee because there is no singular test or method. Having great people makes contracting a less-complicated business. Having bad people can be the death knell of a construction company. It is that important.

Success is between a person's ears. If they think they are successful or not, they are right. We feel some hallmarks exist to judge professional success. Being in the top 25 percent of people who perform your function is one, but having the respect of intelligent people is the ultimate gauge of professional success.

Generations differ in their attitudes. We work with different generations in the construction business and none is better or worse than the other. They simply look at the world differently. Know them and you will have fewer problems with recruiting, hiring, managing, and firing people.

The DiSC personality profile has been an effective tool to uncover the emotional tendencies of people. The analysis has been proven accurate over the decades and it meets the legal requirements for hiring. People are different, even though they may do the same job. Learning approaches to managing people better can make you more effective.

OSHA is a friend to the contractor. It focuses on lessening unsafe behaviors, which leads to fewer accidents and, thus, fewer lost days. OSHA does not try to profit from its fines; in fact, they focus on changing behavior. Fines are only one way OSHA attempts to do that.

You should have additional safety standards to OSHA's guidelines. The payoff is high in many ways: business, personal, and moral.

Negotiating has the highest payoff of any activity for a construction leader. Work at growing and maintaining your skills in this area. When you say "yes," "no," or "pass" at the appropriate time, you can make or save significant dollars and, sometimes, in just a few minutes. All other management activities pale in comparison.

6

Best Practices

Stevens Construction Institute (SCI) queried construction contractors working in the United States concerning 94 industry best practices. This is the limited version of our main library. We held the ranking process open for three months, and gathered respondents from all trades and markets of the construction contracting industry.

We asked each participant to rank each practice we disclosed in importance to "making a consistent profit."

Responses were solicited from three sources:

- Active or inactive clients of our consulting firm
- Association members
- Construction professionals who were neither, but who are actively practicing

Some participants were owners of construction firms, while others were in the employment of a construction firm.

The types of construction firms were as follows:

- **General Contracting Firms, Including Builders.** These firms are characterized as using subcontractors to build most of their work.
- **Specialty Contracting Firms.** These firms are characterized as managing labor, which is directly on their payroll.

The number of employees was segmented into three parts:

- Up to 25 employees
- 26 to 100 employees
- Over 100 employees

The type of construction work engaged range from general to specialty contractors, including over two-dozen trades represented by the 16 divisions of the Construction Specifications Institute (CSI) categories.

The markets they work in are

- Single-family home
- Multifamily
- Commercial/industrial
- Heavy/highway
- Institutional

The number of responses was less than 1,000 individuals. Statistical confidence is not "95 percent or greater." However, the construction industry is highly fragmented and, therefore, statistical confidence is extremely difficult to attain.

We offered 94 best practice statements and asked the participants to rank them in "Importance in Making a Consistent Profit."

SCI's library includes over 200 best practices, but that was not the focus of this exercise. Each professional ranked each best practice in Importance in Making a Consistent Profit. The ranking scale was from 1 (low importance) to 6 (high importance).

We segmented our analysis in three areas:

1. 1–2 is a low-importance best practice.
2. 3–4 is a medium-importance best practice.
3. 5–6 is a high-importance best practice.

We requested comments at the end of the ranking. We received two dozen comments, which were personal and not professional in nature.

Our best practice statements concerned the following areas:

1. Acquiring work
   A. Estimating
   B. Pricing
   C. Bidding
   D. Marketing
2. Building work
   A. Pre-job planning
   B. Job mobilization
   C. Planning the work
   D. Scheduling the work
   E. Executing the work
   F. Closing out the work
3. Financial management
   A. Financial management
   B. Accounting
   C. Costing
   D. Billing
   E. Accounts receivable/payable

CONCLUSIONS

No best practice averaged 1 to 2 in its "importance in making a consistent profit." Only one averaged a 3.0. This translates to mean that all these methods have significant value to all construction contracting firms.

Our analysis discovered that the value of these best practices is clearly based on three factors:

1. Financial—the desire to increase profits
2. Schedule—the need to increase the speed of building
3. Quality—the desire to increase the quality of craft and management work

Financial

Best practices concerning project finance rated highest at 5–6. Best practices for general financial management rated lower.

Schedule

Those processes that sped the project team's work rated highest, while those that only helped an individual work faster were lower.

Quality

Those best practices that improved quality in the face of the client were rated 5 and 6. Those that did not were rated significantly lower.

CHAPTER SUMMARY

We have the opinions of many qualified contractors to support that these processes have value. Best practices represent a series of steps needed to build work and manage a construction firm. We found that there is ample support from the contracting community.

There was no significant correlation of the ranking of best practices to:

1. Type of contractor
2. Type of work
3. Type of market

The greater the number of employees in a company, the higher the importance of best practices. The farther removed the owner is from the following three basic functions, the more the need to have employees follow these best practices. See Figures 6-1, 6-2, and 6-3. The three basic functions are

1. Work acquisition best practices ranking
2. Construction operations best practices ranking
3. Financial management best practices ranking

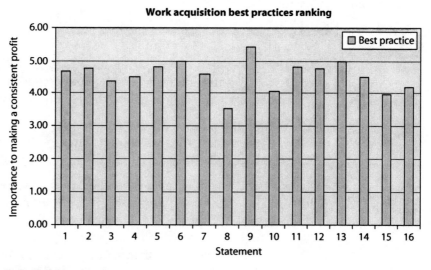

FIGURE 6-1
Work acquisition best practices revolve around two things: accuracy and speed of the work acquisition process (versus being the low bidder).

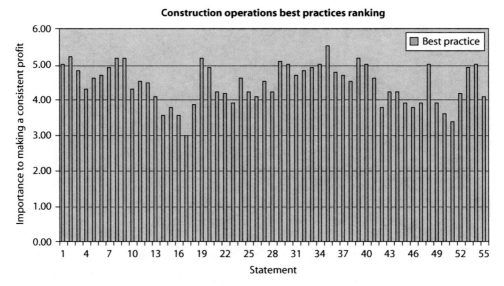

FIGURE 6-2
Construction operations are those practices that are neither work acquisition nor financial management. These practices are all the things that make the projects and the company successful.

Hands-on owners have different effective techniques for their situations. Continuous success by these small companies speaks volumes about the value of individual unique practices.

Most contractors have an entrepreneurial mind-set. They use their knowledge, wits, and gut feel to make their businesses work. These individuals have little need for best practices.

If a construction business is smaller, the value of best practices is lower. The small company size gives the contractor the luxury of direct control of the field and office operations. There is less need for training employees on business approaches to construction. Creating, documenting, or following best practices could lead to a competitive disadvantage; such as employees might leave their employ and use this knowledge against them. Some existing competitors might learn trade secrets. Hence, there is little incentive to follow a formal approach.

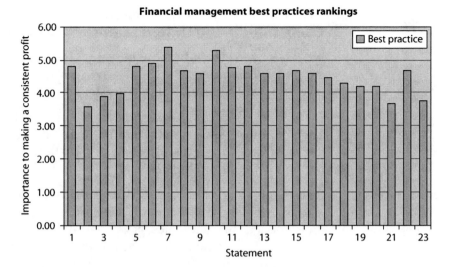

FIGURE 6-3
Financial management best practices cover, in general terms, those items involving office administration and company money management.

For other types of construction leaders, such as

1. Executives of large contracting firms (over 100 employees)
2. Executives whose business requires a complex process approach

our study concluded that there is a high value to knowing and teaching best practices in large or complex businesses. The business steps have to be executed by managers and supervisors. It is essential to keep communication flowing while maintaining speed of process. Thus, the value of best practices is high.

Profitable contractors calculate and know marginal contribution, so they can make informed budget decisions.

Best Practices of Construction Companies in the United States

We have been struck by how best practices are used by both large and small contractors, as well as those in between. Best practices give the user a simple and consistent benefit: a high return on investment (ROI).

This, of course, means that large or small, the contractor is getting the most profit from his investment. Isn't the business of contracting about wealth building?

One of the values of best practices is that we know right behaviors lead to improved results. In any walk of life, such as medical, retail, food service, or academics, it is logical that if a team of people approach a professional situation in the same way, it will produce consistently better outcomes. Communication and speed, among other things, will benefit.

If you want to improve your contracting performance, you and your staff will have to behave differently in those professional situations. (It simply is not sane to act the same and expect better results!) Our best practices are a place to start. Certainly, your best practices are tailored to you. However, taking ones that work for other construction professionals is where I would begin my improvement.

What is startling is that contractors ranked many of these inconsistently. The range was from 4 to 6 points on every question (and our scale was from 1 to 6). This wide perception rank is not easily explained. These variations show that some competitors in the market don't appreciate good process. Your competition is not seeing the value of quicker and more accurate methods. That is good news for you! They are using practices they learned and will not entertain the idea of other good techniques. In other words, some of your competitors "know it all" and don't think there are any better ideas. We were all like that once!

7

Your Last Management Act

Owners of contracting firms are faced with the inevitable. They will not be leaving this Earth alive and breathing. Only astronauts do that consistently, but then, even they return. Some day, a contractor's energy and attitude will wane. Their body and mind will tell them that the business they built needs new leadership. Then, it is time for them to take on a different role in life.

When that time comes, what do you do about transferring ownership? This is often a difficult intellectual and emotional decision. Fortunately, you have several options.

The first option is, sometimes, just a matter of some legal paperwork giving ownership to a son or daughter with a family payout agreement. This is a common occurrence in the construction business.

The second option is, on occasion, employees stepping in as the new stockholders. Again, an agreement has to be sworn to and a cash-payout schedule accepted by both parties. In this transaction, as long as a talented core group owns the majority of stock, it can give the company a new life and a thriving existence for several years.

The third, and most complicated and daunting option, is the third-party buy/sell agreement. In most cases, the buyer and seller do not personally know each other. This leads to a longer transaction process and a somewhat unpredictable ending.

In all these examples, the owner is attempting to accomplish two basic things:

1. Change their relationship to the firm
2. Derive some monetary value for the firm

The transaction between the former and the new owner(s) will be unique. All buying/selling situations have different sets of circumstances and needs by the involved parties.

As previously stated, emotions are part of the equation. The owner who has spent many years nurturing the firm now has to say goodbye. This is not an easy transition. A majority of proposed transactions do not go through due to this reason.

To address this transition, time has to be spent by the selling party thinking about this life change and what they want to do in their future. Walks on the beach or solo vacations are a good idea.

Once the idea of this life change is comfortable, the next hurdle is to think through the transaction, from both the seller's and acquiring party's perspective. All contractors have a fairly clear idea of what they want to happen, but the buyer's perspective is equally important. Remember to ask, "What would I want or accept if I were buying a contracting firm?" Keeping balance in your approach to the negotiation will not prematurely kill it.

Understand that construction firms do not sell at a premium. The going rate is somewhere north of two times earnings, plus book value of assets, which is not a great amount of money. As you can guess, keeping your construction firm until you die makes the most sense. But if your goal is not strictly a financial one, then selling your firm may be your best move later in life.

Contractors Buy Contracting Firms

A majority of transactions occur between like professionals. Yes, sometimes there is the one-off transaction far afield. Money-management firms and public utilities *have* purchased construction companies. These are rare, though; usually only a contractor wants to be in this business (some say it's 9 out of 10). Hence, the search for a buyer is more efficient if pursued with contractors in the population.

The Process of Selling Your Construction Firm

The process of selling your construction firm should be a structured one. A construction-only business broker will know the most effective process.

1. Gather information.

    Here is a list of preliminary information that your broker may require:
    *   Tax returns
    *   Financial statements
    *   Closed job information
    *   Organizational chart
    *   Loan agreements
    *   Employment contracts

2. Begin the interview process.

    The business broker interviews the owner(s) after studying the corporate information. This needs to be accomplished, so the broker knows all the circumstances surrounding the company and can answer any questions about them.

3. Assemble a contact list.

   The business broker assembles a potential buyer list. The owner(s) reviews the list, crosses off those people who are objectionable, and adds people they may know.

4. Make contacts.

   Typically, formal letters are sent to individuals who were identified as potential candidates. The letters are sales-oriented in nature and describe the company and its situation in general terms, so no one can guess which firm it is. After the letters are sent, follow-up is made with phone calls to generate interest.

5. Exchange confidentiality and nondisclosure agreements.

   Once interest is signaled by one or more potential buyers, formal documents memorializing the other side's pledge not to disclose or otherwise disseminate your company information, including that it is for sale. A good agreement will have remedies for violating the document.

6. Send the company book of information to the potential buyer.

   The book of information is created by the business broker. This book discloses the details of the business, its financial status, market share, organization structure, and labor situation, among dozens of other areas. The buyer should be able to decide if the company is of interest. If it is not of interest, the book is returned.

7. Schedule a face-to-face meeting between the seller and the potential buyer.

   This meeting is crucial to establish a relationship and to see if the chemistry is right between the parties. Sometimes this is the only meeting between the two parties and the transaction dies. If both parties feel there is a value to go on further, then another meeting may be held.

8. The potential buyer issues a letter of interest.

   Once a letter of interest is sent to the seller, some steps occur in rapid succession.

9. Proceed with due diligence.

   The buyers have 60 to 90 days to inspect the business they are buying. They go through the books, see the fixed assets, look over the projects, and so forth.

10. Work on a purchase agreement.

    The parties create the purchase agreement that spells out in great detail what is being bought, under what conditions it is being bought, and the amount for which it is being bought.

11. Set a closing date/hold the closing.

The business broker, you, and the other side set a closing date that is fairly close in time—from 90 to 120 days—from the letter of interest.

Three Types of Buyers

The three main types of buyers are

- Strategic buyer
- Economic buyer
- Familial buyer

A *strategic buyer* is someone who is looking for geographic or service expansion. This buyer can be looking in your state. People from the north sometimes buy a firm in the south, or they want to buy a business to expand their service offering. A plumbing firm will purchase an HVAC contractor. Numerous possibilities exist here.

An *economic buyer* is looking for a good price for the value received. They might know they can buy the firm at x amount and it will be worth $2x$ in a few years. Sometimes, they purchase a firm in trouble to capture the workforce. As you know, journeymen are not easy to grow.

A *familial buyer* is someone who knows the owner through a family relationship or who is an employee of the company (company employees are family, too). This kind of transaction is a good first option because this always seems to be a more comfortable situation. This is because the people know each other well, trust is high, and the payment terms are friendlier.

What is the Value of Your Construction Firm?

The value of a construction firm is fairly simple. It is a multiple (e.g., 3 times) of the predictable income stream, plus the value of the assets.

Ascertaining and agreeing on a predictable income stream can be difficult, historical performance not withstanding. The income of a commercial or industrial contractor is based on several factors, including bids, present and future work, and work in process. A residential builder's income might be based on inventory and name recognition, as well as product and economic factors. A service-contracting firm is more straightforward because the business acts more predictably.

A common mistake is to believe that an abnormally great year can be used as the basis for value. It cannot: an average should be taken. Again, think of what you would do as a buyer.

The market determines the multiple (the value of the income stream) and the value of the assets. Similar transactions from the previous years are a good basis for evaluations. Certified professionals in this area are the only ones who can peg the market price fairly. In some cases, each party will hire its own business appraiser, and then negotiate with each other with reports in hand.

The owner has a range of working options after the sale. They can stay involved as leader for a period of time, which gives a smoother transition to the new owner who will need to become familiar with the business. The previous owner knows more about their business than anyone else.

The other end of the spectrum of options is for them to completely remove themselves from the business and, sometimes, people choose this option. As you might think, there has to be some kind of transition, but it can be brief.

The seller should expect to be compensated for time spent working with the new leader(s). If the previous owner stays on as a senior manager, then an earn out is formulated. Typically, an *earn out* contains salary plus bonus, the bonus being a percentage of profits, typically gross margin.

Some Traps

An estimated 90 percent of all proposed transactions don't go through and the reasons are not surprising.

- Owners feel their company is of a greater value than the market will bear.
- The candidate company has no second-in-command to take over. The new owner most often has no one to come in and take charge. They are looking to the candidate company for their next leader.
- There is a profit fade between the initial contact campaign and the closing date. Some owners start leaving the business mentally before the transaction is finished and the financial statement shows it.

An estimated 80 percent of the transactions that do go through are sales to the employees or family members, neither of which can make a cash payment for the business. A payment plan has to be formulated. This means the acquirer will be using your future profits to buy your business. If they fail, you may get your business back.

One caveat to anyone considering selling their firm: Remember, there is no such thing as retirement. Understand that you must be intellectually engaged in something. Not to do so decreases your chance at a long postcontracting life. Additionally, if you talk to others who have sold their companies, you will find there is a certain happiness in doing something challenging or rewarding.

Don't be mistaken. A construction contracting firm is hard to sell. Several factors must come together all at once. Most importantly, the two sides must be willing to negotiate and be reasonable in their demands. Other factors that only complicate the issue are valuation, economic forecasts, business performance, and the regulatory environment. The bottom line is, if the two interests want to, they can make the transaction happen.

Determine the cost of overhead to different departments by using the sales percent, the labor percent, the number of square feet of building space, and so forth instead of judgment. This is a common-sense approach to allocate overhead to different departments or divisions of work.

8

Conclusions

From time to time, people ask my opinion about how best to manage a construction firm. This question has a long answer, but I will attempt to put my recommended approach into words. To be fair, this is better written by the fine people who run profitable construction firms and I have personally known a few of them. This explanation is theirs.

WITH A FIRST-TIME OWNER, A CONSTRUCTION FIRM MUST START SMALL

The first-time owner has to know many small details about how to run a construction business. The business is technical, as well as demanding in time and knowledge. If you are taking over an existing firm, this will be stressful. Because this is an owner/operator business, you have to know it intimately. Going for volume is never a good idea because variable cost can eat you up. If you are just starting out, looking for volume is doubly bad.

YOU MAKE MONEY ON THE COST SIDE

Today, there are more contractors chasing the same amount of work. Margins are thinner. No great premium is paid to any contractor over the market price. So, if you are to make better-than-average profits, the cost side must be reduced. Higher productivity of office and field labor is your greatest opportunity with better business methods and superior technical processes being the best way to realize those gains.

MOST OWNERS MUST BE A "MUD ON THE BOOTS" TYPE

Money is made in the field and the owner has to be there to supervise, work, communicate, and keep their eye on the schedule and financial ball. Reports and e-mails don't tell the owner as much as their feet on the ground.

Today's Contractor Cannot Be Afraid of Technology

E-mail, faxes, and cell phones are a minimum requirement. Not having basic technology is a competitive disadvantage. If you don't have it, competitors will be faster than you. From this point, only add appropriate technology. The shorthand to use in your decision making is:

> Cost Savings + Profit Enhancement over Two Years
> Divided by the Cost of the Technology

This should equal 1 or more. Overall, the speed that computers and other electronic devices produce is undeniable.

Today's Contractor Must Be Financially Conservative

Financial conservatism is a necessary attitude in any construction firm, and this is not different for the new or young contractor. Mistakes and bad clients are a fact of life over a career, so having a monetary cushion in the bank is never a dumb idea. The financial ability to weather the storm is a must because storms happen in the construction industry.

Today's Contractor Must Be a Liberal Thinker

Liberalism is a needed skill of any contractor. Because we don't have many people to choose from and hire, our attitude has to be more tolerant of people's differences than in years past.

Today's Contractor Must Be a Good Risk Manager

As a contractor in today's market, risk management has to be your religion. Keeping risk factors out of contracts, job sites, crews, clients, and the overall business can serve you well. There is no norm in construction risk these days; it is all negotiable. Be active about minimizing or eliminating it.

Today's Contractor Must Believe That Craftsmanship Sells

If you are known for your good craftsmanship, clients will take care of you. Well-built and trouble-free installations enhance reputations. Word is that good contractors are in the minority in today's industry. I believe that. Your customers have other things on their minds. When your finished work doesn't create problems for your clients, they appreciate that. Your customers' friends tell them often enough about their problem contractors, so friends of your customers will seek you out if your client brags about your good craftsmanship.

FOCUS ON THE PROCESS

When you focus on the process, you get to the end of the job quicker without missteps, miscommunication, and, thus, misery. Major processes have to be defined. Insist on a clear definition of processes with your client. Be quietly persistent about getting methods established. Internally, you certainly need to be the agent of change. The more you define your processes and the more you monitor those processes, the better the outcome is for you.

LABOR IS THE OPPORTUNITY

Keeping labor coordinated (better than average), whether this is your labor or that of subcontractors, provides a competitive edge in building work, as well as proposing work. If I were ever to start a construction firm, I would find a labor-intensive specialty-contracting niche and keep the field organized and focused. With an average of 32 percent wasted time in construction, I would have plenty of room for improvement while charging market rates.

USE STATISTICAL METHODS FOR POSITIONING YOUR BUSINESS

Do not rely on luck or gut feel. Long-term the "house" wins unless you know the chances and how to play them. Using sound methods keeps the game simpler. Simplicity means speed, and speed is a constant demand in our industry. Again, good statistical measures keep you from missing problems and opportunities.

NEGOTIATE ALL THINGS

Negotiation is the highest per-hour payoff for any professional. For the construction contractor, it is good news that most things are negotiable.

DOING THE RIGHT THINGS AND HAVING ETHICS MAKE A DIFFERENCE

Being able to "walk in the front door" gives you a powerful advantage. People will recognize you for your ethics in many ways—large and small. Doing the right thing is never cowardly. You will thank yourself for having ethics throughout your career and you can look back at what you've done with pride.

TOMORROW IS ANOTHER DAY: THIS BUSINESS IS NOT LIFE OR DEATH

The construction business is a vehicle to deliver payment to you, so you may enjoy your dreams. It is not a sign of your character.

Do not feel you are a lesser person because of a failure. Life is far too complex to make that conclusion.

It's Not How Much You Make—It's How Much You Save

Your work is not about possessions or prestige. If you are after that as a goal, you are in the wrong industry. Yes, people of modest beginnings have done extremely well financially and they have been able to work with their children in this business. As an aside, the business continues under those same children. This is a gift from generation to generation, both ways.

No One Will Leave This Earth Alive and Breathing

Eventually, you will have to do something with your business. If you take my suggestions seriously, your business will be more organized and more predicable, so it will be more valuable. That is the point.

You Must Have a Business to Sell One

If your construction firm doesn't have a good, documented process and a solid core of employees who work well unsupervised, you don't have a business. You have a job. There will be no premium paid by third parties. In addition, your children will inherit a business that needs your supervision for the first few years, which is not a great prospect for someone who wants to experience other things.

If I were limited to only one sentence to summarize the best piece of contracting advice, it would be this:

Understand the Risk-Reward Curve for Construction

See Chapter 1 for a full explanation. However, your job is to get on *your* correct place on that curve. It is unique to you, just as you have chosen to be a mason, or an electrical, mechanical or general contractor. This is your decision. When you are at the right spot, you will maximize your business and, thus, your personal financial wealth.

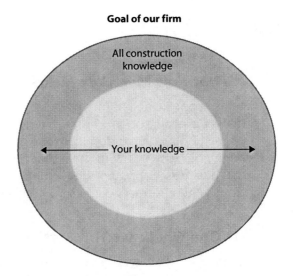

FIGURE 8-1
Only from engaging others can we learn more. The more we know,
the more capable we are as contractors.

I hope you have increased your knowledge of the construction industry from reading this book (see Figure 8-1). My sincere effort is to dispense helpful information to all construction professionals. Please let me know by sending your thoughts to the following:

- mstevens@stevensci.com
- Our free forms: www.stevensci.com and go to "free forms" link
- Our online digest: www.contractorsblog.com
- Our online courses: www.constructioncbt.com

Appendix

Chapter Exercises

CHAPTER 1—THE BUSINESS OF CONTRACTING

1. Give six reasons why the construction industry is considered the best industry for a career.
2. What is the greatest competitive edge a contractor can have?
3. What are the three major business processes that all contractors have to perform?
4. What role does technology play in a contracting business? Why is this role highly important?
5. How is the risk-reward curve different in construction than in general business? Describe the difference and give an example.
6. Name 10 risk factors and describe their negative effect.
7. What risk factors do contractors sometimes choose to have in their business?
8. What are the risk factors on a construction project?
9. Can a construction firm have little risk? How could you do that?

10. What is the trend in construction productivity? Are we more productive? Why or why not?

11. Are supervisor hours/labor hours going lower? Why?

12. Describe best practices in construction contracting. Why are best practices important to a contractor's business?

13. Is there a defined set of best practices that every contractor should use?

14. Do best practices assure a great result in every project? Do they guarantee profits for a contractor every year? Why or why not?

15. What type of software is a good choice for the business of construction contracting? Why?

EXERCISES

1. Using the book as a guide, develop a business plan for a:
   A. $50 million general building contractor
   B. $25 million home builder
   C. $5 million special contractor

   covering all aspects of:

   D. Processes
   E. People
   F. Projects

2. Name and describe a dozen risk factors in a new contracting business, and then discuss how to limit or minimize them.

3. How would you address the issue of the supply/demand curve for construction contracting?

4. Update the trends in productivity numbers and supervisor hours for construction. What is the current trend and what does it mean?

5. State the value of using quantitative methods in managing risk versus reward in construction contracting.

6. What are the positive and negative aspects of technology in construction contracting?

CHAPTER 2—THE ACQUIRE WORK PROCESS

1. Explain the purpose of work acquisition.

2. What role does estimating play in work acquisition?

3. Describe the steps of work acquisition.

4. Is work acquisition more art or science? Why?

5. In what different ways can a contractor determine his installed cost?

6. Explain the pressures to be the low bidder.

7. What is the value of using hours/unit rather than $/unit?

8. What are good uses of a price book or a pricing service?

9. Explain a basic-bid strategy?

10. What factors should you understand in the market to create a bid strategy?

11. Describe the strategy of unbalanced bidding.

12. Name 10 practices that the top estimators use.

13. What is a primary measure to judge the effectiveness of an estimator? Justify this.

14. What kind of work does a single rate of overhead application is effective? Why?

15. How does a dual rate apply? Why is it effective?

16. What is project sizing? How does it apply?

17. What is the tendency when sizing a smaller-than-average project?

18. On what kind of work is a single rate of overhead application effective? Why?

EXERCISES

1. What conditions would you place on your bid proposals?

    A. As a general contractor to an owner? Why?

    B. As a specialty contractor to a general contractor? Why?

2. Fill in a 10-point focused marketing method for the following (Grade each factor and be able to explain each rating.):

   A. Client type—desired types of customers

   B. Work type—desired type of construction work

   C. Geography—desired locations of work

3. Map out an estimating and bidding process for the following types of construction companies. Use the IMPM method (minimum 20 steps).

   A. General contracting

   B. Heavy/highway

   C. Mechanical

4. Create an estimating assembly (math equation) for a quantity take-off. Use the width, depth, and pitch of the roof to determine:

   A. Plywood sheeting

   B. Tar paper

   C. Shingles

   D. Fasteners

CHAPTER 3—THE BUILD WORK PROCESS

1. What phase is the greatest opportunity to save time and cost in a construction project? Why?

2. Which direct cost must a project manager be sensitive to? Why?

3. What are the two primary success factors in judging a construction project?

4. What are two outcomes on a job to judge the effectiveness of a project manager? Why?

5. What is the first step in building a project: scheduling or planning? Why?

6. Name 10 best practices in building work. Explain why each has value to a contractor's business.

7. In what phase of the construction business cycle does the contractor have the most risk and make the most profit?

8. How can the other two phases support this part of the business cycle?

9. What are 10 typically submitted items for a highway contractor?

10. What are 10 items typically submitted to an owner for approval?

11. What measurements are important to monitor in building work? Why?

EXERCISES

1. List 10 key discussion points for a preconstruction conference between an estimator and a project manager; between a project manager and a field manager. Describe each step.

2. Design a short-interval planner for a highway contractor.

3. Design a short-interval planner for a building contractor.

4. List the first 40 tasks that might be in a job management checklist for a:

   A. General building contractor

   B. Water treatment plant contractor

   C. Highway contractor

5. Create an IMP map for a typical CPM schedule for building a 2,000 square-foot home.

CHAPTER 4—THE KEEP TRACK PROCESS

1. What is the purpose of financial management? How does understanding financial management benefit a construction company?

2. List and explain the economic/business characteristics of construction contracting. How are these characteristics different from general business?

3. What is the purpose of job cost reports?

4. What are the primary factors that should be included in a cost report?

5. What is a good measure of productivity in financial terms?

6. What are the two basic incentive programs?

7. What is the primary factor in determining the best of class contractors? Why is this faulty?

8. What are two financial accounts used in construction contracting that are unusual in general business? What is their purpose?

9. What is OCIP and what effect does it have on a contractor's business?

10. What is a superior method to budget in construction? Why?

EXERCISES

1. Calculate the return on investment (ROI) for a project with the following attributes (Use the methodology in the book.):

   A. The labor cost is $20,000.

   B. The material cost is $30,000.

   C. The subcontract is $10,000.

   D. The customer pays you 47 days after he receives your invoice.

   E. The supplier wants payment in 35 days.

   F. The project is three months long.

   G. Costs are incurred evenly for each week of the three-month period.

   H. The overhead is 10 percent.

   I. The profit is 10 percent.

2. Design a job-cost report form for a labor-only contractor. How will this form predict losses earlier? Include an analysis of the cost-to-date and the cost for the current work period, as well as a projection of each item result and the project result.

3. Create a form with five terms and conditions for a purchase order. Justify those terms and conditions.

4. Create an incentive program for a field manager in a company. Do the same for a project manager. Why will the incentive program work? What are its potential weaknesses?

5. Create a budget for the next year for a:

    A. General building contractor

    B. Heavy/highway contractor

    C. Specialty contractor

6. Use the same budget as you created in the previous exercise and split the budget between two divisions of work. Explain the rationale for each budget line.

CHAPTER 5—PEOPLE

1. What are 10 habits to model in dealing with construction personnel?

2. What are the three generations described in the text? How are they different? How are they alike?

3. What are the four DiSC dimensions? What is the strength and weakness of each dimension? Name some employment positions in which each would want to work, for example, in what role would a *D* person want to work? An *I* person? An *S* person? A *C* person?

4. What is the best craft/operator DiSC profile? Why?

5. What are 10 approaches you would use in recruiting? Why?

6. Why can OSHA be viewed as an ally to the construction industry?

7. How can a contractor become more low risk in the eyes of an insurance carrier?

8. How can a contractor reduce the number of incidents and accidents on their construction projects? Describe.

9. In the author's words, what is success?

EXERCISES

1. Write a recruiting plan for a construction company.
2. List construction-related questions you might ask a potential hire. Why?
3. Write a separate 100-word memo for each DiSC personality type to motivate them to work smarter for the week.
4. Write a short safety speech for each generation (described in the book) and motivate them to be safer for the week.
5. Write a 1,000 word speech that you will give at your annual meeting of managers.
   A. Write it to motivate all three generations.
   B. Write it to all four DiSC personalities.
   C. Write it to reflect some of the people practices suggested in the chapter.
   D. Write it to promote the idea of best practices. How would you present it?

CHAPTER 6—BEST PRACTICES

1. How did the author accumulate his best practices? How did he determine their value?
2. Does a best practice guarantee success? Why?
3. Is a best practice a process or a technique? Explain.
4. Why is adoption of best practices critical for a company's success?
5. Is it important to use all best practices without exception? Why, or why not?
6. Are there other best practices in the industry?

EXERCISES

1. Choose 25 best practices you feel work for a general contractor. Do the same for a specialty contractor. Explain why, in your opinion, they have value.

2. Pick 10 best practices and develop a 10-slide training presentation for your new company's employees.

3. Develop an IMP map using 50 best practices for a contracting firm.

4. Write a business process manual using the same 50 best practices.

5. Research three other industries that have standardized best practices. How did the industry collect them? How did they validate them? Are any of these best practices applicable to the construction industry?

Index

CPSIA information can be obtained
at www.ICGtesting.com
Printed in the USA
LVOW09s1323290817
546812LV00009B/137/P